RELIGION IN ACTION

BOOKS BY THE AUTHOR

Religion in Action
Peace, War and You
Character Assassination
Behind Soviet Power
Labor Problems in America (with others)
Capitalism and Its Culture
The Jail Population of Connecticut
The New Russia (with others)
Contemporary Social Movements
Labor Speaks for Itself on Religion
Christianity and Social Adventuring
Introduction to Sociology (with others)
Readings in Sociology (with others)
Business and the Church
Adventuring in World Cooperation
Christian Fellowship Among the Nations (with R. B. Chamberlin)
The Russian Immigrant
The Russians and Ruthenians in America

PARTIAL LIST OF BOOKS

EDITED BY THE AUTHOR

Immigration and Race Attitudes, by Emory S. Bogardus
Introduction to Social Psychology, by Radhakamal Mukerjee
Economics and Ethics, by John A. Hobson
Criminology, by Robert H. Gault
The Concepts of Sociology, by Earle Edward Eubank
The Beginnings of Tomorrow, by Herbert A. Miller
An Introduction to Educational Sociology, by Ross L. Finney and Leslie D. Zeleny
Race Relations, by Willis D. Weatherford and Charles S. Johnson

RELIGION IN ACTION

by
Jerome Davis

Introduction by
E. STANLEY JONES

PHILOSOPHICAL LIBRARY
NEW YORK

Copyright, 1956, by Philosophical Library, Inc.,
15 East 40th Street, New York 16, N.Y.

All rights reserved.

Printed in the United States of America

To all who wish to do the greatest good to the greatest number and who are willing to unite faith and action by fusing their love for God in love for men, I dedicate this book.

Introduction

IN sampling through this book one is struck with several things. One is the amazing amount of apt quotations and stories about people of all ages and all races. They are to the point and gripping.

The other fact that strikes one is that the social and personal sides of religion are blended into a living whole. The social is shot through and through with the personal and the personal is permeated with the social. Life is one and must be dealt with as a whole.

This is a vital book, out of the rich Christian experience of a devoted follower of Christ.

E. STANLEY JONES

Contents

Introduction   vii
Preface   xi

PART I

The Present Social Order

I. Whither Bound	5
II. Religion: Opiate or Dynamic Power?	13
III. Forward with the Prophets	25
IV. Dinosaur Power Is Outmoded	39
V. The Subtle Poisoning of the People	55
VI. Economic Illiteracy	77
VII. The Challenge of Communism	99
VIII. Jesus and Social Christianity	113

PART II

Guide Posts to Progress

IX. Enlarge Your Horizons	127
X. Equality, Justice, and Freedom	137
XI. Economic Democracy	153
XII. The Solidarity of Mankind	167
XIII. Invincible Goodwill	179
XIV. The Test of Action	193

PART III

Changing the Social Order

XV.	Beginning in the Family	205
XVI.	Church and Synagogue Are Indispensable	219
XVII.	"I Was in Prison and You Came to Me"	235
XVIII.	Overcoming the Criminal in Us	247
XIX.	Through Organized Labor	261
XX.	The Democratic Process in the Family of Nations	273
XXI.	What Will You Do With Your Life?	295
Index		317

Preface

THE world is changing. It never stands still. Such factors as the supersonic speed airplane, electricity, atomic power, hydrogen and cobalt bombs, are effecting unbelievable transformations in human life. But vastly more revolutionary in their potentialities are the moral and spiritual forces available to every human personality. To be effective, these *must be applied to life* and it is to stimulate our action in this area that the author has dedicated this book.

The treatment is the culmination of nearly fifty years of study and activity and the conviction that religion and action cannot be separated. The life of prayer leads to love in action and consecrated action leads to prayer. Consequently at the close of each chapter a prayer has been added.

I am indebted to a great many world leaders whose quotations have been used before each chapter. The effort has been to arouse thought, to challenge the conscience and we have not hesitated also to take a kindling spark from relatively unknown thinkers.

I want to thank the experts in many fields who have read these chapters and given me suggestions. None of them are responsible for what is written herein but the book has been immeasurably improved because of their joint efforts. Among the many who have read chapters, I want especially to thank: Prof. Paul E. Scherer of Union Theological Seminary for reading "Dinosaur Power is Outmoded"; Dr. Edward L. Young for reading "The Subtle Poisoning of the People"; Prof. Colston E. Warne of Amherst College for reading "Economic Illiteracy"; Prof. Harlan J. Smith of the Astronomy Department of Yale University for reading "Enlarge Your Horizons"; Prof. John Bennett of Union Theological Seminary for reading "The Challenge of Communism"; Rev. Robert Luccock of the Church of the Redeemer, New Haven, for reading "Church and Synagogue are Indispensable"; Mr. Wilder Foote, Director of the Press and Publications Divi-

xii *Preface*

sion of the United Nations for reading "The Democratic Process in the Family of Nations"; Rev. E. Paul Sylvester of the Edgewood Congregational Church of New Haven for reading "What Will You Do With Your Life?"; Professor Joseph Fletcher for his suggestions; and finally to Dr. E. Stanley Jones for writing the Introduction to this volume. I am also indebted to many others for their encouragement.

J. D.

Part I

The Present Social Order

God hath not given us the spirit of fear; but of power, and love, and a sound mind.

II TIMOTHY 1:7

The art of progress is to preserve order amid change, and to preserve change amid order. Life refuses to be embalmed alive.

ALFRED N. WHITEHEAD

CHAPTER I

Whither Bound

If any one thing can be said to have been proven in human history, it is the universality of change. You who are reading these words are changing. Nations are changing. Civilizations rise and fall. Greek civilization was once the highest in the world. China, centuries ago, considered herself the most advanced nation and contributed gunpowder and many philosophic theories to our common store of knowledge.

Rome rose to commanding eminence only to fall of inner decay. There is considerable evidence to show that all civilizations pass thru a cycle of rise and decay. The feudal system went down, imperialism is on the way out, and slavery is all but ended. There is no reason to think that either capitalism or communism will permanently remain unchanged. Today we must begin to prepare for the new era of tomorrow. We are already entering an age of electronics. What does that presage for the future?

In the past few centuries our social and moral climate has changed far more slowly than our technical skills.

Few people on our earth have really known freedom. Perhaps there have been in the neighborhood of fifty billion people who have lived since the time of Christ. Of these, it is doubtful if even three per cent have lived in freedom. In America we are fortunate to have come out of a heritage of freedom even if it is being dangerously challenged today. The crucial question is: Which way are we heading?

The United States wrote into the Constitution the Bill of Rights, guaranteeing freedom so far as any Constitution could. Our system provides incentives to those who achieve. The condition of the workers has been steadily improving over the years. For example, in 1870 Studebaker workers had a sixty-hour week for which they received only $9.60. But by 1947 they were earning $60.00 for a forty-hour week. In the early 1920's the workers in the United States Steel Corporation had a seven-day week and a twelve-hour day. Today they, too, have a forty-hour week. Gradually the workers have won the right to organize into effective unions, and this has brought high wages and unemployment compensation, besides many other benefits. Today they are beginning to demand an annual wage.

While the condition of the workers has been improving, the corporations have grown bigger. General Motors, for example, operates over one hundred plants. We are working towards a system in the United States in which individual initiative, group organization thru collective bargaining, collective responsibility, and government by the people are all jointly in operation. We even have government ownership thru such projects as the Tennessee Valley Authority where control is decentralized. We are trying to work out a system in which government will be helpful in the economic life without being oppressive. It may be that government operation of a small sector of certain industries may be the only effective obstacle to monopoly. At any rate we have reached the place where too much control of government by big business may be dangerous.

But every society tends to think it is a paragon of virtue, that at least it is civilized and that its enemies or those it does not understand are pagans or devils. Rome considered every one but Romans to be barbarians. One hundred years ago the Japanese nation thought herself superior to all others and that foreigners were devils. When the American Revolution occurred, Great Britain thought our patriots should be shot. We have not advanced far in our ability to view other nations objectively.

The United States now in turn prides herself on being far advanced. "Do we not have the greatest productive mechanism on the globe? Do we not have more automobiles than any one else?" Altho we were the only nation actually to use the atom bomb against an enemy, we think that it is perfectly safe for us to have a stock pile of hydrogen bombs and implements for bacteriological warfare because we will never use them except after being attacked! Altho we take great pride in our own revolutionary history we are fearful of present day revolutions in Europe, Asia, or Africa. "These are different. Are they not against the established forces of law and order?" This in spite of the fact that many of them are opposing much the same imperialism against which our forefathers revolted. The United States has recently had the greatest wave of fear and hysteria in her history.

Because of all this, it becomes dangerous in any society to attack existing prejudices, rationalizations, and stereotypes. Yet this is precisely what the patriots of every age have done, and it is what took Jesus to the cross.

Those whom we call the American Patriots of '76 had experienced political and economic repressions and had a passionate love of liberty —"even unto death." A sense of the worth of the common man was growing steadily as the young Republic passed its fiftieth birthday and continued, with a new and evolving conception of a just and righteous nation.

It is easy not to sense the great changes that have taken place in our native country. From 1775 to 1875 we won our independence politically, financially, and even culturally. We completed the conquest of a Continent and we abolished slavery.

Today we have become a World Power and both economically and militarily it is recognized that we are in the lead of the nations in the world. We have a great deal to be proud of. The Statue of Liberty in New York harbor typifies our belief in freedom for all, the motto "In God We Trust" carried on many of our coins typifies our heritage of religious belief. Our great technological progress has brought us to the forefront of mechanical development. On the whole we live more luxuriously, if not comfortably, than any other people on the globe.

Still our liberty has been tarnished when, as the American Civil Liberties Union says, at one time we refused to let Chinese citizens go back to China, or let some of the representatives from England, accredited as Non-governmental Observers to the United Nations, have the freedom of New York City.

The pastor of the Vine Street Christian Church of Nashville, Tennessee, asks these questions:

Is it God we trust when we listen to those who say our salvation hinges on technical science and the art of mass murder?

Is it God we trust when we rest our hope for peace in political action and organization?

We might add, Is it God we trust when we spend over seven times as much on tobacco and liquor as we do on religion? Is it God we trust when, in the *Saturday Review of Literature* (Feb. 6, 1954), it can be said: "Historically the American people long ago abandoned their traditional scruples about intervening in the affairs of other peoples?"

I have faith in America. I am inspired by our great historic record for liberty and justice. I can wholeheartedly subscribe to the traditions of our great Republic and the principles for which it stands, "one nation indivisible, with liberty and justice for all." But I believe that the price of liberty is eternal vigilance. The greatest safeguard to progressive implementation of justice with liberty is when the bulk of the citizens believe sincerely in religion and *practice their faith*.

We believe the real patriot is the one who tries to make his country better than it is, and the real traitor is the one who, while parroting his loyalty, in practise denies to some one else the very principles of liberty, equality, and fraternity in which he pretends to believe. It is in this faith that this book has been written and in the hope that it may stimulate us to move forward on the pathway to happiness, justice and freedom for all mankind.

Let us then examine critically some of the characteristics of our present social order, to see if we can get any new insights on what changes should be advanced or retarded. Before we do this let us turn to religion itself to see if it has today any guiding principles which will help our analysis and aid us in changing our own lives.

Perhaps we shall find that the greatest moment in life is when we *persistently begin to say yes to God*.

Prayer

O God of Love, we humbly confess our weaknesses both as individuals and as a nation. Forgive us our failures, our selfishness, and our common tendency to self-righteousness. We ask Thy pardon wherever we have failed to follow Thy will for us or for our country. Purge from our hearts our complacency with things as they are.

We know that all things, both ourselves and our nation, are in process of change. Help us to see the ways to advance towards Thee and Thy righteousness rather than towards temporal and ulterior ends. Above all, guard us from indifference and cynicism towards the problems of our time. May Thy light and truth so dominate our lives that we may say, "I can do all things through Christ which strengtheneth me." So help us God. Amen.

The Bible has been the Magna Charta of the poor and the oppressed.

T. H. Huxley

The heart of his heart was religion. But no man shares his life with God whose religion does not flow out, naturally and without effort, into all relations of his life and reconstruct everything that it touches.

Walter Rauschenbusch

May we help forward the coming of social justice! Our place ought always to be beside the poor and the humble, those who labour and perish . . .

We find ourselves at a point in the history of the world when the peoples, oppressed and sacrificed as they have been for a number of centuries, are organizing themselves for their defence against an exploitation which is becoming more and more humiliating and cruel.

Romain Rolland in *Message of the East,* Vol. XXVI, No. 2.

CHAPTER II

Religion:
Opiate or Dynamic Power?

THE world has been telescoped into a small community where we are all next door neighbors. It makes no difference whether we have sensed the full implications of what has happened, the revolution with all its consequences has taken place. Yes, and it is playing with fire to be indifferent to others who are in need anywhere in the world. If wealth in one little family group, say the United States of America, callously remains indifferent to dismal poverty in another, say Africa, danger looms. Over a billion people of Asia, Africa, and Latin America are waking up. They refuse to sit silent while they are exploited or remain in darkness. They want an end of colonialism, landlordism and ignorance *and they want it now*. When history is written in the next century this new revolutionary feeling will rank very much higher in importance than our little quarrels about Communism and the police state. We will be judged by the concrete *steps we have taken* to help forward or retard the aspirations of our brothers in Asia and Africa. Our fulminations against Communism will not count heavily in our favor.

Now true religion should be a dynamic, powerful force making us go out into the entire world helping our brothers and sisters overthrow landlordism, exploitation, poverty, ignorance and disease; on the other hand religion can be an opiate which leaves us indifferent and smug in the comfortable church to which we belong. Sometimes the members of a great cathedral, a synagogue or a church may have a faith, but they seem paralyzed from translating it into the community and national life. Frank Laubach, one of our great missionary leaders, has this to say about what we have actually been doing: "The so-called 'Christian Nations' have had a really tremendous crusade—but it was to go forth and exploit the world for profit, *not* to save it. Lured by gold and not by zeal for the kingdom of God, 'Christians' have spread all over the world to take what they could get."[1] The most powerful bulwark against Communism is a *vital, active* Faith; the greatest peril is a spiritual vacuum.

The problem confronting the world is essentially: freedom vs. colonialism, hunger vs. plenty, ignorance vs. knowledge, war vs. peace and spiritual power vs. selfish indifference. Some way, somehow, society must be saved from the moral rot and social disintegration which ever threaten to engulf us.

Religion in the churches and synagogues can be ever so beautiful, with the most awe inspiring music, deep worded prayers, and the most wonderful mosaic windows and still lull the believer into the mistaken belief that the symbols and the spiritual trappings are all he really needs. Thus many a nominal Christian becomes a pagan in business or in any other endeavor in which he may be engaged.

Down through all history religion has been either an opiate or it has been a dynamic power, sometimes far greater than the hydrogen or cobalt bomb. When the Children of Israel bowed before a graven image of stone, it was an opiate; when they began to accept and practice the ten commandments, it became more dynamic.

When Martin Luther reached the age of twenty-two, his father desired him to become a lawyer. Had he done so his religion would in all probability have been an opiate but Martin Luther refused and went into the Cloister where his religion became dynamic and eventually he challenged the Papacy and began the series of courageous responses to inner convictions which resulted in the Reformation.

Albert Schweitzer might have remained a musician all his life, but religion was like a dynamic force ever leading him on to new and outgiving adventures. It was eventually to take him as a medical missionary to Africa where he would have a life of service within the spiritual ideal of justice and brotherhood for even the most needy outcast. For him reverence for life is love in action. On receiving the Nobel Peace Prize in 1954 Schweitzer said,

[1] Frank C. Laubach, *Wake Up or Blow Up,* New York, 1951, p. 26.

"What is important is that we should recognize jointly that we are guilty of inhumanity. The horror of this experience [two world wars] should shake us out of our torpor, so that we turn our will and our hopes toward the coming of an era in which war will be no more. That will and that hope can have only one result: The attainment, by a new spirit, of that higher reason which could deter us from making deadly use of the power which is at our disposal." No man could say that who has not made his religion dynamic.

Johann Sebastian Bach, perhaps the greatest universal composer in human history, was for twenty-seven years director of music at a church in Leipzig, Germany. If religion to him had been merely a means to make a living he would have probably lived, like so many other organists, relatively unknown. But Bach tried to make God the center of his life. He was determined to reflect through his music the spiritual power of the divine. He wanted to light a candle for God in the heart of every soul that heard his music. As a result Bach's music has spread around the world and long after his death, is inspiring millions to catch a fleeting glimpse of divine love and power.

Sir Wilfred Grenfell while in Medical School in London was fired by a spark from Dwight L. Moody. He decided to devote his life to the service of God. The result was that all up and down the Coast of Labrador, hospitals, orphan asylums, schools and churches are a testimonial to his religious power. When the writer toured the Coast of Labrador with him we were aground three times, on fire once, once we lost our anchor and once a great iceberg crashed up against us and deposited tons of ice on board. On asking a Newfoundland fisherman what he thought of Dr. Grenfell, he replied, "There'll be more folks as'll miss the doctor when he dies than'll miss King George." Yet Grenfell's whole life was fired by a spark from the anvil of another great soul who at seventeen years of age in Boston decided to give his entire life to God.

An entire book could be filled with the adventures of men and women who were transformed once they surrendered their entire selves to God and His power.

Here, for example, is a student at Cambridge University in England known by his fellows as "Bill, the cynic." Yet underneath he had a spark of faith for when he had offended a friend he wrote, "I know that I am hard, proud, scornful, bitter and insulting very often and always selfish; but I don't like you to treat me as though I wasn't trying to do a bit better."

Later on he went with Captain Scott as physician on the ill-fated expedition to the South Pole. As they lay dying in the snow Captain Scott wrote this about him, "I should like you to know how splendid he was at the end. Everlastingly cheerful and ready to sacrifice himself for others. His eyes have a comfortable blue look of hope and his mind is peaceful with the satisfaction of his faith in regarding himself a part of the scheme of the Almighty."

A sociological study could be made of the action pattern of those who genuinely took the dynamic power of religion and let it transform their lives. A partial study, incomplete though it is, brings out the following points which could be supplemented by many others. If we care to transform our religion from that of passivity, and stereotyped conformity to the pattern of those about us, perhaps these behavior patterns which emerged from the study may be stimulating.

1. Start the day in prayer but don't let it be a form, these leaders *lived their prayers*.

Everyone of the great prophetic leaders depended more on God than they did on themselves alone, and it gave them a courage and power which was irresistible.

2. The greatest leaders seemed to start *by reforming themselves first*. They were quite ready to admit their own mistakes. Albert Einstein, for instance, confessed that prior to the Nazi accession of power he had opposed the churches. Said he, "Being a lover of freedom, when the revolution came to Germany, I looked to the universities to defend it, knowing that they always boasted of their devotion to the cause of truth; but no, the universities immediately were silenced. Then I looked to the great editors of the newspapers whose flaming editorials in days gone by had proclaimed their love of freedom; but they like the universities were silenced in a few short weeks ... Only the church stood squarely across the path of Hitler's campaign for suppressing truth. I never had any special interest in the church before, but now I felt a great affection and admiration because the church alone had had the courage and persistence to stand for intellectual truth and moral freedom. I am forced thus to con-

fess that what I once despised I now praise unreservedly."

3. In general, they tried to *help every person they met beginning with those they saw daily and extending to all*. Jesus helped the woman taken in adultery although the law of the day said she should be stoned to death. In doing so he made the crowd realize that they also were guilty in their hearts.

After one of his meetings the famous evangelist, Dwight Moody, was approached by a locomotive engineer who said he had decided to go as a missionary and convert the heathen. Moody replied to him, "Is your fireman a Christian?" "I don't know. I never asked him," the engineer replied. "Well," said Moody, "why don't you start with your fireman?"

4. *Keep first things first by recognizing that every minute of your time belongs to God and Society*. The world-famous Archbishop Temple of England once said Christians "must undertake the heroic, intellectual and practical task of giving to spiritual faith a living content over against the immensely effective 'this worldliness' of Marxism and secular humanism." This means that Christians have to be more effective servants of God every minute of their lives than the Communists are to their ideal. No one could watch Sir Wilfred Grenfell of Labrador piloting his hospital ship through the icebergs in the early morning, ministering to his patients in a little fishing village all afternoon and speaking at a church in the evening without recognizing that his life was demonstrating his message.

5. Another rule that seems to hold true for all great religious leaders is: AIM TO GIVE NOT GET.

The greatest religious leaders have not amassed fortunes. Nearly every one of them has been poor in this world's goods. Mahatma Gandhi of India is a good illustration. Although he started as a successful lawyer he gave away all his money and ended up penniless. Apparently the injunction of Jesus has held true down through the ages, "It is harder for a rich man to enter into the Kingdom of Heaven than it is for a camel to go through a needle's eye." Conversely those who have spiritual wealth do not have material riches.

6. The sixth rule dominating these men's lives is: *Perfect Love casteth out fear*.

Joseph Neshima was born in Japan when it was death to be a Christian and death to leave the island empire. When Neshima became a Christian he cast out fear. He determined to leave Japan and study in America. Without even telling his parents he went out to an American boat. The Captain threatened to send him ashore. Neshima simply knelt on the deck and prayed to God. This melted the Captain's heart; he allowed the boy to stay. He graduated from Amherst, then from the theological seminary and lived to found the largest Christian University in Japan.

How often we see nominal Christians in America who are afraid even to sign petitions they believe in or to join organizations working for the public good.

7. *See the other fellow's point of view, not merely your own.*

Again and again great Christian missionaries will point out to us the viewpoint of the native people among whom they work even when it is directly at variance with Western ideas. Both John R. Mott, the missionary statesman and Frank C. Laubach whose effort has helped millions to read their own languages, repeatedly point out the other nation's viewpoint. Laubach, for instance, says: "Our losing the world to Communism is our own fault wholly because we are blind to the situation ... The bottom four-fifths of the world are going Communist because they are hungry, terribly unhappy, and grimly determined to raise out of their destitution ... They love us when we help them, they hate us when we don't."[2]

Christians everywhere should be less ready to mouth the criticisms and hatreds of the press and radio towards other nations and more ready to follow Christ in trying to understand and love even our enemies.

8. These great leaders exemplify this rule: *Always Be a Doer Not Simply a Dreamer*.

Take the case of Xavier, a student in the University of Paris in the Sixteenth Century. He loved to have a good time and didn't bother much about religion but when at length the Christian revelation came to him in all its seriousness he changed his whole life pattern. Every minute became precious. He did not know it but he only had ten years to live. He blazed a trail for the faith in the vast Portuguese-

[2] Ibid, p. 101 ff.

Indian Empire beginning in 1542. He was the first to preach Christ to the Japanese and was trying to enter China when he died in 1552 and has gone down in history as St. Francis Xavier.

Remember how the devil tempts the good man in *The Screwtape Letters*. He comments, "That great thing is to prevent his doing anything. As long as he does not convert it into action, it does not matter how much he thinks about . . . repentance. Let the brute wallow in it . . . The more often he feels without acting, the less he will ever be able to act, and, in the long run, the less he will be able to feel."[3]

9. *Don't be Provincial, Be World-Minded.*

Dr. John R. Mott after his conversion, might have remained relatively unknown had he not become world-minded. He coined the phrase, "The Evangelization of the World in This Generation." The inspiration from his life and work has reverberated around the world. In referring to Russian Communism, this great leader told the writer, "I am so busy trying to help the people of Russia and aid their religious life that I do not waste time in long diatribes against their Communist rulers."

10. Another rule of these leaders seems to be: WHEN YOU GET A VISION SHARE IT.

This has been true of all the prophets. It was true of John the Baptist and it has been true of all great religious leaders of our time. They have shouted their message from the house tops. But how many ordinary church members fail to share their Christian beliefs with anyone. Even many of the ministers are fearful of their Boards and tone down their message. When the writer urged a prominent minister in New England to take a stand in favor of union labor and better conditions for the workers, he replied, "What would you do if you believed in following Jesus Christ but none of your church Board believed in Him at all?" Other ministers have actually broken down and wept in telling why they cannot speak the vision that God has given them. "We have to think of the fate and welfare of our wives and children," they confessed. How different this is from John Calvin, and Faustus Socinius, who spoke the truth as God gave them to see the truth even when it involved persecution and danger.

The same is true of Karl Barth, a great religious leader of Switzer-

---

[3] Lewis, C. S. *The Screwtape Letters*, p. 69.

land, who was exiled when the Nazis came to power. Walter Rauschenbusch in the United States is another great religious leader who shared his vision with the world. In fact we can say that all of the greatest religious leaders have spoken what they considered to be God's truth fearlessly.

11. NEVER STAND STILL

When one gets in a comfortable spot or in a rut, it is easy to stand still. These leaders never did that. One vision led to another, one mission of mercy led to a whole series. Did Gandhi ever rest content with his previous achievements, or John R. Mott or any of the prophets? No, they all pushed on as did Francis of Assisi and George Fox, the Founder of the Society of Friends. In fact, Fox was imprisoned eight times before his death.

12. *Cultivate a Constant Dependence on Strength From God.*

If we take all the distinguished men who have delivered the Lyman Beecher lectures at Yale University Divinity School since its inception, now over eighty, in all, we would find in the by and large that if there is any one characteristic that is common to most of them it is a constant dependence on God. In fact the more spiritual intensity a preacher or prophet has, the more effective his work seems to be, provided he has the other qualities which are necessary.

We are living in a world which is steadily increasing its command over material things. As we thus increase our knowledge of science, we should make certain that our spiritual resources are growing even more rapidly. Prayer can do this more than any other force that we know. Its power is illimitable. For those of us who want to make our lives effective to the maximum, let us catch the contagion from other great souls. Let us refuse to accept religion as an opiate to lull us into complacency and stereotyped thinking. Let us rather accept religion as an invitation to launch out into a new dimension, a dimension where love and truth are fused into spiritual power.

Prayer

Place upon us, we pray, the responsibility to make our faith dynamic. Send us out in a ceaseless quest to find Thee, the source of all power. We thank Thee for the irresistible incentives which come into every life which is tuned to the spirit of Jesus Christ.

We are grateful for all those in human history who have led others to rise above the conventional standards of their time. Help us to rise above prejudice, suspicion and hate. May we be able so to reflect Thy love that it may unfailingly pass on to others with whom we daily associate.

Grant unto us persuasiveness, persistence and a sympathetic heart of goodwill as we go out into the highways and byways of life to serve Thee.

The road we travel is long, but at the end lies the grail of peace. And in the valley of peace we see the faint outlines of a new world, fertile and strong. . . . I believe that man stands on the eve of his greatest day. I know, too, that that day is not a gift but a prize; that we shall not reach it until we have won it.

ADLAI STEVENSON

The Tribe of the Helpers

The ways of the world are full of haste and turmoil;
I will sing of the tribe of the helpers who travel in peace.

He that turneth from the road to rescue another
Turneth toward his goal;
He shall arrive in time by the foot-path of mercy,
God will be his guide.

He that taketh up the burden of the fainting
Lighteneth his own load;
The Almighty will put his arms underneath him,
He shall lean upon the Lord.

He that speaketh comfortable words to mourners
Healeth his own hurt:
In time of grief they will come to his remembrance,
God will use them for balm.

He that careth for a wounded brother
Watcheth not alone:
There are three in the darkness together,
And the third is the Lord.

Blessed is the way of the helpers,
The companions of the Lord.

DR. HENRY VAN DYKE, *The Poems of Henry Van Dyke,* Scribner's 1911, p. 377.

CHAPTER III

Forward with the Prophets

EVERYONE seems to think he knows what religion is but for that very reason the term is a little vague. For example, a person can be said to be religious when he goes to church or synagogue and yet in reality he may be irreligious and merely conforming. On the other hand a person may be religious even without such attendance.

Sometimes it is said that a person is religious if he believes in God but this is only one aspect of being religious. According to the old traditions even the Devil is supposed to believe in God. Nor is a person completely religious merely because he does a good deed.

Some people call religion an instinct but this is hardly a definition. Another mistake is to say that being religious is to follow our own denominational faith alone. Others make the meaning so broad that it loses all point. They say, "Anyone who prays is religious."

Still others confuse religion with ethics, but it may be possible to be ethical and not religious. Sometimes we define religion in terms which are too narrow to take in all varieties of religious experience. Therefore instead of defining religion to include all forms from the primitive worshippers of fire down to present day existentialism, let us rather ask what is the highest form of religion. Each reader can make his own formulation but we will venture the following: *True religion is exemplified by anyone who has faith in a higher power which makes for righteousness; and who day by day increasingly manifests an invincible spirit of goodwill in action towards all men.* This is usually the result of a personal relation between man and God— man to God and God to man.

Now, man's world has changed and shrunk. Through a technological revolution old means of communication have been superseded. The radio, television and the jet plane have annihilated space. But in some ways we haven't changed much. We still have fears and hates; we still slaughter each other with scant thought of higher methods of dealing with conflict. Selfishness still raises its ugly head in the market place and in all the four corners of the earth.

Bergan Evans in *The Natural History of Nonsense* has this to say.[1]

We may be through with the past, but the past is not through with us. Ideas of the Stone Age exist side by side with the latest scientific thought. Only a fraction of mankind has emerged from the Dark Ages, and in the most lucid brains, as Logan Pearsall Smith has said, we come upon nests of caterpillars! Seemingly sane men entrust their wealth to star gazers and their health to witch doctors. Giant planes throb thru the stratosphere but half their passengers are wearing magic amulets and are protected from harm by voodoo incantations. Hotels boast of express elevators and a telephone in every room but omit thirteen from all floors and room numbers lest their guests be ill at ease.

Altho society does lip service to love, good-will and justice, all over the world there exists its negation—discrimination. In the southern states of the United States, Negroes are not allowed in the best hotels and restaurants and even while riding on the bus have to be separated from whites. Too often some such incident as this has happened: A Negro testifying against a sheriff who has done some evil deed, is not safe even in another state, and may be extradited and shot to death by the sheriff; with little done about it.

A man may be a great inventor, a great scientist and yet at the center of his life where dedication to working with God in his universe could provide invincible resources, there is human weakness. For example, the inventor of Frequency Modulation, and the superheterodyne receiving circuit, and one of the nation's leading radio pioneers, killed himself by jumping from the thirteenth floor in New York City in 1954.

All of which shows that the world needs the spiritual dynamic power of Moses and the prophets desperately, even if that was demonstrated thousands of years ago. Of course, there were false prophets in those days, just as there are today, who spoke to please those in

[1] P. 5.

power. But there were others who spoke in clear, forthright tones against the iniquities of the time. They had lofty spiritual insights. We need their voice today.

The belief that a religious leader cannot rise above the thought pattern of his era and his people is shown as absurd by the prophets of the Old Testament. When the Jewish tribes first came into Palestine they began to do reverence to a foreign god, Baal, who was supposed to help their crops to be fruitful. When the land was finally conquered by Saul and David, all the Jews did was to begin to call the Baal rites and ceremonies which they had been practising "ceremonies for Jehovah." Some of the religious rites to the god Baal involved immoral practises supposed to aid fertility. Hosea struck out against all this saying it was only a camouflaged Baalism. He urged the people to return to the pure and undefiled love of Jehovah. He portrayed the genuine religion of Jehovah as love for all that was good, and unalterable opposition to all that was evil and wicked. In other words, God's favor could only be obtained by the highest ethical conduct on the part of men, not by practising what was pleasing to their men of power.

Some of the later prophets continued to denounce the religion of sacrifices and forms, rather than genuinely ethical behavior. They saw clearly that corrupt government and depraved rulers might threaten the very existence of the state itself. Consequently there were those who even spoke out against their own rulers. Of course, the overwhelming majority of those called "prophets" at the time, championed the status quo and declared that all was "sweetness and light." They denounced such prophetic leaders as Micah, Amos and Hosea as "false prophets," or in effect, "Apostles of Discord." Time was to prove who were right, and history has shown that Amos and Hosea were on the side of a God of righteousness. Later on Jeremiah was to say, "In the prophets of Jerusalem I have seen a horrible thing . . . they strengthen the hands of evil doers, so that no one turns from his evil way." (Jer. 23:14) But it must not be forgotten that as long as the Jewish nation stood, so long were the prophets of doom denounced and condemned by the great majority. In the centuries following, we often find a similar situation and even in our own day those who tell of evil conditions and condemn great military spending and the reign of great corporations may be called "subversive" or "fellow travellers."

When the Jews were driven into exile, then the prophets of optimism were shown to have been deceptive, blind leaders of the blind. Ezekiel at the time of national collapse and the capture of Jerusalem, declared to the people that it was not God who had betrayed them but that they had betrayed God. Their defeat was the natural consequence of their guilt. Ezekiel said that the Jewish people go to the synagogue all right, they listen to the words of God, "but they will not obey them; for with their mouths they make a show of love, but their minds are set upon their selfish gain." (Ezek. 33:30–33)

Most religious believers revere the Bible and the prophets but they seldom ask, "What would it really mean if I should follow a prophetic policy for our time?" Social betterment appears to follow three specific steps. First, there is agitation; second, there is legislative enactment; and finally there must be education, if the new program is to succeed. The agitator precedes the legislator. William Lloyd Garrison pleaded for freedom for the slaves long before Lincoln secured the legal enactment of it. Even after enactment, a law may fail unless there is adequate education of the public. This is true in many of our traffic laws. It may be illegal to drive while under the influence of liquor but unless the public is educated the statute is a dead letter. This is why the National Safety Council has continually to spend time and money all over the nation changing the way people's minds work.

In the Bible the prophets Amos, Micah, Isaiah and Jeremiah were the agitators. Here are some of their general exhortations:

Seek justice, relieve the oppressed. (Isa. 1:17.)
Execute ye justice and righteousness, and deliver the spoiled out of the hand of the oppressor; and do no wrong, do no violence. (Jer. 22:3.)
Rescue the poor and needy; deliver them out of the hand of the wicked. (Ps. 82:4.)

A great many passages are directed to the lawyers, as is the following:

Open thy mouth, judge righteously, and plead the cause of the poor and needy. (Prov. 31:9.)

Nehemiah attacked the holders of mortgages, who were too severe with their tenants in these words:

Would ye sell your brethren? . . . Restore, I pray you to them, even this day, their fields, their vineyards, their oliveyards, and their houses, also the hundred pieces of silver and the corn, the wine and the oil, that ye exact of them. (Nehemiah 5:11.)

Sometimes the prophets denounced an entire nation:

The people of the land have used oppression, and exercised robbery, and have wronged the poor and the needy, and have oppressed the stranger unlawfully. (Ezek. 22:29.)

The prophets did not hesitate to condemn the rulers and leaders of the people as in the following two passages:

The Lord will enter into judgment
With the elders of His people, and the Prince thereof;
It is ye that have eaten up the vineyard;
The spoil of the poor is in your houses.
What mean ye that ye crush my people,
And grind the face of the poor? (Isaiah 3:14, 15.)
Woe unto them that decree unrighteous decrees,
And to the writers that write iniquity;
To turn aside the needy from judgment,
And to take away the right of the poor of my people,
That widows may be their spoil,
And that they may make the fatherless their prey! (Isaiah 10:1, 2.)

The wealthy come in for special castigation:

Through the pride of the wicked the poor is hotly pursued . . .
He lieth in wait in a secret place as a lion in his lair,
He lieth in wait to catch the poor;
He doth catch the poor, when he draweth him up in his net. (Ps. 10:2, 9.)

Shall not all the workers of iniquity know it,
Who eat up my people as they eat up bread? . . .
Ye would put to shame the counsel of the poor. (Ps. 14:4, 6.)

The wicked have drawn out the sword, and have bent their bow;
To cast down the poor and needy. (Ps. 37:14.)

Naturally the prophets attacked what were serious evils in the day of the particular prophet. For example, here are some denunciations of the practise of compelling poor people to mortgage some article before they could get a loan:

Thou hast taken pledges of thy brother for nought, and stripped the naked of their clothing. (Job 22:6.)
They drive away the ass of the fatherless, take the widow's ox for a pledge. (Job 24:3.)
There are those who snatch the fatherless child from the breast, and take in pledge the infant of the poor. (Job 24:9.)
I was very angry . . . and said to them: You are exacting interest each from his brother . . . Return to them this very day their fields, their vineyards, their olive orchards and their houses. (Nehemiah 5:6, 7, 11.)

Naturally the seizure of property for unpaid loans was violently attacked:

Woe to those who join house to house, who add field to field. (Isa. 5:8.)
They covet fields, and seize them; and houses and take them away. (Mic. 2:2.)
He hath violently taken away a house. (Job 20:19.)
They violently take away flocks. (Job 24:2.)

As in the recent case of Negroes in the South or of natives in South Africa, in Biblical days there was a method of foreclosing the body of the living person and forcing him into labor. Amos has this to say about such practise:

For three transgressions of Israel, and for four, I will not revoke the punishment; because they sell the righteous for silver and the needy for a pair of shoes—they that trample the head of the poor into the dust of the earth. (Amos 2:6, 7.)

Amos also denounces injustice in our modern practise of share-cropping:

Therefore because you trample upon the poor and take from him exactions of wheat, you have built houses of hewn stone, but you shall not dwell in them. (Amos 5:11.)

Nearly all the prophets castigated profiteering which is a very modern and contemporary evil:

> Hear this, you who trample upon the needy, and bring the poor of the land to an end . . . and deal deceitfully with false balances, that we may buy the poor for silver and the needy for a pair of sandals, and sell the refuse of the wheat? (Amos 8:4–6.)

The prophets are protectors of the poor against the men of wealth and power:

> Rob not the weak because he is weak, neither crush the poor in the gate. (Prov. 22:22.)
>
> He that oppresseth the poor blasphemeth his Maker. (Prov. 14.31.)

In the United States today we have those who believe in more and better T.V.A.'s, in more public ownership of power projects. We have those who believe that organized labor should get a yearly wage the same as business executives do. We have those who believe in socialized medicine and increased social security and a host of other measures. Then there are those who are bitterly opposed to public ownership, to cooperatives and to organized labor. There is little doubt where the prophets of old would stand in this division. They would protest against injustice and oppression and stand squarely beside the poor and against selfishness which flowers in exploitation and riches.

Today ministers often are told to keep out of controversial areas. They must steer clear of great social issues or they will lose their "spiritual power." On the other hand one of our greatest students of the prophets concludes, "Confine religion to the personal, it grows rancid, morbid."[1]

It is sometimes charged that ministers who preach the "social gospel" are too optimistic. If the truth were told they are generally pessimistic. Similarly the prophets in the Old Testaments were prophets of doom. Amos predicted the fall of the Northern kingdom and the exile of the people. The modern social prophet may declare that if we continue our trust in military might, atomic and hydrogen bombs, and our backing of imperialism and landlordism, Communism will continue to win around the world. The prophetic preacher may

---

[1] George Adams Smith—*The Book of the Twelve Prophets* I, p. 25.

even say that if profit, materialism and selfish gain continue to dominate our policies, disaster will strike even the wealthiest country in the world.

The greatest stress of the prophets was on righteousness. They insisted that one could genuinely worship God only by a *right life.* Any substitute for righteousness was harmful, even sacrificial ritual. "I desire goodness and not sacrifice," was Hosea's warning.[2] Like the blast of a trumpet, Micah in these words contrasts ceremonial religion with inner righteousness: "Shall I come before him with burnt offerings, with calves a year old? Will the Lord be pleased with thousands of rams, with ten thousands of rivers of oil? Shall I give my first-born for my transgression, the fruit of my body for the sin of my soul? He has showed you, O man, what is good; and what doth the Lord require of you but to do justice, and to love kindness, and to walk humbly with your God?"[3]

After wars and disasters not unlike in some degree, what has happened in modern times, Isaiah warns the nation that they must reform and make restitution, that unless they do, God will avert his face from their hypocritical worship. "When you spread forth your hands I will hide my eyes from you; even though you make many prayers, I will not listen; your hands are full of blood. Wash yourselves; make yourselves clean; remove the evil of your doings from before my eyes; cease to do evil, learn to do good; seek justice, correct oppression; defend the fatherless, plead for the widow."[4]

We do not have the sacrificial system of the Old Testament. Our modern method is to go to church every week, cushioned comfortably, listen to a beautiful choir rendering sacred music, sing songs, kneel in prayer, contribute to a collection, listen to a noble and, we hope, inspiring message and return home satisfied. The prophets insisted on self-sacrificing action. They demanded action on the great moral problems of the day. Religion and ethics, they proclaimed, are inseparable. Yet President Eisenhower's Budget for the year 1954 while not as large as the Truman Budget still has some $65.6 billion or 68% for war preparations, 22% for fixed charges (largely payments

[2] Hosea 6:6.
[3] Micah 6:6-8.
[4] Isaiah 1:15-17.

on past wars), roughly 5% for the cost of government and 5% for all the rest of the needs of the people.

Christmas is the birthday of the Christ. Here we celebrate the anniversary of the Prince of Peace. Yet what do we do specifically on that great day for the cause of peace? Our country may be fighting in Korea, we may be spending more money than ever before in human history for armaments; what do we do "to turn spears into ploughshares" at the Christmas season? Do we send out messages urging that our military budget be cut, that we seek disarmament, that we use greater skill towards solving world problems thru creative methods involved in the injunction "love our enemies"? Some may do this but usually we have instead, a beautifully lighted Christmas tree loaded with decorations and toys. We give and receive gifts from our friends. We celebrate with a glorious Christmas dinner. In a word, we have a good time for ourselves, our friends and relatives but we seldom stop to ask, "What can we do at this Christmastide to change the public morality? What can we do to stop the riotous expenditures for instruments of force and violence which are eating like a cancer into international goodwill? What can we do to stop imperialism, poverty, landlordism in Asia, Africa or elsewhere?"

The evils which the prophets denounced were not only personal, but extraordinary in their social and national impact. The prophets did not so much laud the man of temperance and chastity, as the crusader for social righteousness. They thundered against *injustice and oppression* in every form. They proclaimed the truth that if the nation had a low morality, if the nation were backing military power instead of God, if the nation were embarked on the pathway of materialism and selfishness, then, private virtue alone would not save the individual. He *must* attack the national evils. He must fight for the poor and the oppressed.

In our day the world is smaller in point of time than was the Kingdom of Judah in the days of the prophets. The Bible says that if one member suffers, all members suffer. This is true of our entire little planet today. Therefore, we are charged before God to redeem the world and every part of it from sin, from poverty, from exploitation, from ignorance, from imperialism. It is to the credit of the church that we have a vast missionary movement whose total effect is incalculable. Nevertheless too often we have been blind, indifferent, or we think it unwise to attack the gross injustice now being practised in South Africa on the natives, for instance. It is more than doubtful, also, if we can mend social evils by declaring war on a foreign power. The history of the past two thousand years has seemed to indicate that for every problem this alleviates, scores of new ones are created. Neither is preparedness the way out. We can prepare millions of bayonets. The only thing we cannot do is sit on them. Military preparedness is more likely to become the master rather than the servant of the people.

The fact of the matter is, then, that the prophets are very modern. We, too, have our poverty, our loan sharks, our racial discrimination, our profiteering by malefactors of great wealth. In America in the interest of the common people everywhere we probably do need compulsory health insurance or some form of socialized medicine, more effective social security, better provisions for education and recreation, the preservation of civil liberties, the prevention of unemployment, the abolition of sales tax on necessities, and the end of racial discrimination.

In South Africa we have conditions where eighty per cent of the people do not have the vote and where thousands are dragged away into involuntary slavery. We have been largely indifferent, if not perpetuating imperialism in Indo-China and other countries, even supplying arms and ammunition to crush the aspirations of the overwhelming mass of the people. Let us support the religious leaders that are standing up for the rights of the people as the prophets did in the days of the Old Testament. Too often today as in the past they are castigated by those in power. McCarthyism may call them Communists or fellow travellers. Today we stand in danger of selling great public enterprises of natural power to the highest bidder, of turning over atomic power developed by the people's money, to private interests. We are in a period when great corporations rule in the seats of the mighty. We need great prophetic religious leaders who will make their religion live in terms of justice and liberty not in mere platitudinous words and prayers of comfort.

Prayer

O God, we thank Thee for the prophets of every age who have galvanized men into action. Develop in us a stalwart righteousness that we may do for our time what they did for theirs. Save us from the conventional morality that believes in the piling up of wealth, and make us alert to search for opportunities to help others. Save us from the tyranny of the nonessential and the injurious and set us on the pathway of doing good like our Master.

Guard us from breaking faith with the highest visions that Thou hast vouchsafed to us in moments of our greatest spiritual power. Help us to undertake big things in partnership with Thee but may we ever remember that it's the quality of our deeds—not their size that counts. Show us what we can do to make our community, our nation and the world a better place for men to live in. Help us to realize that good resolutions alone do not feed the hungry, clothe the naked and bring peace to the world. May we be ready to act with our whole lives to bring happiness to all men everywhere beginning in our own homes. So help us to follow in the footsteps of the prophets that we may be partners with Thee in all we do For Jesus's sake. Amen.

There never was a good war or a bad peace.
>	BENJAMIN FRANKLIN

Force is no remedy.
>	JOHN BRIGHT in Speech on the Irish Troubles (1880)

There has never been a war yet which, if the facts had been put calmly before the ordinary folk, could not have been prevented. The common man is the greatest protection against war.
>	ERNEST BEVIN, in the House of Commons, 1945

America must offer the world a positive program. It must never accept, as a final fact, the division between East and West.
>	JAN MASARYK, 1947

We are not going to get involved militarily in any way on the island of Formosa. So far as I know, no responsible person in the government, no military man has ever believed that we should involve our forces in the island . . . We are honorable and decent people. We do not put forward words, as propagandists do in other countries to serve their advantage, only to throw them overboard when some change in events makes the position difficult for us.
>	SECRETARY OF STATE DEAN ACHESON, Jan. 5, 1950

In spite of all evidence to the contrary, the things that divide the world are trivial as compared with things that unite it.
>	RAYMOND FOSDICK

We forget that all men are brothers and members of the same great human family, that other nations have an equal right with us both to life and to prosperity, that it is never lawful nor even wise to dissociate morality from the affairs of practical life.
>	POPE PIUS XI

What we [the United States] do have to prove to the world is that we can help a country without destroying it. If the Air Force demolishes the roads, bridges, public utilities and factories of all Korea, the "victory" when it comes will indeed be Pyrrhic. Even if the operation is successful the patient will be dead.

WALTER LIPPMANN

At what point, then, is the approach of danger to be expected? I answer, if it ever reaches us, it must spring up among us. It cannot come from abroad. If destruction be our lot, we must ourselves be its author and finisher. As a nation of freemen, we must live through all time, or die by suicide.

ABRAHAM LINCOLN, 1837

CHAPTER IV

Dinosaur Power Is Outmoded

Two thousand years ago Jesus spoke in ringing tones that war, militarism, and extermination of the enemy were not the way to peace, happiness or morality. Today, after all the lessons of history, mankind has not yet learned to heed his words. Indeed, it would not be too much to say that War is now our deadliest disease. Our best generals have long recognized the futility of war. General Sherman said, "I am tired and sick of war. Its glory is all moonshine. It is only those who have neither fired a shot nor heard the shrieks and groans of the wounded who cry aloud for blood, more vengeance, more desolation. War is Hell." General H. H. Arnold says, "War is like fire, you prevent a fire or you can try and put it out, but you can't 'win' a fire, because fire is destruction." If you prefer General Douglas MacArthur, here is what he says, "You cannot control war; you can only abolish it. Those who shrug this off as idealistic are the real enemies of freedom—the real war mongers." Sir John Slessor, Marshal of the British Royal Air Force declares, "Today there is not the remotest chance of anyone winning a war." He says the time has now arrived that Winston Churchill predicted, ". . . When the advance of destructive weapons enables everyone to kill everybody else, no one will want to kill anybody at all." In most wars of the past disease killed far more than military arms. The influenza epidemic of 1918–9 killed 20 million people. The last war left 80% of the children of Europe tubercular.

World War III, if it comes, will probably slaughter more millions through its hydrogen and cobalt explosions than have died in all the wars in which man has been engaged since the birth of Christ.

The history of the Twentieth Century has been largely a record of man's warfare. Professor Sorokin maintains that wars are increasing in frequency, certainly they are more costly, more devastating and more deadly. Now, as the United Nations Charter says, wars begin in the minds of men and it is in the minds of men we must begin to build peace. The minds of men must be conditioned and trained to produce the bases of peaceful living. But so many Americans have already made up their minds. The deadly propaganda in radio, television and the press continuously do their work. Many Americans believe that the rulers of the Soviet Union are the villains and that if it were not for them, war would end. This was not true in World War I nor was it true in World War II. The fact is that the United States along with other nations of the world invaded the Soviet Union after World War I. Soviet Russia has never invaded the United States.

If it is said that peace would have been assured if Russia had lived up to her agreements after World War II, James P. Warburg, the banker and writer, maintains this assertion is false. He declares that these "past agreements have been given widely differing interpretations in Moscow and Washington; but they have been violated by all the signatories, to the point where they have become, to all intents and purposes, dead-letter covenants. If these agreements were to be enforced, the United States would be compelled to reverse some of its own major policies such as those relating to German and Japanese rearmament, the intended modification of the Italian peace treaty and our present plans regarding Formosa."[1]

On August 6, 1945 a man in an airplane dropped an atomic bomb and 80,000 men, women and children were annihilated. Of the 300 doctors in the city 260 were wiped out along with 1800 of the 2400 nurses and 26 of the 33 fire stations. The fact that the city was one of the centers of Christian missionary work is an ironical commentary on the effect of war.

Of course, since then we have developed bombs one thousand times more powerful. We do not know how effective bacteriological warfare would be. Prof. M. I. Oliphant long ago declared that a single gas attack with radio-active poisons would end all life over a radius of 1,000 miles.[2] Dr. Brock Chisholm says a new substance enables us

[1] James P. Warburg, *How to Co-Exist*, p. 208.
[2] The *Christian Century*, Dec. 5, 1945.

to destroy all of mankind with only seven ounces. We now know something of the terrible destructiveness of the hydrogen and cobalt bombs.

In 1952 a test hydrogen bomb exploded in the Marshall Islands. It tore a hole in the floor of the ocean a mile in diameter and 175 feet in depth. The Chairman of the Senate-House Atomic Energy Committee, W. Sterling Cole, declared that if the blast had been touched off in a modern city, it would have completely devastated an area three miles in all directions from the point of explosion. In addition, he declared, it would have blanketed an area up to 150 square miles.[3] If the bomb were exploded in New York City, for instance, it would have sunk and obliterated the whole mid-town area. In 1954 the hydrogen bomb was dropped with even more devastating effects.

Dr. Ralph E. Lapp, one of the developers of the first atom bomb, says that one hydrogen bomb if exploded close to the ground in Maryland, for instance, would jeopardize all lives over an area of 10,000 square miles. He believes twenty-eight well-placed hydrogen bombs would endanger the lives of fifty million United States citizens.[4]

In 1955, Bertrand Russell released an appeal to the world signed by Albert Einstein before his death and other noted scientists from many nations which read:

"In view of the fact that in any future world war nuclear weapons will certainly be employed, and that such weapons threaten the continued existence of mankind, we urge the governments of the world to realize, and to acknowledge publicly, that their purposes cannot be furthered by a world war, and we urge them, consequently, to find peaceful means for the settlement of all matters of dispute between them."

Unfortunately, our thinking has not kept pace with technological progress. We are still tied to outworn policies and tend to use new developments for war and preparation for war. The new weapons in some ways make us more irresponsible. The aviator of push-button warfare hardly realizes the awful massacre which he is inflicting on innocent men, women and children. What must be the attitude of pagan peoples to a Christianity which fails to condemn such weapons if, in fact, it does not sanction them? In the early days the pagan world

[3] The New York *Herald Tribune,* Feb. 18, 1954, p. 1.
[4] New York *Journal American,* Feb. 11, 1955, p. 5.

watched in amazement saying: "How these Christians love one another." Today they would probably say "How these Christians hate one another."

We tried in World War I to fight "to make the world safe for democracy," but it actually brought in Communism and Hitlerism. In World War II we were supposed to overthrow dictatorship and usher in freedom from want and fear. Actually it resulted in more dictatorship rather than less, and the United States, which won the conflict, has more fear than ever before in its history. Instead of peace we have been waging a "cold war" ever since the end of hostilities. In other words, we have embarked on the dubious policy of "perpetual war for perpetual peace." Mankind has achieved miracles in scientific production. We have the means to abolish poverty and want. But still we face the paradox that actually there is more poverty, more suffering in the world today than ever before in history. The reason for this unbelievably strange situation is that more and more of our wealth and our technology instead of removing the causes of war are being used for rearmament around the world which makes for more conflict. The United States which is the wealthiest country on the planet is spending some eighty percent of its income for wars—past, present and future.

By spending our time, our thought, and billions of dollars we have established air bases completely surrounding the Soviet Union. Our latest military aid to Pakistan insures a military air base within some six hundred miles of the capital of the Soviet Union, Moscow. This move will guarantee continued military preparation in Russia out of fear of atomic attack from us. Certainly all our air bases make it possible for us to launch a devastating attack if that should prove "necessary." In Japan alone the United States has some 56 bases, much to the discomfiture of the Japanese. So desperate is the situation thought to be by those in power that although we wrote into the Japanese Constitution only a few years ago that she should remain unarmed we are now doing our utmost to have her break and repudiate the very constitution which we wrote. Japan, the only modern nation to repudiate militarism, is thus being rearmed. The United States is exerting similar influence on Germany. Russia, having been devastated by Germany in World War II, is desperately fearful of a rearmed Reich, but the United States is determined to have Germany a partner in a European Army. Instead of producing health and moral power by these moves the world seems rather to be sinking into feverish rearmament, mental intimidation, and periodic waves of fear.

Professor Norman J. Whitney, of Syracuse University, a member of the Executive Committee of the American Friends Service Committee, asked his students in 1954 to interview the Korean veterans on the campus. Here were Americans who had fought for what many had been taught to believe was a great moral conflict; yet note the conclusions of the veterans as written by one Catholic student: "America is gradually losing its moral perspective and spiritual fibre. Ironically enough, morality and spirituality are the two things we have most prided ourselves upon, but like so many virtues, they have become extinct in practice . . . Our children are continually exposed to the tritely sophisticated adulteries of movies and magazines, the hollow, hackneyed reverberations of radio and television, and to the moronic jinglets of the jukebox. As a logical consequence they spend their lives living externally, and remain inwardly hollow men."[5]

In the war in French Indochina the United States contributed $800,000,000 a year, but the conflict cost the French over 7 billions. The United States sent in planes and technicians to perpetuate imperialism and prevent democracy,—according to the view of the Indian government. The ruler of the country we backed did not have the support of his people. The highest claim for support of Bao Dai, the ruler of Vietnam, by the people of the country was twenty per cent.[6] In other words, the rebels whom we fought had the support of perhaps eighty percent of all the people. What becomes of American pretensions of genuinely favoring democracy when they support a dictatorship against the will of the people? In addition, the actual government of Bao Dai was graft-ridden and corrupt. A four-deputy commission of the French National Assembly even accused the French bureaucracy of establishing a "virtual dictatorship" in Vietnam.[7] It is probable that this war and the policy we followed there actually strengthened Communism. A Vietnamese summed up the verdict of

[5] *Friends Intelligencer*, Feb. 20, 1954, p. 105.
[6] *New York Times*, Nov. 8, 1953.
[7] *The Crisis*, Feb. 1954, p. 81.

his people by saying, "I have always despised the whites. I considered them as moral savages." In Kenya, South Africa, the British are trying to exterminate the Mau Mau by a military struggle. The result has been almost complete failure. R. H. S. Crossman, writing in the *New Statesman and Nation,* declares, "Mau Mau has shaken the settlers out of their escapism into a bewildered realization that they have chosen to make their lives among millions of Africans, who possess the power to destroy them, and whose minds they have never bothered to begin to understand . . . So far repression has aggravated the disease."

The fact of the matter is that it does not pay us to enter a World War today even if we could win it. Both sides would be armed with the hydrogen bomb and other deadly weapons. Harrison S. Brown, professor of chemistry in Chicago, believes that Russia with the hydrogen bomb might be able to destroy most of the higher forms of life in the United States. To be sure, America might be able to do the same in Russia, but the United States is far more exposed to such an attack than is the Soviet Union. Thus another World War would mean the annihilation of the vast bulk of the people on both sides.

Let us face the fact that it is far harder to wage peace than it is to wage war. We might as well recognize that down through the ages there have been two ways of solving difficulties, tensions, fears. One is to use brute force to conquer and kill, the other is to use mutual aid or cooperation to win and help. In the past both methods may have perpetuated a species; but one thing is indisputable, the dinosaur is gone. His heavy armor, his brute power, did not save him, and he finally went down and out. Will it not be the same with our civilization if we continue to trust in military power and armaments?

It is our contention that we are now in a period where World War has been outmoded. The atom, hydrogen, and cobalt bomb have become so dangerous that war, instead of solving life's problems, increases them in a geometric ratio.

If we desire good physical health, we have to do the things that make for health. We cannot perpetually violate the laws of hygiene, or the laws of nature, without paying a price. It is possible to drink ourselves to death, even eat ourselves into the grave. Tuberculosis, colon bacilli, infected water, poverty, ignorance, undulant fever, filth, malarial mosquitoes and influenza germs are extremely dangerous to life. Similarly if we want health in the international field we have to do the things that make for sound international relations. Racial discrimination, imperialism, puppet rulers, poverty, ignorance, fear, landlordism and militarism are all detrimental. None of them is favorable to health in the international arena, and several existing in conjunction are extremely dangerous symptoms.

America is in grave danger but the danger arises not so much from Communist espionage or Soviet conspiracy as it does from our *fear and hysteria*. We are in a pathological frame of mind. When we begin to use *character assassination* on a former President of the United States and when even the Republican *Herald Tribune* can say of McCarthy's interrogation of General Zwicker, "Under severe party pressure, the Secretary of the Army surrendered to a Senator who had humiliated and bullied an Army general and who had spread the most infamous insinuations touching the Army's very loyalty and patriotism,"[8] then we can be certain that we are socially ill. After prolonged debate the Senate finally condemned McCarthy but it failed to censure him for his treatment of General Zwicker. As Vera Dean, Editor of the Foreign Policy Association says, our danger "is due to our own state of mind—to the confusion, distrust, lack of confidence and inner vacillation created in our midst by fear of the world we live in . . . as the childish dreams of glory have grown dim this anxiety has generated a moral crisis which causes many of us to lash out at our fellow citizens, to seek for scapegoats, to castigate our allies the moment they do not agree with us 100%."[9]

What must we do to be saved? We must regain our sanity and see the world steadily and see it whole. We need to follow the moral injunctions of the prophets and of Jesus. In a real sense we need psychiatric treatment. We must no longer live in a dream world, but face the sobering fact that no amount of military build-up will stop Communism as long as feudalism, colonialism, ignorance, and poverty continue. These things will cause upheaval now just as certainly as they did when our forefathers revolted from England.

If we fear change because it might jeopardize our financial secur-

[8] See editorial in N.Y. *Herald Tribune*, Feb. 25, 1954.
[9] See article in *Christian Century*, Feb. 3, 1954.

ity, we shall continue to support leaders who in the hour of trial will collapse. This we have already done in supporting Chiang Kai-shek in China, Franco in Spain, and Bao Dai in Vietnam. What then should we do?

First, we should probably recognize that to some extent we are suffering from schizophrenia. We are unable to choose between alternatives. Are we to trade with the Soviet Union or not? Are we to support dictators like Franco or not? Are we to demand that Germany and Japan rearm, and, if so, how far should they rearm? Are we to support any regime that is backed by the majority of her population no matter how violently we disagree with them? Perhaps it would be wiser to trade with all the peoples, even with those behind the Iron Curtain. Perhaps in the long run we shall have to recognize even a new regime in China, just as, long ago, the world had to recognize a regime called "red" in its day on the virgin American continent.

Second, we must accept the fact that the United States should not dictate decisions throughout the world, but should genuinely make them with other nations by majority vote, even if our way does not prevail. We should never try to force our way on others by monetary bribes or threats.

Third, instead of relying on the atom and hydrogen bombs and overwhelming military power, we might try reliance on the mightiest weapons which man has tested and proved down through the centuries. What are these? Are they not truth and love? But the cynic will retort, "This is visionary and impractical. You can't change human nature. The entire history of man is war." Many Americans agree with the German General who said, "Perpetual peace is a dream, not even a beautiful dream."

But the greatest prophets as well as Jesus and Buddha all held to reliance on spiritual and moral force. Indeed, Jesus' teaching about truth and goodness so maddened the authorities of his day that they crucified him but that only made the eventual acceptance of his ideas more certain. Today all over the United States we nominally bow down in reverence before the prophets or before Jesus. At least we do lip service to them. All through the country huge synagogues and cathedrals testify to our nominal allegiance to the greatest truths proclaimed in all human history. Yet in our feverish rearmament, in our subservience to the God of War, we are in reality negating the very teaching which we pretend to serve.

Perhaps some one may retort to all this, "Yes, but the majority of the people in America really believe that militarism and war are necessary." Granted that this may be so, the question still remains whether or not this conviction is sound or is a snare and a delusion? In an atomic age should we trust in militarism to the tune of eighty percent of our budget? Are we living up to our highest moral and spiritual insights? Are we facing the realities of the revolutionary atomic era?

We have already quoted from military leaders who cast doubt on reliance on war as a method. That a wide segment of informed opinion believes that World War is now obsolete is shown by the following extracts from the address of General Douglas MacArthur given under the sponsorship of the American Legion in California in 1955.[10]

". . . War has become a Frankenstein to destroy both sides. No longer is it the weapon of adventure whereby a short cut to international power and wealth—a place in the sun—can be gained. If you lose, you are annihilated. If you win, you stand only to lose. No longer does it possess the chance of the winner of a duel—it contains rather the germs of double suicide. Science has clearly out-moded it as a feasible arbiter. . . .

"The hundred of billions of dollars now spent in mutual preparedness could conceivably abolish poverty from the face of the globe. It would accomplish even more than this; it would at one stroke reduce the international tension that seems so insurmountable now to matters of more probable solution. For instance, the complex problems of German rearmament, of preventive war, of satellite dominance by major powers, of Universal Military Service, of unconscionable taxation, of nuclear development for industry, of freer exchange of goods and people, of foreign aid, indeed, of all issues involving the application of armed force. . . .

"Sooner or later the world, if it is to survive, must reach this decision. The only question is, when? Must we fight again before we learn? When will some great figure in power have sufficient imagination and moral courage to translate this universal wish—which is

[10] Delivered in Los Angeles, Jan. 26, 1955.

rapidly becoming a universal necessity—into actuality? We are in a new era. The old methods and solutions no longer suffice. We must have new thoughts, new ideas, new concepts, just as did our venerated forefathers when they faced a new world. We must break out of the strait jacket of the past. There must always be one to lead and we should be that one. We should now proclaim our readiness to abolish war in concert with the great powers of the world. The result will be magical . . . .

"Whatever betides, the ultimate fate of the Far East—and indeed the world—will not be settled by force of arms. We may all be practically annihilated—but war can no longer be an arbiter of survival."

It is time to face facts not illusions. World War in our modern age is a complete delusion. It is an anachronism. Suppose we try to prevent Communism in China by the hydrogen bomb, what would happen? Even if we won the war, it seems likely that Communism would spread much farther than it has yet done. For Communism thrives on suffering, poverty and dislocation.

Suppose industrial workers, in the days of the twelve-hour day and the seven-day week, had said that it was necessary to attack and kill their employers in order to get fair play, what would have happened? The whole cause of justice would have been set back for generations. Instead, the workers used the strike, a relatively non-violent weapon, where workers merely withheld their labor. Note carefully that in strikes the workers and their families must sacrifice and suffer. Strikes mean hunger for the children and wives of the strikers. Yet in the long run it was these non-violent techniques which won the day. Perhaps Nehru, in his mediating rôle in world affairs, has been rendering all humanity an essential service.

It seems probable that the world is suffering from radical mental disorders. What it needs is not armaments and threats but courageous, love-filled strategies and lives with the power of truth behind them. Perhaps we should really act on the faith that we must *overcome evil by good*. Christ tried it in Palestine, and we have been bowing in reverence before him ever since. Gandhi tried it in India; and it "worked"!

If the great powers continue to take the military path, each will go on arming for defense against the other until the whole world becomes a vast armed camp; and we shall all go bankrupt or be annihilated. Alternatively, we can follow the way of intelligence instead of armaments and use positive measures for friendship even with our enemies, including trade and disarmament. Everyone is afraid to do this because of fear that they will be attacked and conquered. And so the vicious system goes on. We need mental and moral therapy and the conviction that it is better to be brave and unarmed than it is to be armed and afraid.

It is obvious that an unarmed man has more courage than an armed man. For as Gandhi said "If you are so brave that you can throw away your armaments and stand before the world unarmed, you are brave indeed."

Now this argument does not imply that we should not work to get agreement for disarmament. Russia has repeatedly offered to reduce her armaments. But we always see a flaw in the proposal. Perhaps it would be better to agree. Naturally, we should also try to get world government and support the United Nations, in other words, cultivate world loyalty. Let us abandon narrow nationalism. Let us encourage interchange of the peoples of different races and nations. But let us remember in the long run that we have to face up to the challenge of whether or not we wish to follow Christ's law of love and truth. If we really decide to follow His way then we can hardly use atom, hydrogen, or cobalt bombs, not to mention bacteriological warfare and all-out war. Reliance on world warfare is as outmoded as the stagecoach or the bow and arrow. Let us go bravely forward into the atomic age trusting in moral and spiritual values and renouncing the lethal weapons of mass murder.

In conclusion we cannot do better than refresh our minds with a few quotations from Gandhi who in the future will tower above most of the so called "great" men of our time. Gandhi said, "Look after the means and the end will take care of itself." "The free world we enjoy is less than that of a passenger on a crowded deck." "Instead of defiling the soul and relinquishing the truth by stooping to the enemy's level of violence, revenge and hatred, you must raise him to your level by non-violence, suffering and love. Instead of attacking his body, you must attack his soul. Instead of killing him, you must redeem the truth that lies deep within him. If anyone suffer it must be yourself."

Gandhi's message to the missionaries was simple:

"First, I would suggest that all of you Christian missionaries must begin to live more like Jesus Christ. Second, practice your religion without adulterating it, or toning it down. Third, emphasize Love and make it your working force, for Love is central in Christianity. Fourth, study the non-Christian religions more sympathetically to find the good that is within them in order to have a more sympathetic approach to the people."

Lord Louis Mountbatten, the last British Viceroy of India, summed up the verdict of history when he said at the time of Gandhi's death, "What 50,000 well-equipped soldiers could not do, the Mahatma has done. He has brought peace."

The Bible says, "Seek ye first the kingdom of God and His righteousness." Shall we follow the road to peace or shall we go forward along the broad highway of the self-righteousness of power which inevitably leads to a "self-righteous" war and destruction?

Prayer

O God of love, who dost ever lead us toward the ways of peace and brotherhood, help us to understand the full meaning and significance of the fact that Thou hast made of one blood all nations of men to dwell on the face of the earth.

Forgive us our sins, that we have trusted in the God of War. When we say we would have no other gods but Thee, and then spend most of our national revenue on preparations for war, teach us to understand that we are negating our faith. Forgive us, we beseech Thee, for relying on the righteousness of power rather than on the power of righteousness.

O God of all mankind, unite in opposition to the demon of war all those who genuinely love Thee and claim the name of Christian. Give us the courage to stand with Thee against all the forces of men who consciously or unknowingly would ignore Thy teaching about the consequences of war through the centuries. Help us really to practise Thy word, that we should love our enemies.

Grant us the courage genuinely to work at building a warless world here and now, and guard us against using false alibis for postponing such action. Help us not to be so much concerned about building mighty military forces, but rather to be willing to spend our treasure in removing the causes of war.

Our Father, take from our hearts the selfishness, the acquisitiveness, and the hypocrisy which are the seeds of war. Help us not only to see our own sins first, but always to love our neighbors as ourselves.

Above all, grant us not to seek the approval of man, but in all things to do Thy will, so that we may play our part through Thy help in building a world of brotherhood and peace.

IF there be any among us who wish to dissolve this union, or change its republican form, let them stand undisturbed, as monuments of the safety with which error of opinion may be tolerated where reason is left free to combat it.
PRESIDENT THOMAS JEFFERSON, 1801

Yet every day in this country men and women are being deprived of their livelihood, or at least their reputations, by unsubstantiated charges. These charges are then treated as facts in further charges against their relatives or associates. We do not throw people into jail because they are alleged to differ with the official dogma. We throw them out of work and do our best to create the impression that they are subversive and hence dangerous, not only to the state, but also to everybody who comes near them.
ROBERT M. HUTCHINS, Chancellor of the University of Chicago, 1949

The growing practise of character assassinations is already curbing free speech and it is threatening all our other freedoms. I dare say there are people here today who have reached the point where they are afraid to explore a new idea. . . . Slander, lies, character assassination—these things are a threat to every single citizen everywhere in this country. When even one American—who has done nothing wrong—is forced by fear to shut his mind and close his mouth, then all Americans are in peril.
PRESIDENT HARRY S. TRUMAN to the American Legion in 1951

I think it is high time for the United States Senate and its members to do some soul searching—for us to weigh our consciences—on the way we are performing our duty to the people of America, on the way we are using or abusing our individual powers and privileges. I think that it is high time we remembered that the Constitution, as amended, speaks not only of freedom of speech but also of trial by jury instead of trial by accusation....

Those of us who shout the loudest about Americanism in making character assassinations are all too frequently those who, by their own words and acts, ignore some of the basic principles of Americanism: namely, the right to criticize; the right to hold unpopular beliefs; the right to protest; the right of independent thought. The exercise of these rights should not cost one single American citizen his reputation or his right to a livelihood, nor should he be in danger of losing his reputation or his right to a livelihood merely because he happens to know someone who holds unpopular beliefs—who of us doesn't?

SENATOR MARGARET CHASE SMITH
Excerpt from *The Nation*, Dec. 1953.

CHAPTER V

The Subtle Poisoning of the People

THE American people are being poisoned in three major ways. First, and perhaps least important, is through the air we breathe. Medical authorities who have investigated the subject believe many communities have air which contains dangerous quantities of chemicals known to be irritating and as such possibly influential in the causation of cancer and tuberculosis. This form of poisoning varies in different sections of the country. Robert M. Hutchins, formerly Chancellor of the University of Chicago, writing in the *Nation* in 1954, states the problem in Los Angeles as follows:[1] "Last Saturday the visibility in Pasadena was four blocks. The spectators at the Santa Anita race track could not see the well-tended horses until they reached the finish line. The same condition prevailed over most of Los Angeles County, a territory in which four million people are living. It has prevailed at more frequent and for longer periods in the last ten years, and its dark and poisonous quality grows worse from month to month. Everybody knows what causes it. Nobody believes that anything will be done about it. The most elementary requirement of human life, air, is one that the people of Los Angeles County must apparently reconcile themselves to going without."

In New York City, in a period of a decade the air pollution has increased 40 per cent. Dr. Paul Kotin made some studies in coöperation with the University of Southern California. He is convinced that the exhaust from gasoline engines contains carcinogenic chemicals. The density of this carbon monoxide gas is about twice that of air, so that it settles in an invisible layer through which people in our cities walk. It is estimated that in New York City alone a total of one billion one

[1] *The Nation,* Feb. 20, 1954.

hundred million gallons of gasoline are burned on the streets each year. A study made by the United States Public Health Service shows that the dust-laden air in eight different cities across the country caused cancer in animals. After an actual count it was found that 176 tons of solid matter was deposited on a single square mile of Manhattan in a month. Included in this material was half a ton of cancer-producing tars. It has also been shown that persons living in the heart of industrialized Manchester, England, die on an average ten years earlier than the general average (*The National Public Gazette*, April 1954).

In St. Louis, before remedial legislation was passed, the United States Weather Bureau recorded 716½ hours of moderate and thick smoke during the heating season. This was reduced 72.5% when laws were passed to curb it.

Nashville, Tennessee has somewhat similar bad smoke. Why are not the conditions remedied? Well, measures have been proposed which would largely curb this evil in Nashville, but they are vigorously opposed by some of the coal companies, laundries and dry cleaners who stand to gain by the present system. Yet the mayor of St. Louis, where they have banned the inferior grades of coal, maintains that they have saved fourteen million dollars a year by the elimination of the bad smoke, not to mention the vast saving in health. America is geared to an economy of profit-making rather than health first.

The second form of poisoning is through our food and drink. Not long ago the author was instrumental in having biopsies made on dead bodies chosen at random in New York City. If some one was hit by an automobile and killed, his body might be used. Out of thirty dead bodies examined, twenty-eight had significant amounts of DDT. This poisoning is cumulative. DDT sprays used to be recommended by the U.S. Department of Agriculture for use in cow barns. The result was that the poison went into the milk. Now this is frowned on, but still DDT and other poisonous sprays are being used on vegetables and fruits and there seems little doubt that the majority of the American people are being poisoned to some degree in this way. In fact DDT is used so widely in agriculture that we probably could get some in almost every meal we eat. Dr. Wayland J. Hayes, Jr., Chief of the Toxicology Section of the United States Public Health Service's communicable disease center in Savannah made a study of restaurant meals. There was not a single meal analyzed which did not contain DDT. On the average the amount in three daily meals equalled 184 micrograms.[2] A young girl attending a university in Pennsylvania was reported to have died following the eating of sprayed apples, and another death was reported from eating asparagus at Northwestern University. The New Hampshire Agricultural Experiment Station has reported that a half a pint of strawberries may carry as much as 8 mg. of oxide of arsenic (Savage, *Food Poisoning*). Schlink in *Eat, Drink and be Wary* maintains that practically all fruits and vegetables now contain arsenic and lead. Of course, it is extremely rare for a person to die after eating sprayed vegetables, but it is quite likely that many of us are slowly absorbing poison.

About a half century ago Dr. Harvey W. Wiley and others helped to secure the enactment of the *Pure Food and Drug Act*. Justice William O. Douglas says:[3] "Dr. Wiley submitted twelve healthy young men (dubbed the 'poison squad') to tests to show that preservatives used in food were harmful to health. In other studies, it was shown how from an average breakfast one got eight doses of harmful chemicals and dyes, at lunch, sixteen, at dinner, sixteen. In patent medicines, one often got poisons or habit-forming drugs."

Unfortunately in spite of protective laws we still have far too much of this with us. It was only in 1955 that the Pure Food and Drug Act finally debarred certain types of dyes on oranges and in candy. Yet the *Herald of Health* in 1949 declared, "Fruits and vegetables obtained in the open market today are literally reeking with poison." While this may be too extreme, the magazine *Prevention* is constantly giving somewhat similar evidence. J. I. Rodale, the editor of this magazine, cited a case in California where the fumes from a poison spray used on an olive grove killed 1200 sheep.[4] Keepers of bees lost so many of their hives when blossoms were sprayed that the law was changed to require previous notification to all bee keepers in the vicinity. The *New York Herald Tribune* reported that in Germany "insecticide E-605" costing ten cents had been used "in almost 100

[2] New York *Times Magazine,* Jan. 16, 1955, p. 38.
[3] Douglas, William O., *An Almanac of Liberty,* 1954, p. 379.
[4] Tensen, A. H., *How to Eat Safely in a Poisoned World,* p. 40.

murders and suicides. A Mrs. Lehman, who was convicted of murder, sprinkled a little insecticide in her husband's milk to kill him. Later she got rid of her father-in-law by placing some in his yogurt."[5]

The extent of the food poisoning in the United States is unbelievable. Take this heading in the Nashville paper in 1954,[6] "Six Found Stricken of Food Poison." They ate baked ham taken from the refrigerator and within one hour were desperately sick. The physician reported that they were victims of "paint fumes."

Not long ago it was found that coumarin, a substance used in artificial vanilla flavoring all over the United States, was injurious. It was decided to prohibit its use. Nevertheless some of the commercial companies continued to use their supply until it was gone. The Food and Drug Administration at Washington reported the testimony of the pharmacologist who tested coumarin in 1953 as follows:

"The average oral fatal dose of coumarin in male white rats was about 0.2 gram per kilogram of body weight. In a 4-week feeding test in male rats 0.02% coumarin in the diet caused some growth retardation but no increased mortality; 0.1% caused greater growth retardation but no effect on mortality either. As little as 0.1 gram per kilogram of body weight per day produced severe liver damage within 5 to 22 days in 9 dogs. Death occurred in 2 of the 9 dogs following 8 such 0.1 gram per kilogram per day doses. This dose in the dog corresponds to a dietary concentration of 0.13%."[7] Bread softeners have been found to be injurious and it seems that if the truth were known a considerable number of canned and processed food products have harmful substances in them. In a previous chapter we have mentioned the danger from the excessive use of cigarettes. But here we simply state, cigarettes are one of the irritants which increase cancer. In 1956 roughly 25,000 citizens of the United States will die of lung cancer. Smoking will be a factor in some 95 per cent of the cases.[8]

The fact is we are not as socially intelligent as we think. Professor A. J. Carlson, Former President of the American Association For

[5] N.Y. *Herald Tribune,* Sept. 23, 1954.

[6] *The Nashville Tennessean,* Feb. 23, 1954.

[7] Letter to author from J. E. Kirk, Assistant to the Commissioner of the Food and Drug Administration, June 18, 1954.

[8] Ochsner, Alton, *Smoking and Cancer,* Messner, 1954.

the Advancement of Science says, "Modern industry poisons our lakes, our rivers, and our coast line waters so as to reduce food from these sources."[9]

Many Americans feel from statistical evidence that we have made great progress in prolonging life. Certainly we have cut down infant mortality. All this is true. Tuberculosis has dropped since 1859 from a death rate of 444 per 100,000 of the population to 36. Appendicitis, diphtheria, measles, pneumonia, rheumatic fever, scarlet fever, and whooping cough have all declined.

How is it, then, that vast numbers of people are starving in various areas of the world? Dr. Thomas Parran, Surgeon General of the United States, has this to say: "We have learned of the virtues of milk and green vegetables; of the fish and liver oils, so rich in vitamins A and D; of the vitamin C of citrus fruits. In spite of this, every survey, by whatever method and wherever conducted, shows that malnutrition of many types is widespread and serious among the American people. We eat over-refined foods, with most of the natural values processed out of them. Because of this, many well-to-do Americans who can eat what they like are so badly fed as to be physically inferior and mentally dull." The Bible says, "Why spend your money on what is not food; your earnings on what never satisfies?" (Is. 55-2).

The Institute of Pennsylvania State College, where President Eisenhower's brother is president, recently published a six-year survey on health which showed that out of 2,511 adults and children only two were free from evidences of malnutrition. Of the entire number only eight had no tooth decay and over half were anemic. Sixty per cent of the children were six months behind in skeletal growth, yet hardly any recognized their condition.

The chronic or degenerative diseases are now the ones which are taking an alarming toll of the American people. These include heart disease, cancer, and arthritis which cripples some ten millions. Heart disease is the most widespread killer. If we include all diseases called "cardiovascular" involving the heart and arteries, they cause over half the deaths in the country. Many experts believe that a fatty alcohol, cholesterol, is part of the difficulty and it seems probable that diet can have some effect.

[9] *A Fifteenth Anniversary Report from Consumers Union,* 1951, p. 37.

Cancer kills about 225,000 in the United States every year, so that in the neighborhood of 22,000,000 now living will die of the disease. Over a million Americans die each year from these two causes (heart disease and cancer), with an additional ten millions crippled by arthritis. In the face of this appalling situation one would think that intelligent, rational human beings would devote vast sums for research on how to prevent these ailments. But in the United States, although we are increasing such funds, they are pitifully small.[10] To some degree the amount appropriated could be said to be a measure of our intelligence. Prior to World War II the United States did not spend more than twenty million dollars for medical research, and of this the United States Public Health Service put up two million. Today we are spending upwards of $190,000,000, with about half coming from pharmaceutical firms. This sounds impressive, but compare it with our military expenditures. "Where thy treasure is there will thy heart be also." The total sum spent for medical research is less than one-third of one per cent of the national defense budget. This proportion would be far worse if we include the expenditures for previous wars. The cost of one airplane carrier alone is 235 million dollars, some 45 million more than we spend on this medical research in an entire year. The House of Representatives' Commerce Committee reported in 1954 that even the scientific advances we have made are not being fully applied for the prevention of our major diseases. The Committee reported that half of the cancer cases could be cured but are not. "Tuberculosis," it declared, "could be virtually eliminated." It stated that the "visible and hideous costs of disease are catastrophic in human as well as economic terms . . . for the nation as a whole they constitute a serious threat to continued progress along the path leading to strength and security." The Committee concluded, "The cases of cancer alone that were diagnosed in 1953 have been estimated to cost society $12,000,000,000 in lost goods and services."

The Committee declared that we could rehabilitate the blind but are largely failing to do so today.

What can be done to promote good health with very little money is

[10] On the other hand vast sums of money are spent on palliatives. The aspirin consumption in the United States is 42,000,000 tablets every 24 hours. We use annually enough sedatives and sleeping pills to put every U.S. citizen to sleep for 20 days.

demonstrated by the work of the World Health Organization. When a cholera epidemic broke out in Egypt, it spread at the rate of 1,000 cases a day, yet it was stopped cold in six weeks and did not spread abroad, a feat unparalleled in medical history. How was this done? Seventeen countries, including the United States and the Soviet Union, sent in thirty-two tons of anti-cholera vaccine. The World Health Organization, supported by sixty-four nations, receives only $5,000,-000 a year. In contrast to the military budget this is infinitesimal.

Many believe that one cause of the increase of degenerative diseases lies with the agriculturalists, the soil chemists, the food processors, and the peddlers of food products. Dr. James McLester, Professor of Medicine at the University of Alabama, for instance, says, "No greater catastrophe comes to man than the loss of efficiency, the lack of initiative, and the mental depressions which accompany nutritive failure." Dr. Henry Trautmann brings this home when he says, "The use of potent insecticides, weedicides, in agriculture, and the use of potent chemicals in the food industry are contributing factors to our disease problems. Foodless food may satisfy the profit motive but can never satisfy the tissues."

Recently one company devised an insecticide which entered the sap of the plant so it could not be washed away. When asked what happens if a person eats the plant they advised against human consumption! But who guarantees that farmers will not use it, if it is profitable to do so?

After an exhaustive scientific analysis, Mrs. Field in her recent book concludes, "We have about 23,000,000 people in the United States suffering from some form of prolonged illness of whom 1,500,000 are permanent invalids."[11]

Dr. Royal Lee of the Lee Foundation for Nutritional Research says, "Since practically all the cereal products found in human diets are degerminated at the factory to keep out bug infestation, it is quite clear to any rational person why the incidence of heart disease has increased with the sale of such cereal products. It is clear too why heart disease is so uncommon in parts of the world where these food frauds are fortunately not used."

Dr. Morton Biskind, in the *American Journal of Digestive Dis-*

[11] Field, Minna, *Patients are People,* Columbia University, 1953.

62   *Religion in Action*

eases, declares that "no matter how lethal a poison may be for all forms of animal life, if it doesn't kill human beings instantly (we think) it is safe." Dr. Biskind declares our use of insecticides is "the most intensive campaign of mass poisoning in known human history."[12]

All of this is said not to prove the cause of disease but to urge that if we were intelligent we would spend adequate sums for medical research. As long as we do not do this while we spend billions for preparation for suicidal mass murder called "military preparedness," we cannot claim a high degree of rationality let alone moral power. But let us turn to another area where we need even more vigilance.

By far the most dangerous form of poisoning is that of the minds of men. The eye and ear stimuli, if controlled, can largely shape the thinking of the people. We know that they are so controlled in the dictator countries, but we have not yet grasped the important fact that to a considerable extent these stimuli are being warped and directed even in the United States. Of course, we must recognize that any mind tends to be partially controlled by the self's own interests or by its commitments and loyalties. This makes it easy to warp our thinking if it is in the direction of our selfish interest. The path of truth has been a circuitous and tortuous one.

What we need in the press is a truthful, comprehensive, and intelligent account of the major events of our time, so that there is full access to the day's actions. We should have the arguments pro and con on controversial issues. The most important recent study of the freedom of the press was that undertaken by Chicago University and largely financed by *Time,* Inc. After an exhaustive study and spending over $200,000, the report concluded that the freedom of the press is in danger for three reasons:

1. The press is now a medium of mass communication but the proportion of the people that can express their opinions through it has greatly decreased.
2. The few who control it have not provided a service adequate to the needs of society.
3. "Those who direct the machinery of the press have engaged from time to time in practices which the society condemns."

[12] See article by R. G. Martin in *Harper's,* April 1955, "How much poison are we eating?"

The Subtle Poisoning of the People 63

In a section on the bias of the owners of the press the report has this to say. "The agencies of mass communication are big business and the owners are big businessmen. The American consumers just prior to the war paid the forty thousand mass communication establishments nearly two and a half billion dollars for their services, representing one dollar out of every twenty-seven spent that year for goods and services. . . . The press is connected with other big business through the advertising of these businesses, upon which it depends for the major part of its revenue. The owners of the press, like the owners of other big businesses, are bank directors, bank borrowers and heavy taxpayers in the upper brackets." Erwin D. Canham, editor of the *Christian Science Monitor*, lists at the head of the shortcomings of the press its upper-bracket ownership. In other words, the virus of commercialism endangers the health of our minds as well as of our bodies. We have come a long distance since the days when a competing press fought for the attention of men's minds. Today in eleven out of every twelve cities there is no competing press. The Commission on Freedom of the Press reports. "Altogether, 40 per cent of the estimated total daily newspaper circulation of forty-eight million is noncompetitive. . . . Rival newspapers exist only in the larger cities" . . . "The right of free public expression has therefore lost its earlier reality."

The result is that the Newspaper Publishers Association condemned the Child Labor Amendment when it was up for approval. The press in general has shown great bias against cooperatives, against food and drug regulation, against Federal Trade Commission orders designed to suppress fraudulent advertising. Some time ago Leo C. Rosten, making a scientific study on a fellowship, sent a questionnaire to one hundred Washington correspondents about bias in the press. He found that they admitted our news was colored.[1]

Herbert Brucker, editor of the Hartford *Courant*, has well summarized what has happened. "Every newspaper, every editor, and every editorial writer is constantly subjected to a myriad of pressures . . . pressures of the status quo, the economic forces of the community, the closeness of the (paper's) ownership to one side or another in the local political and social push and pull."

[1] Leo C. Rosten, *The Washington Correspondents*.

The control of the radio by the big advertisers is even more complete. Says the report, "Fewer than a hundred and fifty advertisers now provide all but three or four per cent of the income of the radio networks, and fewer than fifty provide half the total."[2] The concentration of radio sponsorship is even worse, "in 1943 one eighth of N.B.C.'s business came from one advertiser, two advertisers supplied one-fourth and ten advertisers 60% of N.B.C.'s income." Roughly the same proportion held for the A.B.C. network.

No wonder so many liberal commentators are left off the air. Of course, the American Federation of Labor can keep a commentator speaking by paying the necessary fee to the radio chain, but how many organizations are in a position to do this?

In television there is even less chance to get liberal ideas on the air. Furthermore, the prevalence of television has still further reduced the number of Americans who read books. Nearly every study of the moving picture industry and the comics show that they are actually demoralizing in much of their influence and too often promote crime among the young.

The noted British writer, Gunther Stein, summarizes his verdict on the American mass communication media as follows:

The very combination of all those gushing pipelines into the people's minds makes the system so surprisingly effective in a society which, as a whole, is still far from political and economic literacy. Whatever corner of their minds one medium may not reach and adjust to the requirements of the economic order, another will gradually conquer. Whatever bias or illusion, tabu or fear the constant hammering of one may not be able to establish, the endless drumming of another eventually will. For most Americans, in the long run there is no escape from the captive audience. One may switch on one's radio only for music or the news but one cannot help hearing the commercial, ideological by-pay that infiltrates every programme. (Gunther Stein, *The World the Dollar Built*, 1953, p. 50.)

The warping effect of the eye and ear stimuli, the slanted direction of the press, the radio, the television, the moving pictures and the comics is really surprising. We shall take up the effect of the comics again in a later chapter, but let us now consider the effects of all these

[2] The Commission on Freedom of the Press, University of Chicago Press, 1947, p. 63.

stimuli. If one should throw a lot of iron filings on a table, they would be scattered in irregular disorder. Now wave a powerful magnet over the table always in the same direction, just above the iron filings. What happens? The filings arrange themselves in one major direction. This is exactly what tends to happen to our minds because of the slanted direction of the organs of communication. To have balanced opinions we must get two sides of every question, not just the one which is orthodox in our country, in our newspapers, on our radio.

About one-third of the world population live under a dictatorship, which muzzles communication. In these countries, newspapers, magazines, books, radio, television, and movies must all accord with the official line or they are suppressed. In the United States the big organs of public opinion live under a fluctuating control of big business, freedom, like credit at the bank, tends to disappear when it is most needed. Even in ordinary times there may be pressure on professors who champion unpopular causes. Here, for instance, is an extract from the life of John Henry Gray, formerly President of the American Economic Association, as published in the Harvard Class Book; yet all this occurred long before the present wave of hysteria.

At Northwestern and Minnesota I was under constant fire for my economic, social and political views, many of which have been generally accepted. The others must shortly be accepted if American civilization is not soon to disappear. The records of the Board show a motion made by a sitting judge to dismiss me 'for criticizing the United States Constitution.' It was not carried.

At the University of Minnesota, Pierce Butler (later of the United States Supreme Court), the leading corporation lawyer of the State, was dominant member of the Board of Regents. He seemed always opposed to any investigation or discussion of economic questions as if the duty of a professor were merely to teach, apparently from a 'safe' textbook. He opposed me and my department in every turn.

In 1909 when I started extension work at the University of Minnesota, I lectured chiefly on Cooperatives. I soon received a notice from the President to meet with him and a Committee of the Chamber of Commerce to discuss the extension work. The Committee minced no words. They said that my work was injuring their business and that they had the power to stop it. Either we must stop talking cooperatives all over the state or they would cut off the university appropriations.

The President then drafted a resolution by which we were to explain the cooperative movement but *not to advocate it*. Such a subterfuge did not appeal to me and I dropped out of the extension work.

In spite of all these controls the people do think. When Franklin Roosevelt ran for the Presidency, three-fourths of the press were against him; yet he won.

Compared with where we might be as an intelligent thinking people, we are probably very backward. Bergen Evans in *The Natural History of Nonsense* has this to say about going counter to popular voodoo:

Until about a hundred years ago rational men lived like spies in an enemy country. They never walked abroad unless disguised in irony or allegory. To have revealed their true selves would have been fatal.

Today their status is more that of guerrillas. They snipe from cover, ambush stragglers, harass retreating rearguards, cut communications and now and then execute swift forays against detached units of the enemy. But they dare not yet risk an open engagement with the main force; they would be massacred.

Of course this is not true of the prophets of our time, men like Gandhi, or Bishop McConnell, or Father Ryan of the Catholic Church, or Stephen S. Wise of the Jewish Free Synagogue.

Justice Holmes of the United States Supreme Court puts it this way: "I say to you in all sadness of conviction that to think great thoughts you must be heroes as well as idealists." To say today what Thomas Jefferson once said would endanger imprisonment: "The moral right of rebellion is the life blood of the community."

The fact is that every one is born into a cultural environment of customs, beliefs, attitudes, and ways of thinking. The cultural tradition embraces the child at birth and gradually gives him language, beliefs, attitudes. Consequently the conscience of people depends to some degree on their culture. An American conscience is different from a Chinese one. Now if the eye and ear stimuli are largely stacked one way, it increases the chance for fear, hysteria, and mistaken notions to become ingrained.

Albert Schweitzer, the noted missionary statesman, inveighs against the propaganda forces of our time because they make the people lose

The Subtle Poisoning of the People 67

the power to think. We are circumscribed on all sides, he believes, by advertising and propaganda. In a sense we become mere suggestible automata, losing the power to think independently. In addition science has become so specialized that we often passively accept truth on authority rather than think independently for ourselves. Schweitzer concludes, "Renunciation of thinking is a declaration of spiritual bankruptcy."

This is what has been happening in the fifties in the United States. The country has been the victim of a dangerous witch hunt. We must stand guard against legalized lynching.

Congressional committees condemn individuals if they have ever spoken before a radical or a Communist group. If it can be shown that the meeting later passed a "bad" resolution, then they are guilty for this too. How absurd this is can be seen by a simple illustration. Not so long ago Senator Knowland, Republican majority leader in the Senate addressed a woman's group. Afterwards the meeting passed a resolution opposing statehood for Hawaii. In a few days Senator Knowland was asked if he was responsible for passage of the resolution. He replied that all he did was speak at the meeting and that the resolution did not represent his views. However, if a poor professor had been up before the Un-American Activities Committee in a similar situation for speaking to a radical group, he would have been blasted from coast to coast.

The Alsop brothers [13] have shown how ridiculous the methods of loyalty investigations have been. Thousands of people have been dismissed from the government at Washington and it has been estimated that a few may have once belonged to a radical organization. The Alsop brothers proposed that the record of John Foster Dulles, our Secretary of State, should be examined to see if he does not have similar connections. They found that he had recommended in writing the recognition of Red China, that he was closely identified with the Institute of Pacific Relations, that for a long time he had a sympathetic association with Alger Hiss (later convicted and sent to prison), that he even recommended him for an important post of great national influence. Finally they brought out that John Foster Dulles even failed

[13] New York *Herald Tribune,* March 10, 1954.

to propose the discharge of Hiss when he was exposed by the Un-American Activities Committee. All this is not derogatory to John Foster Dulles, but it would be far more than enough to secure the dismissal of any ordinary State Department employee in the present era of hysteria.

John B. Oakes, in the lead article in the New York *Times Magazine*, tells of a Republican Congressman who wants to resign because he cannot tell the truth without being called a Communist. He says, "The evidence increases daily that it would have been the part of wisdom and safety to have joined nothing, said nothing, written nothing, associated with nobody that could possibly have caused embarrassment in the future." He quotes the Superintendent of Schools as saying, "I hope nobody will leave this room today thinking that teachers are not afraid. Of course, they are. They are afraid to discuss controversial issues in the classrooms. They are afraid of community pressures."[14]

Elmer Davis, distinguished columnist for the American Broadcasting Company and Director of the Office of War Information during World War II, says:

> The present attack on the freedom of the mind is the worst America has ever had to face since the days of the Alien and Sedition Acts of 1798. . . . Most of the men who profess to be attacking Communism now are really gunning for people who are not reactionaries nor Communists either; but want to do their own thinking, and cling to the right of American citizens to say what they think. . . . As for Senator McCarthy he has been candid enough to admit that when he gets around to the colleges he will pay less attention to Communists than to what he calls Communist thinkers; and has made it clear that his definition of a Communist is a man who criticizes McCarthy.

Elmer Davis adds, "If Communism ever was a serious danger in this country—which I doubt—it is no longer."

Robert M. Hutchins, formerly of the University of Chicago, declares, "Education is impossible in many parts of the United States today because free inquiry and free discussion are impossible. In these communities the teacher of economics, history or political science cannot teach. . . . In Los Angeles, Houston and Pawtucket a teacher

[14] New York *Times Magazine*, March 7, 1954.

would hesitate to mention UNESCO" and probably would fear to mention the United Nations (see *Look Magazine,* March 9, 1954).

Through all history men have been afraid of books. In Moscow, some books were kept under lock and key in the library. Of course, all books are dangerous, and any librarian has dynamite under his care! Some Congressional leaders want 30,000 books removed from overseas libraries. In Indiana the story of Robin Hood was suppressed as subversive. In Alabama in 1953 they passed a law which requires that the publisher of every text-book submit a statement that the author is or is not a known advocate of Communism or a Marxist socialist or that he is not a member of any Communist front organization listed by the Attorney General. Now the Council of American Soviet Friendship is on the Attorney General's list. Twelve years ago it was addressed by Governor Lehman, Mayor La Guardia, President William Green, Professor MacMahon of Notre Dame, and it was sponsored by Harold Ickes, Judge Learned Hand, and Dean Christian Gauss. All of these individuals might, then, be characterized by some as "fellow travellers." Should, then, Alabama libraries debar books by any of these authors?

The terrible fear which has been awakened in the people is so great that in a test made by a Wisconsin newspaper on July 4, 1951, only one out of 122 people interviewed dared to sign the Declaration of Independence. Most of those said it was "for fear of the consequences." A woman reading the Declaration of Independence said, "That may be the Russian declaration of independence but you can't tell me it is ours." The first man interviewed said, "You can't get me to sign that, I'm trying to get a loyalty clearance for a government job." Another said, "I see you are using the old Communist trick—putting God's name in a radical petition." One said, "Get the hell out of here with that Communist stuff. . . ." In all, twenty persons asked the reporter whether he was a Communist.

Another poll taken in Wisconsin in 1954 found that more than half of those interviewed thought that the government should forbid some people (naturally those with whom they disagree) from holding public meetings and making speeches, and a third thought there should be restrictions on the freedom of the press. Professor John F. Caughey of the University of California, commenting on this says that people like that are not afraid of Communism—they are afraid of Americanism!

So great is the hysteria that people afflicted with paranoia now imagine their neighbors are Communists instead of something else. In Battle Creek, Michigan, for instance, the mother of six children was shot to death by a man of twenty-eight presumably suffering from dementia, who said "she was the biggest Communist in the world." Police said she has absolutely no connection with Communism. It was all due to the fear complex of our time.[15]

The President of the American Psychiatric Association warned his colleagues against "contagion by hostility and anxiety, forces which history have shown to be far more destructive of human life than any plague." He urged every citizen to speak out against the fearmongers. Said he, "Those who will not in these days speak out against error and hate may never speak again in freedom's name."

Mrs. Eugene Meyer, the wife of the chairman of the Board of *The Washington Post*, speaking before the Ohio chapter of the American Association of University Professors in 1954, said that all of our freedoms are being threatened today. "Our congressional investigators are seeking to curb all expression of opinion." Turning to academic freedom she declared that the nation's entire education system is being subjected to "repression and intimidation."[16]

Senator Herbert Lehman, speaking before Unitarians in the nation's Capital, said: "These inquisitors have exposed the nation to confusion and dissension at home, and to contumely and ridicule abroad. . . . demagogues have seized false banners of anti-communism and launched a wholesale attack against the very sinews of our power to oppose communism. They have invented strange new techniques and devices—the multiple untruth, the splattering smear, the trial by headline, the intimidation by innuendo, the grisly blackmail by threat of subpoena, all these and many more. . . . New words and phrases have been introduced into the language—sly substitutes for the word traitor and traitorous—like Fifth Amendment Communist, soft towards communism, Communist stooge, special affinity for communist causes—

[15] The Washington *Evening Star*, July 12, 1954.
[16] N.Y. *Herald Tribune*, Feb. 28, 1954.

The Subtle Poisoning of the People 71

words and phrases vague in meaning but specific and tragic in their effect." (N.Y. *Herald Tribune,* Feb. 28, 1954.)

Former Secretary of the Air Forces, Thomas K. Finletter, added a devastating attack against the inquisitors by saying, "A government composed of people paralyzed with fear because of the invasion of their rights is not going to be a very good government."

John Stuart Mill long ago wrote, "That which seems the height of absurdity to one generation often becomes the height of wisdom to the next."

It is an extremely dangerous situation when the American people are subjected to propaganda and an epidemic of fear. All through history on occasions men have been killed for ideas which a later generation accepted as law. The Puritans were heretics in England and to escape persecution they came to America where they, in turn, burned witches and exiled Roger Williams.

Here is an actual letter showing how Cotton Mather and the religious leaders in America wished to deal with Quakers in 1682:

To ye Aged and Beloved Mr. John Higginson: There be now at sea a ship called Welcome which has on board 100 or more heretics and malignants called Quakers, with Mr. Penn, who is the scamp at the head of them. The General Court has accordingly given sacred orders to Master Malachi Bascott, of the brig Porpoise to waylay said Welcome slyly as near the Cape of Cod as may be, and make captive of the same Penn and his ungodly crew, so that the Lord may be glorified and not mocked on the soil of this new country with the heathen worship of these people. Much spoil can be made selling the whole lot to Barbadoes where slaves fetch good prices in rum and sugar, and we shall not only do the Lord great good by punishing the wicked, but we shall make great good for the minister and his people.

Yours in the bowels of Christ
Cotton Mather

In the early part of this century American radicals had a rough time of it with strikes, lockouts, court injunctions, arrests, jail terms, and assault. What were they striving for? Laws such as old age pensions, government housing, the nine hour day, and the recognition of trade unions!

How do we protect ourselves from such hysteria? Let me give you a homely illustration. Why do we brush our teeth or rinse out our mouths at night? Is it not to clean out the "garbage" which has accumulated there during the day, much of it even reasonably good food? Yes, it may be good if properly digested, but if left in the mouth to decay it may cause cavities and eventually severe pain may necessitate having a tooth extracted. Now what do we do with the mental garbage that we accumulate every day from the press, the radio, and television? This may be all right if properly digested. But, if not, do we use any method to cleanse our minds? We should ask ourselves: What has been poured into my mind today? Is it honest? Is it true? Has it been propaganda? Has it been filth? Has it been properly digested? What are the opposition arguments to those I heard today? This is the only way we will reach the truth on the great issues of the day; indeed, it is the only way to prevent our minds from becoming mental garbage cans full of a host of decaying and unassimilated ideas.

The General Council of the Presbyterian Church (U.S.A.) recently adopted a resolution calling attention to the ways in which Congressional investigations were threatening American life. It was written by President John A. Mackay of Princeton Theological Seminary. It says in part, "As a result of this there is growing up over against Communism a fanatical negativism. Totally devoid of any constructive program of action, this negativism is in danger of leading the American mind into a spiritual vacuum. Our national house cleansed of one demon, would invite by its very emptiness the entrance of seven others. In the case of a national crisis this emptiness could, in the high-sounding name of security, be occupied with ease by a fascist tyranny." In short, there can be no peace until reason, understanding, and real facts have a greater part in our mental processes than mere emotions fed by ignorance and prejudice. All of this demands freedom for all men everywhere to think as the truth leads them.

Another defense against the poisoning of our people is a return to a reliance on God and His Truth, on prayer, and on moral power. We must try to be good neighbors to all, even our enemies, as Christ and the prophets taught. This is a hard road but it leads to moral power, integrity, and friendship, and it almost certainly prevents poisoning and hate.

Prayer

O Father of Love, we thank Thee for the chance that is ours to resist all that is harmful to Thy children everywhere. Inspire us to add our small share to the building of freedom and health in our own communities. Help us to strive both individually and collectively for "whatsoever things are true, whatsoever things are honorable, whatsoever things are just, whatsoever things are pure, whatsoever things are lovely, whatsoever things are of good report."

We realize the imperfections of our nation and of our world, but with Thy help all things are possible. Keep us worry-free because we have tried to do the best we know. Guard us from cynicism. Let us be Thy instruments in positive acts of kindness. Put the smile of the radiance of truth on our faces. Help us to do our best and leave the rest with Thee.   Amen.

The tombstones of a good many people should read: "Died at thirty, buried at sixty."

> NICHOLAS MURRAY BUTLER, President of
> Columbia University

I see in the future a crisis arising that unnerves me and causes me to tremble for the safety of my country. As a result of the war, corporations have been enthroned and an era of corruption in high places will follow, and the money power of the country will endeavor to prolong its reign by working on the prejudices of the people until all wealth is aggravated in a few hands and the Republic is destroyed . . ."

> REPUBLICAN PRESIDENT ABRAHAM LINCOLN, 1864

It was time to say something, for the representatives of predatory wealth, of wealth accumulated on a giant scale by iniquity, by wrongdoing in many forms, by plain swindling, by oppressing wage-workers, by manipulating securities, by unfair and unwholesome competition and by stockjobbing, in short, by conduct abhorrent to every man of ordinarily decent conscience. . . . From the railroad rate law to the pure food law, every measure for honesty in business that has been pressed during the last six years, has been opposed by these men, on its passage and in its administration, with every resource that bitter and unscrupulous craft could suggest, and the command of almost unlimited money. These men do not themselves speak or write; they hire others to do their bidding.

> REPUBLICAN PRESIDENT THEODORE ROOSEVELT,
> Jan. 2, 1908 (*Autobiography,* pp. 451–2)

Samuel Gompers was right when he said that the effort to secure justice for the working man means a fight. It does. It means a long, unending fight. I have seen the truth of that in my experience, too.

It is an unending fight because the forces of reaction never give up. They have money and they have power, and they never really believe that the people ought to govern themselves. They are always trying to turn the control of the country over to a privileged few.

DEMOCRATIC PRESIDENT HARRY S. TRUMAN,
Oct. 27, 1951

There are plenty to follow our Lord half way, but not the other half.

MEISTER ECKHART

> He is a path, if any be misled;
> He is a robe, if any naked be;
> If any chance to hunger, He is bread;
> If any be a bondsman, He is free;
> If any be but weak; how strong is He!

GILES FLETCHER

CHAPTER VI

Economic Illiteracy

THE economic order should serve the Kingdom of God. The Preamble to the Constitution states: "We the people of the United States, in order to . . . *promote the general welfare* . . . do ordain and establish this Constitution." Have we really been scrupulously careful to promote the public welfare? Have we shown great wisdom and intelligence in our economic system? Every generation tends to believe its own economic order is good. This has held true of feudalism, slavery, and the acquisitive society. But we all know in our hearts that the present social order does not attain to the standards of God.

Stuart Chase, the eminent writer, maintains that a visitor from another planet looking at our behavior after the financial crash of 1929 would have thought us "mad." He insists that looking at the American world in 1929 the planetary visitor would have seen factories, railroads, stores, farms, operating normally and nearly everyone busily employed. But what a change in the situation in 1932?

"Millions of men have thrown down their tools and left their machines and conveyer belts in the factories; they drift about the streets doing nothing. The farmers' crops, harvested with such labor, lie rotting in the fields or on railroad sidings. People are being evicted from their homes by the thousands in both city and country. . . . Factories close one wing, then another, then bank their fires together. Mines flood with water, ships are tied up at the docks, freight cars and trucks go into storage. Long lines of men move slowly up to gloomy buildings with signs saying 'soup kitchen' or 'Employment Agency,' is it any wonder the observer thinks we have gone mad?"[1]

Now if the observer were to look at the world in the Fifties he

[1] Stuart Chase, *Harper's Magazine,* Oct. 1942.

would see that the United States produces enormous amounts but spends roughly 85 per cent of its governmental revenue for wars, past, present or future. Other nations are starving while food belonging to the United States is rotting in storage. The entire world is split into two rival camps each calling the other vile names. We are normally at peace but actually using a substantial segment of our productive power for armaments and military air bases. The observer would probably still conclude we were just a bit demented. This feeling would be strongly reinforced if he read the statement of the late Harold L. Ickes, who was Secretary of the Interior in the President's Cabinet. As far back as 1949 he wrote: "Fear of Communism is a great, open spigot that drains billions from the U.S. Treasury faster than they can be accumulated. Our scientists pervert their truth-questioning minds in a search for surer means of annihilation. But while we fume at the totalitarianism that is Communism, we prepare to embrace the totalitarianism fascism that also sought to destroy the freedom without which life would be too shameful to be worthwhile. We propose a garden hose for the feeble, corrupt Chiang Kai-shek gang to turn upon the unquenchable conflagration that is sweeping China. *Per contra*, we send warships to Spain to salute a fascist dictator who has destroyed the liberties of his people."[2]

Although in 1954 the United States was supposed to be in an era of prosperity and the President had stated there were no genuine signs of depression, by the middle of the year the President of the American Federation of Labor maintained the unemployed numbered over five million. By 1955 the government had a deficit of $9,249,000,000 for the first half of the fiscal year. This in spite of the President's campaign pledge to balance the budget. As we shall see in subsequent chapters the Prophets and Jesus castigated wealth and economic exploitation. They maintained that *only what is right is practical*. What would Jesus have said about our armament race? Would he have endorsed the idea that we must be practical, compromise our conscience, and drop atom and hydrogen bombs to snuff out whole populations?

Now a strong case can be made out for capitalism. We have in the United States the greatest productive capacity in the world. It provides automobiles, movies, television and clothing in abundance. The sys-

[2] Harold L. Ickes, *New Republic*, Oct. 17, 1949.

tem is flexible and brings to the top men of real ability. Inventions and the production of things are stimulated. Professor Adolph A. Berle, Jr. maintains that the American corporation now has a conscience and thinks of its duty to the public as well as to the stockholder.[3]

America which contains perhaps only six and a half per cent of the world's population makes some fifty-five per cent of all the steel, produces seventy per cent of the oil, produces some sixty per cent of the manufactured goods, grows about half the cotton and raises one third of the grain of the world. It is safe to say that the United States has roughly forty-five per cent of all the income of the world.

Yet we know that mere material prosperity is not enough. What we desperately need is a spiritual and moral foundation for our life. Not only the individual but every business should be a channel of spiritual power. Charles Malik, the distinguished Minister of Lebanon to the United States has this to say, "To the superficial observer who is unable to penetrate to the core of love and truth which is still at the heart of the West, there is little to choose between the soulless materialism of the West and the militant materialism of the East. . . . If your only export is a distant reputation for wealth and prosperity and order, you cannot lead. Nor can you really lead if you send forth to others only expert advice and technical assistance. To be able to lead and save yourself and others you must above everything else address their mind and soul."[4] But have we done this enough?

The working class is isolated from the capitalist class. They go to different sections of the city to live, belong to different clubs and churches. It is very hard for the millionaire to understand the feelings of the worker living in the slum.

Of course, in theory the poor worker can become the great capitalist. In theory the system provides for freedom of enterprise. Today workers who are effectively organized, as long as they can keep employed, benefit by high wages if they are in the right factory or area.

America was founded on the basis of individualism. This worked well while our natural resources were undeveloped and we inhabited a virgin continent but now our American society has become an inter-

[3] Berle, A. A., *The 20th Century Capitalist Revolution*, 1954.
[4] A statement made before the Political Committee of the General Assembly of the United Nations, Nov. 23, 1949.

acting whole. The old individualism has tried to hang society together on the basis of dollars and profits. This worked well as long as we were individual communities but today we are a nation of 160,000,000 people living in an interdependent urban society. The fact of the matter is the whole world has become so small in point of time that we are now part of one small planetary society. It is no longer possible for any of us to say "each for himself and the devil take the hindermost."

An outstanding feature of the capitalistic system is the profit motive. Yet there is a wide consensus among Christians calling for its subordination to a more moral motivation. For example, a statement by Protestant, Catholic and Jewish leaders called "Pattern for Economic Justice" says, "The profit motive must be subordinated to the moral law. To make the profit motive the guiding principle in economic life is to violate the order which God himself has established."

There are disquieting signs that we are not highly intelligent in the economic area, perhaps not even literate.

For instance, we are increasing the national debt towards the three hundred billions mark, an astronomical figure that the citizen cannot understand, but the interest alone comes to $6,475,000,000.[5]

Again and again the attempt has been made to free natural gas rates from Federal control. This would cost the consumers over $160,000,000 annually. In 1955, this was blocked largely through the efforts of Senator Douglas, altho the natural gas producers spent in lobbying in the first half of the year alone, $67,851. In fact lobbying by the big financial interests is a potent power in defeating the will of the people and counting nationwide radio, television and advertising programs runs up into the hundreds of millions.

We have been subsidizing farmers to keep them prosperous until we have on hand vast quantities of food which are spoiling. Although the people are eating oleomargarine at perhaps one-fourth of what they would have to pay for butter, the government continues to keep up the price of butter. Vast quantities are purchased by the government until now we have thousands of tons which are in danger of

[5] Letter to the author from the Treasury Department, January 31, 1955, showing interest for the fiscal year 1955.

spoiling in our store houses.[6] We have devised some plans for selling some of this to the Orient but apparently are unwilling to sell to Russia who could use it. In spite of the billions of dollars of farm support, the Agricultural Department announces that the income for the average farmer in the United States for 1953 was only $852. The United States has purchased millions of dollars worth of dried milk which it is now giving to the farmers at far below cost to feed to the cows. This should eventually result in far more powdered milk which the government can purchase and again give back to the cows!!

Apparently the chief way we keep our economic machine going without a depression is to spend vast sums on supplies for the military. If we were intelligent enough we could spend more for worthwhile projects such as schools and hospitals.

We profess to believe in individualism and free competition while we slap on high tariffs and give subsidies to firms that will enlarge their plants. Actually we have had since the war a two billion dollar tax amortization "give away" program whereby business can build huge industrial plants and charge it to their taxes.

Reports of the Kefauver Committee, the Temporary National Economic Committee and the La Follette Committee and other investigations of lobbying have shown how monopoly has thrived in the United States. The late Secretary Harold L. Ickes has said that our great corporations are controlled by a handful of men who don't even own the corporations.[7] The Cabinet of the United States under the Eisenhower Administration is made up largely of representatives of big financial interests. By way of contrast one has only to look at the poverty of the organization of the consumers' interests to sense what is happening. The big corporations are getting smarter. As Tawney has remarked, "The great beasts of the jungle do not hunt by daylight." They try to hide their monopoly power, but if they are indicted, they can usually have the prosecution dropped through one influence or another. As we

[6] In 1954 the Commodity Credit Corporation had 466 million pounds of butter on hand.

[7] *The Secret Diary of Harold L. Ickes* Vol. II, p. 62. President Franklin D. Roosevelt declared that the power of money is so great in the United States that "Give me ten million dollars and I can prevent any amendment to the Constitution from being ratified." *Ibid.,* p. 65.

have seen in the previous chapter, the private interests are increasingly able to manipulate public opinion.

Again our economic illiteracy is shown by our standard of values. A moment's reflection will show how warped and distorted this is. We pay a national baseball player from $60,000 to $80,000 a year while the average country school teacher makes only $1,500 a year. Baseball is rendering a service to the nation but is it more important than the education of our children? One of our best comedians makes a million dollars a year. Is it more important to make the nation laugh than it is to make the nation think?

We have used the land so recklessly that it is being exhausted. We have allowed our wild birds to be shot in such quantities that duck and wildfowl are now nonexistent in many places.

We could not enforce Prohibition because people violated the law and lawlessness corrodes justice in almost every large city. Paid lobbyists at our nation's capital receive more money to block or change legislation than do the legislators who write the laws. All of this is indicative of the fact that we still have economic illiteracy. Too bad that we cannot read *now* what the future historian will write about our age?

Too often the United States Government and the corporations have been backing outworn social structures around the world,—feudalism, landlordism, dictatorship and injustice. This was clearly true in French Indo-China where until recently we have been backing corruption and reaction against the wishes of the masses of the people. William Worthy in an article for the National Association for the Advancement of Colored People entitled "Our Disgrace in Indo-China" concludes, "This, then, is the dangerous pass to which we have been brought by the enormous, the imperial, the war-making power of white America."[8] Let us hope that America will now change her policy and support genuine home rule in Indo-China.

We are also doing little or nothing to stop the terrible conditions in South Africa. Just consider the situation briefly as summarized by the famous author Allan Paton: "There are *not many* white people in Africa, perhaps five million in a continental population of one hun-

[8] *The Crisis,* Feb. 1954, p. 82.

dred and fifty million (Northern Rhodesia has three per cent white and Kenya one per cent) . . . the influence of a dominant one per cent, even, is 'immense.' The white man brought *everything:* guns, books, learning, disease, liquors, religion,—there was no plan or project; the things just came. It was only when the damage had been done that white men stood back aghast, seeing that they had destroyed a way of life which, whatever its faults, was *superior to that which succeeded it.*"[9]

In Angola all native black boys are conscripted and forced to work in factories or mines unless they have graduated from high school. "The present government has made it clear that the African is not to expect the vote *ever*." "At any time of the day or night an African must be able to show his 'Pass' to any policeman otherwise he is jailed." Ruth Seabury, Educational Secretary of the Congregational Church, says that she has never seen such slums anywhere in the world as the Africans are forced to live in. She concludes, "Why shouldn't these people hate the white man with a terrible and rising tide of hatred?"

Now just what is the *power structure* in the United States? Long ago when the United States Steel Corporation was formed, President Hadley of Yale said that unless some way could be found to curb the trusts, there would be "an emperor in Washington within twenty-five years."[10] His alarm was not completely unfounded.

Today some 250 giant corporations control roughly two-thirds of the nation's manufacturing and 135 own half the industrial assets of the country. The Federal Trade Commission reports that the largest 113 own 46 per cent of the total capital of all manufacturing. We are now in an era of billionaire corporations. In 1953 this consisted of 22 banks, 13 life insurance companies, 17 industrial companies, six railroads, three other financial corporations, four utilities and one retail giant. Their total assets in 1953 came to almost $175 billions. The eight main financial groups in the country controlled some 70% of this total as follows:[11]

[9] *Envelope Series,* The American Board of Commissioners for Foreign Missions, Spring, 1953, p. 11, 17, 18.
[10] Marquis W. Childs and Douglas Cater, *Ethics in a Business Society,* p. 104.
[11] Labor Research Association, *Billionaire Corporations,* 1954, pp. 13–15.

Financial Group	No. of Companies	Assets
Morgan First National	12	$50,300,000,000
Rockefeller	9	36,800,000,000
Du Pont	3	8,100,000,000
Chicago	4	7,800,000,000
Boston	3	6,600,000,000
Kuhn, Loeb	3	5,800,000,000
Mellon	3	4,700,000,000
Cleveland	1	1,300,000,000

An examination of the Board of Directors of these companies shows that each of 127 men hold directorships in two or more of the billion dollar corporations. As far back as 1949 nine billionaire corporations had a total sales income of $21 billion, half as much as the combined Federal Government revenue. Attorney General Tom C. Clark in 1949 told Congress, "Today monopoly power in this nation is to be found in those industries controlled by a few large companies—the Big Threes or the Big Fours—following policies and practices which avoid any real competition among themselves and which at the same time enable them to maintain their dominant position."[12]

A study of the Twentieth Century Fund in 1948 showed that cartels regulate the sales of 86.9 per cent of all minerals, 47.4 per cent of the agricultural products and 42.7 per cent of all manufactures although these may include some inter-governmental syndicates. Naturally the big business concerns take the lead in determining how much is produced and exported. As Charles E. Wilson, former President of General Motors and Secretary of Defense, said in a Congressional Hearing these business leaders tend to believe that whatever is good for the big corporations is good for the people. In fact Senator Joseph C. O'Mahoney speaking to the American Bar Association in 1947 declared, "The modern corporation, in some instances, has become more powerful even than the state." General Motors alone in 1953 set a total sales record of $10,028,000,000 and net income was $558,-721,179. Still corporation leaders are not adverse to further tax relief!

Professor Edward H. Carr of England maintains: "Before the end of the nineteenth century, organized groups of capitalists were exer-

[12] Gunther Stein, *The World the Dollar Built*, p. 32.

cising a predominant influence on the political life of all advanced countries" and in the United States "The new economic power had the field to itself." He maintains that the two great American political parties were "cleverly constructed combinations of economic group interests, dependent for their financial maintenance on those interests and struggling on their behalf for the control of the political machine."[13]

Because there is some truth to Professor Carr's charge the Federal Government hesitates to prosecute to a conclusion these big financial combines. Besides, they contribute heavily to political campaigns through their officers and others. From a practical standpoint, the government's legal staff is hardly on a par with that of the big corporations because not enough money is voted by Congress for the enforcement of the antitrust laws. Even when the government starts a suit against a company as it did against Du Pont in 1949 nothing usually comes of it in the end. On March 17, 1954 the suit against the four major meat-packing companies filed in 1948 was dropped, the Attorney General of the United States saying he was convinced there was "no possibility of dissolution of the companies."

The talk about vast numbers of the people owning the corporations means very little. The Brookings Institution found that only one out of every sixteen persons in America owned any stock at all and only 8 per cent of these owned more than $480 worth. Small stockholders have almost no say in running the business. Sumner H. Schlichter of Harvard said in 1949, "The directorates of most corporations consist almost entirely of officials of other corporations, plus a few so-called 'capitalists,' that is men who own large investments but do not directly administer enterprises."[14]

In the United States there are also some three and one-half million small business concerns but they do not have much control or power. During the first six and one-half years after World War II over two million small firms died. Actually three out of every ten new small enterprises die within the first year and roughly another two die in the next two years. Only about a quarter live for six years or more.

Some may say, well at any rate the working class has enormously

[13] Carr, Edward H., *Conditions of Peace*, Macmillan, 1947, pp. 23–29.
[14] *Fortune Magazine*, Sept., 1949.

advanced in the past fifty years. While there is much that can be said for this theory in reality its purchasing power has only increased about 38% if we take the data from the Census of Manufacturers and the Bureau of Labor Statistics on price changes.[15]

Year	Output	Employment	Output per wker	Wages & Salaries	Av. Annual earnings empl. wkers	Index of Price	Av. real purch. power	Relative position of wker
1899	100	100	100	100	100	100	100	100
1909	158	139	114	169	122	129	94	82
1919	222	191	116	518	271	235	115	99
1929	364	190	192	587	309	232	133	69
1939	373	187	199	490	262	188	139	70
1947	649	281	231	1530	544	413	133	58
1952	669	286	269	2119	741	537	138	51

The people who prepared this table believe that since productivity has risen to 269 the relative position of the worker in the economy has declined seriously. Whether or not we accept this position, we certainly have not produced a "utopia" for the factory workers.

But the reader may feel the present capitalistic system is the best the world has ever seen, therefore, it is immortal. Every generation tends to think its own dominant system will last. The writer was in Tsaristic Russia just before it collapsed. The nobility were sure it would endure long after capitalism had vanished.

THE ETHICS OF *The Economic Order*

We must beware of accepting beliefs merely because they are the dominant opinions of the status quo. In 1939 Professor Lynd of Columbia University made a study of Middletown which listed some 172 beliefs held by the majority of the people. Stuart Chase in 1948 in a book called "The Proper Study of Mankind" estimates that "about one hundred were rendered obsolete in whole or in part by the march of events." Here are some of the beliefs which were proved false: 1—The open shop is the American way of life, 2—Nothing can be done to stop depressions, 3—Every man for himself is the right and necessary law of the business world, 4—It is a man's own fault if he is dependent in

[15] Victor Perlo, *The Income 'Revolution'*, 1954, p. 55.

his old age, 5—The government should not interfere in the economic affairs of the people.

Now today it is held that the capitalistic-competitive system will be with us forever but this assumption may not be true any more than arguments for slavery were right a century ago. Let us compare, therefore, the arguments used 100 or more years ago with the arguments used now for our competitive economic system.

Underlying Basic Claims

FOR SLAVERY | FOR CAPITALISM

Arthur Lee, Virginia slaveholder, declared that the habitations of the Negroes are "palaces compared with the peasants of Scotland or Ireland."[15a]

People live very much better and are happier under capitalism than under any other way of life.

Gov. S. D. Miller in his message to the South Carolina Legislature in 1829, "Slavery is not a national evil; on the contrary, it is a national benefit." George Fitzhugh argued that slavery would exist through all eternity.

Capitalism is the best order ever invented by man and will endure forever.

Economic Factors

"Slavery has ever been the stepping ladder by which countries have passed from barbarism to civilization."[16]

The competitive system has made the United States the wealthiest nation on the earth.

(Slavery) "A great blessing to both of the races . . . one of the main sources of the unbounded prosperity."[17]

Without the incomes of the rich where would we get savings for capital investment?

The slaves are better off than hired labor. "The slave has no anxieties from want, misfortune or disability."[18]

Our workers have automobiles, television and more luxuries than in any other country.

[15a] Lee, Arthur, *An Essay*, p. 25.
[16] *Notes on the Origin and Necessity of Slavery*, (Charleston, 1826), p. 6.
[17] Senator John C. Calhoun, *Congressional Globe*, 25th Cong. 3rd Session, p. 177 (Feb. 18, 1839).
[18] W. S. Jenkins, *Pro-Slavery Thought in the Old South*, p. 298.

The laws once sanctioned slavery and it would be a breach of faith to wrest that property from its owners.

Compulsion is necessary to force labor to produce wealth.

Slavery is the means whereby the white man will conquer and improve the world.

Evils are not inherent in slavery; they are mere incidents.

Slavery "the most safe and stable basis for free institutions in the world."[19]

"I think slavery as much a correlative of liberty as cold is of heat."[20] It gives plenty, security and liberty for the Negro. Slavery will preserve free institutions from the growth of revolution.

Abolitionists are revolutionists plotting insurrection and thus are Communists.

Public ownership robs private owners, including widows and orphans, of their property.

Labor works best under the spur of necessity.

America's destiny is to spread the blessings of competitive enterprise around the globe.

Regulated competition will eliminate any weaknesses in laissez-faire competition.

Capitalism really gives workers freedom and equality of opportunity.

Free competitive enterprise is the economic basis of freedom of worship, education and government. They are inseparable and indivisible. Free competitive enterprise will prevent the growth of revolution in America.

Opponents of competitive enterprise are supporters of revolution and are Communist sympathizers.

Religion and Moral Factors

God has set different orders and degrees of men in this world.

God decreed slavery and sanctioned it in the Bible. Neither the prophets nor Christ opposed it.

God brought the slaves to us and we have to accept them as a trust from Him.

God has endowed some men with the ability to accumulate wealth.

It is curious to observe how through the wise and beneficent hand of providence, men do the greatest service to the public when they are thinking of nothing but their own gain.

The rights of the laboring man will be cared for by the Christian men to whom God in His infinite

---

[19] Senator Calhoun, *Congressional Globe,* 25th Cong. 2nd Session, Appendix pp. 61–2, (Jan. 10, 1838).
[20] W. H. Roane, Richmond *Enquirer,* Feb. 4, 1832.

Slavery enables Christians to exercise more of the virtues of mercy and kindness.	wisdom has given control of the property interest of the country. What is good for the corporations is good for the people. Public welfare is replacing the virtue of Christian charity.

Biological and Sociological Factors

Negroes are biologically a different species from white men.	Owners and workers are a different class. "The nature of man establishes the doctrine of the elite."
Slavery is as much a natural phenomenon as the origin of species.	"The survival of the fittest is the natural law of life and a material standard of values . . ."[21]

Since the arguments about slavery have been proved false, it is quite conceivable that time may prove some of the arguments used to support our economic competitive system false.

Henry Demarest Lloyd has said in *Wealth Against Commonwealth,* "When it comes to know the facts, the human heart can no more endure monopoly than American slavery or Roman empire." Arnold Toynbee said, "The Twentieth Century will be remembered not as the age of the atomic bomb, or as the conflict between Christianity and communism, but as the first age in history in which man thought it practical to distribute all the benefits of civilization to all men." Of course, we haven't done this yet. We distribute taxation to all. If even a fifteen cent article is purchased in a grocery store in Tennessee, a one cent tax is paid!

Actually one out of four Americans who died in the post-war years could have lived longer. What was killing them was chiefly poverty.[22]

Are not the following some of the goals we should strive for?

Social Motives	Political Motives	Economic Motives
Freedom	Liberty	Opportunity
Justice	Equality	Security
Brotherhood	Fraternity	Partnership

[21] James W. Prothro, *Dollar Decade,* 1954, p. 209.
[22] Gunther Stein, *The World the Dollar Built,* New York, 1953, p. 164.

If we had economic security we should probably have (1) everyone an owner of productive property (2) opportunity for full employment for everyone able to work (3) everyone receiving an equitable share in the national income.

In the family one would not permit a bigger boy to reach across the table at meal time and grab all he could lay his hands on leaving not enough for his small brothers and sisters. Yet such actions are permitted by society in the working of its economic system. Dr. E. Stanley Jones says the same equitable system we use in family relationships should be applied in community, state, nation and the world.

Today the common people who do not have much money are encouraged to do installment buying, until now their debt has risen to twenty-two billion.

To summarize
1. Our present economic system is unstable—think of the record of booms and depressions
2. The system is not equitable

Thornstein Veblin once wrote "The highest achievement in business is the nearest approach to getting something for nothing."

Here was the picture economically in the U.S. in 1953 from Federal Reserve Board sources.

The wealthiest tenth get 31% of national income, have 45% of savings and 65% of liquid assets.

The poorest tenth get 1% of the national income, 1% of savings and have no liquid assets.

The upper half of the people get 77% of the national income, have 84% of savings and 99% of liquid assets.

The lower half get 23% income, have 16% of the savings and have 1% of the liquid assets.

The Federal Reserve Board and the University of Michigan's survey research center have made an annual survey of consumer finances.[23] Grouping 55 million families by income before taxes in 1953 this survey shows:

[23] Federal Reserve Bulletin, June, July, 1954.

1953
Distribution of **MONEY INCOME** among American families

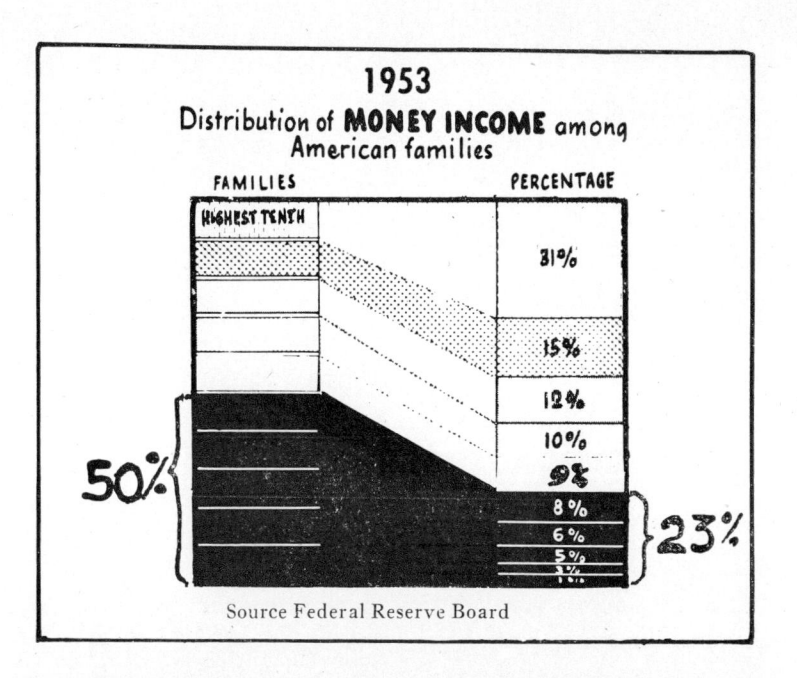

FAMILIES | PERCENTAGE

HIGHEST TENTH — 31%

15%
12%
10%
9%
8%
6%
5%

50% { ... } 23%

Source Federal Reserve Board

DISTRIBUTION OF TOTAL LIQUID ASSETS*
Early 1954

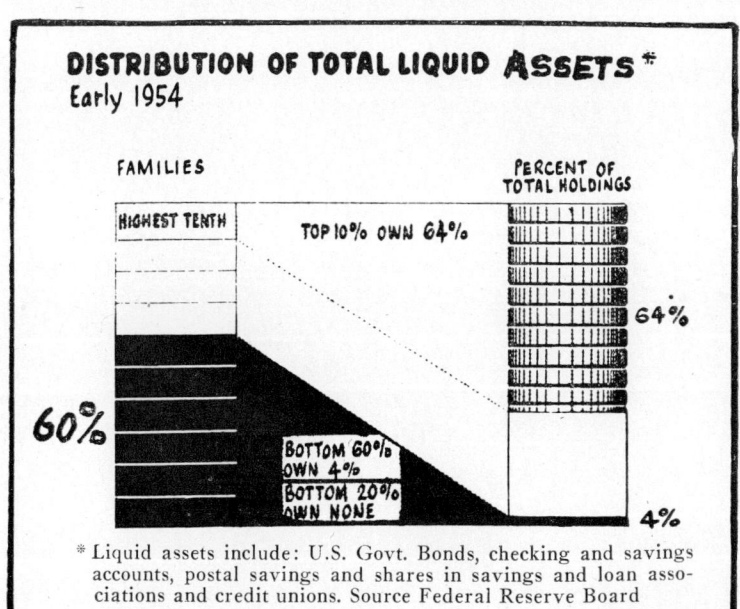

FAMILIES | PERCENT OF TOTAL HOLDINGS

HIGHEST TENTH — TOP 10% OWN 64%

64%

60%

BOTTOM 60% OWN 4%
BOTTOM 20% OWN NONE

4%

*Liquid assets include: U.S. Govt. Bonds, checking and savings accounts, postal savings and shares in savings and loan associations and credit unions. Source Federal Reserve Board

Economic Illiteracy

5,500,000	families	(10%)	received	less	than	$ 1,000	
12,650,000	"	(23%)	"	"	"	2,000	
20,350,000	"	(37%)	"	"	"	3,000	
29,150,000	"	(53%)	"	"	"	4,000	
37,950,000	"	(69%)	"	"	"	5,000	
49,500,000	"	(90%)	"	"	"	7,000	
5,500,000	"	(10%)	"	"	"	7,500	or over
2,750,000	"	(5%)	"	"	"	10,000	or over
1,100,000	"	(2%)	"	"	"	15,000	or over

Half these families received annually less than $3,780, and half received more. The Federal Reserve Board found that in 1954, when it made its survey, 14,300,000 families had no liquid assets at all such as, "all types of U.S. Government bonds, checking accounts, savings accounts in banks, postal savings, and shares in savings and loan associations and credit unions." On the other hand the ten per cent with the largest incomes had 64% of the liquid assets of all families.*

Is a system with such contrasts of income just or unjust? E. R. Bowen, former Secretary of the Consumers Cooperative League of the U.S.A. calls it "social robbery."

Edwin Markham wrote a little poem:

> Two things, said Kant, fill me with breathless awe:
> The starry heavens and the moral law.
> But I know a thing more awful and obscure
> The long, long patience of the plundered poor.

3. Our system is so precariously balanced that it seems as if we maintain prosperity by war or military preparations. The government is continually giving business subsidies and as a result of this and military spending we have already run up the national debt to astronomical proportions.

4. The present corporation system is undemocratic. Wealthy owners of stock can frequently control even if they have a very small proportion of the total stock issued. On the other hand, the widely scattered owners of the majority of the stock find it difficult to take action. The Consumers Cooperative Movement which gives a vote per person is far more democratic.

5. The present economic system leads to monopoly.

* See facing page.

The Senate Committee Report issued after World War II entitled "United States vs. Economic Concentration and Monopoly," shows in cases of some commodities 85% are produced by one company.

6. The present system often results in imperialism or the exploitation of backward people. The way out is not Communism and dictatorship, but we must move in the direction of an economy based on a more sustained effort to promote the public welfare as in the cooperative movement, for instance.

Under the present order even some of the successful may become casualties. A printed slip presented to its guests by a Hotel Court, in Florida reads:

"In 1923 a very important meeting was held at the Edgewater Beach Hotel in Chicago. Attending this meeting were eight of the world's most successful financiers. Those were:

The President of the largest independent steel company
The President of the largest utility company
The greatest wheat speculator
The President of the New York Stock Exchange
A member of the President's Cabinet
The greatest "bear" in Wall Street
Head of the World's greatest monopoly
President of the Bank of International Settlements

"Certainly we must admit that here were gathered a group of the world's most successful men. At least, men who had found the secret of "making money." Twenty-five years later let us see where these men are:

"The President of the largest independent steel company—Charles Schwab—died a bankrupt and lived on borrowed money for five years before his death.

The President of the greatest utility company—Samuel Insull—died a fugitive from justice and penniless in a foreign land.

The greatest wheat speculator—Arthur Cutten—died abroad—insolvent.

The president of the New York Stock Exchange—Richard Whitney—was recently released from Sing Sing penitentiary.

The member of the President's cabinet was pardoned from prison so he could die at home.

The greatest "bear" in Wall Street—Jesse Livermore—died a suicide.

The head of the greatest monopoly—Ivar Krueger—died a suicide.

The President of the Bank of International Settlements—Leon Fraser—died a suicide."

All of these men learned well the art of making money, but not one of them learned how to live.

Can you imagine eight of the great religious leaders of the United States having a similar fate? Apparently working for others in God's service is better than building corporate structures for financial gain.

Another example is that of Terry J. Druggan who died in March, 1954. The Internal Revenue Board estimated that at the peak of his career he was making $1,500,000 a year. Even when he went to jail for bootlegging he lived in luxury. He simply "bought" his keepers. He not only conducted his business affairs in jail garbed in silk clothes, but he was stepping out evenings in a dinner jacket to make the rounds of the night clubs. This only cost him $2,000 a month paid to the jailer. Yet when he died of a chronic heart ailment, stomach ulcers and asthma at fifty-two, he was penniless. He typified the alliance between corruption and business. He was manager of seven breweries for Al Capone and ran another for himself at full scale even when it was padlocked by the government.[24]

From these illustrations we must conclude that making money is hardly a sufficient test of success in any society. We do not mean to imply that a great many of our financial leaders have not got satisfaction out of life. But there is much evidence to show that many finally realized happiness by giving their money away to worthwhile projects, witness Carnegie, Rockefeller, Kresge, Ford, to mention only a few.

If we were highly intelligent in economic affairs, would we not plan so that all peoples in the world had the chance to earn the necessities of life? Would we pile up huge surpluses of food subsidized by the government while other peoples were starving? Would we promote and perpetuate imperialism and economic exploitation?

It seems much more likely that we would reduce the vast sums now being spent on armaments and air bases all around the world and would

[24] New York *Herald Tribune*, March 6, 1954.

use these for rational planning for the development of the natural resources of the world. It seems probable that there would be a trend towards having the economy owned by those who use it as in the cooperative movement. We should also have an economy with a stable secure subsistence for all, not one of "booms and busts" at periodic intervals as at present. We should not waste and destroy our natural resources.

Dr. Paul Sears, Chairman of the Conservation Program at Yale University, has this to say about present politics: "The raging waters of today are the price of waving fields of grain, of forests destroyed, of roads and cities thrown together with no far-seeing plan. To an eye trained to read the landscape, this tragic disaster of flood has but one meaning. Our continent is sick. The floods of today boiling over a land stripped of its cover and so robbed of its moisture that wells must sink from twelve to sixty feet deeper than ever before to strike water. This land is covered by a network of highways which defy natural drainage patterns. How far must suffering and misery go before we see that even in the day of vast cities and powerful machines the good earth is our mother and that, if we destroy ourselves."[25]

Professor Prothro in his recent book *Dollar Decade,* which has an Introduction by Professor Alpheus T. Mason of Princeton, says by way of conclusion, "On occasion the exclusive concern of business organizations for property reaches virtually paranoiac proportions. Programs as innocuous as old age pensions and unemployment compensation—subsequently to be accepted by business itself—are viewed as revolutionary moves calculated to destroy the institution of private property."[26]

To summarize consider the following statement from the Committee on the Church and International Affairs adopted by the General Council of the United Church of Canada in 1952, in which it condemns materialism as a stumbling block:

"North American materialism, however, has less favorable aspects. Because this continent's peoples have emerged as World War II victors they are tempted to use power irresponsibly. And there are evidences that this is the situation. For example, the United States pro-

---

[25] Gilbert, Clinton Wallace, *The Mirror of Washington,* also checked with Dr. Sears for its relevance in 1955.
[26] Prothro, James W., Dollar Decade, 1954, p. 240.

gramme of aid to Europe was primarily non-military in character. Today, however, its civilian part is only 12 per cent compared to its military section of 88 per cent. Further, the total aid programme is sometimes used by the United States to force an alignment of Western European nations in accord with American policy.

"The power plays of the United States are paralleled by displays of pride. This pride is regarded by many nations as arrogance. They think the United States has imperialistic ambitions. Thus many people abroad suspect the American people. Others are bitter and some hate both them and us because of pride.

"The world's poor deplore North America's wasteful ways. They think this continent is a profligate one whose people take too many of the essentials of life to satisfy their selfishness. They say North America has priced many important commodities so high that poor nations cannot buy from her. Many people overseas have other doubts about this continent. They view North American movies and hear her radio programmes and think the people of this continent are headed for paganism."[27]

[27] *The Church and International Affairs,* The United Church of Canada.

Prayer

Our Father, forgive us for our concentration on material success. Help us to grow to maturity in our economic life. Aid us to become "literate" in the moral aspects of the economic order which we create. We realize in our hearts that a different world cannot be built by indifferent people. We are grateful for the words of inspiration and help that come down to us from the prophets and from Jesus. Help us to apply them in our own lives not just listen to them. We thank Thee for the chance to reshape and remold our lives each day towards truth and righteousness. Help us to catch the fleeting aspirations, the kindling desires, the new opportunities, that come to us as we go about our daily duties. May we not be indifferent to the evils of our social order. Guard us from forgetfulness, from concentration on our own desires or conventional entanglements which make us unconsciously forget Thy cause. Challenge us to dedicated hard work, recognizing that if economic sins exist in the fabric of society we cannot evade or shirk our responsibility. Teach us that we are partners in the sins of our age. Beget within us more and more of the spirit of the Master whom we would serve. And so let our light shine before men that they also may irresistibly do more good in their lives. We pray humbly and earnestly that little by little our society may be transformed into Thy society of justice, peace and goodwill.   Amen.

In thus forcing us once again to search our hearts, communism is doing us Westerners a valuable, though unintentional, spiritual service; for to skate on the surface of spiritual life is an unhealthy and unhappy way of living; and a spiritually "emancipated" Western man has been living this superficial life ever since he discarded Christianity.

> ARNOLD TOYNBEE, The New York *Times Magazine,* Dec. 26, 1954.

As president of the National Negro Congress, I saw Communists, rank and file members, as well as so-called leaders, who resorted to the most abject groveling, the most undignified concealment of their personal convictions and the grossest denial of the ordinary principles of decency when their party bosses cracked the whip.

It is the grossest travesty upon truth to say that these miserable cowards and hirelings have been raised 'to the full dignity of mankind.'

> MAX YERGEN, *The Crisis,* no. 487, p. 570

While we must fearlessly reject, as we did, what we think wrong, we must be prepared to acknowledge what is good, and I think particularly the solid progress which Russia has made since the devastating war, and the extraordinary development from an agricultural to an industrial country with a higher standard of living than it has ever known in the past . . .

Russia is intensely frightened of a rearmed Germany. It is my opinion that nothing is more likely to precipitate an early war than the real belief that Germany will again become a great military power. That is something that the West could trade in at this moment in return for freeing the whole of Germany from any sort of foreign control.

> PAUL S. CADBURY, Vice-President of Cadbury Brothers, Ltd. England and member of the British Quaker Mission to Moscow, 1951

Our liaison with Russia has always been as close and intimate as necessary to meet any situation at any particular moment. They have given me the information I desired willingly and cheerfully. I am completely satisfied.
>   Gen. Dwight Eisenhower, during World War II

Today we are faced with the pre-eminent fact that, if civilization is to survive, we must cultivate the science of human relationships—the ability *of all peoples, of all kinds*, to live together and work together in the same world, at peace.
>   The last words of Franklin Delano Roosevelt

An entire nation has stopped everything else to hunt Communists and to fear Communism. And so obsessed has America become with this search that she is in grave danger of losing her way of life, not so much to communism itself as to fear of Communism.
>   Murray D. Lincoln, President of the Cooperative League of the United States

Communism is "foredoomed to failure" because it does not accept God, but no negative program against it will be successful.

Ideas are on the march, forces are abroad whose time has come. They cannot be repressed and they will bring unjust orders to an end . . . All forms of feudalism . . . are foredoomed. So too are all forms of imperialism . . . Many of the revolutionary forces of our time are in great part the judgment of God upon human selfishness and complacency, and upon man's forgetfulness of man.
>   The General Council of the Presbyterian Church, Oct. 21, 1953.

CHAPTER VII

The Challenge of Communism

THE Western World has been greatly alarmed about the spread of Communism, as over a third of the world's population has fallen under its sway. There are undoubtedly great dangers in Communism but it is an oversimplification to blame all our evils on this one scapegoat. The adoption of a communist devil-theory to explain the whole world crisis simply blinds us to the complexity of the problems we face. We should rather ask why does communism keep spreading? Why do the exploited masses embrace it?

You shall know the truth and the truth shall make you free. The free man is unafraid. The American tradition upholds in Milton's forceful phrase, "the liberty to know, to think, to believe and to utter freely, according to conscience." There is a danger that Americans may be misled by a caricature of Communism and thus not know how to oppose it effectively.

It so happens that the author went to Russia almost forty years ago under the Tsar's regime, has visited the country often and has been following the situation closely ever since. In Turkestan, where he was first working for the American Y.M.C.A. under the Tsar, some ninety per cent of the people were illiterate. In the first prison camp to which he was assigned seventy-five were dying every single day. The Tsar's secret service shadowed him twenty-four hours a day and even slept in the same room at night.

Remaining in Russia all through the period in which the Bolsheviks consolidated their power the author was strongly opposed to Communism. He did not believe in their brutality towards the old propertied and aristocratic classes.

He could never agree with Communistic theory. It accepts the metaphysics of Karl Marx which views all history as solely the interplay of economic forces. Actually there is a spiritual power at work in the universe that affects individuals and history.

In the third place, the Communists believe that the end justifies the means. They are quite willing to overthrow democracy by any means if they can secure the triumph of Communism.

In the fourth place, the Communists hold as a goal the "dictatorship of the proletariat." This they believe is the exact opposite of what prevails in the capitalistic countries where the rich are viewed as the dictators. In theory the Communists believe that after the power of the rich is broken and the masses are ruling, the state should "wither away." Actually, instead, they have built up a highly centralized and disciplined party organization which in the end seems likely to make the dictatorship of the party leaders endure for decades. Within the party certain individuals rose to the top and became the real rulers. Stalin exiled Trotsky and executed many of his other rivals. Certain of the actions of the party were undoubtedly against the wishes of the majority of the people. For example, when collectivization was forced upon the peasantry it is almost certain that if an honest vote had been taken the overwhelming majority would have opposed it. True, in theory, the Communists believe in "freedom of discussion, and unity in action" but in actual practice criticism of the highest decisions of the party is tabu. Lenin called this principle *democratic centralism,* in other words freedom of criticism was allowed as long as it did not undermine or negate an action already decided on by the highest organs of the party. For those who believe in liberty and freedom without any *ands, ifs* and *buts,* it is hard to see how this doctrine can usher in true liberty.

In the fifth place, the Communists tolerate only one political party, their own. To be sure, they permit non-party candidates to be nominated but since they cannot have the backing of a national political machine they operate under a severe handicap. In a genuine democracy it is essential to permit *all* parties to function.

In the early days of the Revolution in Russia the party congress was supposed to meet every year and was the supreme power but as time went on it met less frequently. In 1934 the rule was changed to a meeting once every three years but when that regulation was adopted it had not met for three and one-half years and the next Congress did not meet for five years. In 1917 there were only about 23,600 party members but by 1946, if we include its auxiliaries, it included some 32 millions or roughly one-sixth of the population, still far from a majority.

In the sixth place, the Communists do not sufficiently safeguard the rights of the individual. The author watched individual after individual arrested for mere criticism of the state or suspicion. The policy of "guilt by association" is followed. If a man is found to be disloyal, then all his friends are suspect. If an organization is listed as disloyal, then membership in it may cause arrest or loss of position.

In the seventh place, the Communist regime is sometimes callously indifferent to the fate of individuals or groups, if they go against "necessary" measures. Party theory is based on justice for the industrial worker and has often been cruelly unjust to the peasant. Communists do not believe in the infinite worth of each personality. Professor Frederick L. Schuman describes the famine in the Ukraine in 1932–33 in these words:

Most of the victims, the number of whom cannot be ascertained in the absence of any official or accurate information, were kulaks who had refused to sow their fields or had destroyed their crops. Observation in the villages suggests that this portion of the peasantry was left to starve by the authorities and the collective farmers as a more or less deliberate policy. Large numbers were deported to labor camps where some died of malnutrition and disease and others were rehabilitated into useful citizens. The human cost of "class war in the villages" was horrible and heavy. The Party appeared less disturbed by dead kulaks than by dead cows. The former were "class enemies."[1]

There was also terror during the Revolution but it must always be remembered that the terror of the reactionary elements was usually even worse. Wherever a dictatorial government tried to suppress Communism, if later the Communists captured the power, the red terror struck back in full force.

It is also true that at least two of those who headed the Russian G.P.U. or Secret Service were put to death by the Communists themselves. The most recent example was that of Beria who had several times

[1] Schuman, F. L., *Soviet Politics*, 1946, p. 219. For a popular statement of the U.S. State Department view see *Let Freedom Ring*, Publication 4443, also speeches of John Foster Dulles.

received the Lenin medal for his great services to Communism. Therefore, it would be fair to say that even from Communist records there have been terrible crimes and injustices practiced in the Communist secret service.

Again, Communist countries rigidly restrict those who can get passports to leave the country even for a visit. Many people are afraid to write friends abroad because of the fear that they may become suspects.

Eighth, the trade unions in Russia are dominated by Communists. The right to strike is often made illegal.

In the ninth place, the official Communist position is that of atheism. For years they carried on vigorous anti-religious propaganda. Since World War II this atheistic propaganda had been reduced but still the Communists oppose religion.

It would be possible to write volumes on the negative side of Soviet Communism but it is only fair to present a more balanced picture.

The Revolution in Russia was a reaction against the Tsar's tyranny. It is an effort to secure the realization of more equal justice in society. What are some of the positive factors? First of all, the author found that many of the Communists were sincere fanatics who believe they were working for the good of all.

Education has been vastly improved. Under the Tsar's regime in Turkestan, for instance, where over ninety per cent of the people were illiterate, today all except the elderly can read and write. Libraries have been established. There have been many cultural advances such as a vast increase of theatres, orchestras, athletic events. Today in the Soviet Union, we find over eight thousand newspapers with a total circulation of over forty million. One thousand five hundred periodicals are printed and in 1953, 850 million copies of books were issued. It goes without saying that much of this is loaded with propaganda. The educational preparation of students in the sciences however, is of a very high order and far more are being trained than in America. Some of our United States Ambassadors have maintained that the cultural level of recreation as shown in the theatre and in music surpasses our own. In any case it has to be admitted that there has been an advance in culture for the common man.

In the Tsar's tyranny many of the lowest class had scant opportunity for medical aid. Today medicine is free to all. Naturally doctors in a capitalistic economy may not like the system but it is clear that free medicine in Russia is infinitely ahead of the system prevalent under the Tsar's tyranny.

The economic life has been taken over by the government. All the basic means of production and distribution are owned and operated by the state. Cooperatives are allowed; but the individual is not permitted to hire labor for his private gain. Many of the Russian people seem to like this. The experts at Harvard University questioning Russian refugees who had escaped from behind "the Iron Curtain," reported that the majority thought the system of state ownership was good. What they objected to most of all was the secret police and the danger of arrest. Personal acquisitiveness is severely restricted in the Soviet Union. While the bureaucracy is better off than the mass of the people, the extremes are infinitely less than under the Tsar's regime. A successive series of five year plans are supposed to build up the economic life of the country so that the common man will eventually have far more of the good things of life. Over a forty year period, there is little question that on the economic front the Communists have made a remarkable advance.

The workers are far better off today. Where before they may have worked twelve to fifteen hours a day on starvation wages, now they are not working over eight and have enough to live on even if it does not come up to American standards. In electrification, under the Soviets as much has been done in one month as the Tsar's regime did in five years and the peasants are gradually getting electricity. The Russian people do not compare their lot with Americans, they compare their condition with what they used to have.

Now this brings us to the question, is it possible to negotiate with the Communist rulers? The entire record of over a third of a century proves it is possible but difficult. When the author was in charge of the Y.M.C.A. in Russia he proposed that the Association send a steamer down the Volga River. American authorities declared permission would never be granted. Actually the Communists provided the steamer free, and the American Y.M.C.A. equipped it with ministers, Association workers, and religious pamphlets. The steamer stopped wherever it pleased and the Y.M.C.A. was publicly thanked by the Foreign Minister on its return. Later when there was a truce with Germany, the author proposed that we send over United States propaganda into the German lines. Again the U.S. Ambassador predicted that permission could never be secured but it was and the propaganda went over the line into Germany. Some said Lenin would never agree to continue to fight Germany but Col. Raymond Robins, head of the American Red Cross, secured such agreement with Lenin on condition that America would aid the Communists. America refused and the deal fell through.

In 1921 after the United States had fought the Communists on Russian soil and then abandoned intervention, Sherwood Eddy of the Y.M.C.A. sent the author to Moscow to find out if the Russians would accept American aid. The mission was successful and Hoover directed the relief to Russia. In World War II it was said the Russians would never permit American air bases on Russian soil but finally there were three such air depots in Russia. Negotiation is possible but it has to be in the interest of Russia just as it has to be in the interest of America. There must be give and take on both sides.

In the United States many politicians seem to feel that Communism is the greatest danger of the age. Even if this were true there would still be the question of how to meet the crisis. But perhaps it would be more accurate to say that even if Communism were non-existent we would face the rising tide of the exploited and the poverty-stricken people the world over. Therefore it would be truer to say that we are facing a moral crisis. In essence the crucial question is, will we build one world for the benefit of all the people or shall we go on perpetuating landlordism, imperialism, racial discrimination, poverty, hunger and disease? That is the real challenge before mankind. Unless we meet it we can never win against Communism.

Most Americans, if they were asked what was the real cause of the trouble in the world, might be inclined to answer, with the one word, "Russia." The average Communist if he were asked the same question would probably retort, "The capitalist-imperialist powers of the West." The fact is that both are partially right. The real difficulty is *all of us*. We are selfish, we often see through a mirror darkly, we are all prejudiced by the culture in which we live, we all make rationalizations to justify *our* way, *our* beliefs, *our* dogmas.

Now in reality the world has been passing through three great revolutions simultaneously, one is the abolition of distance. The radio, the television and the jet plane have made the whole world one little back door community. This is a *technological* revolution.

In the second place, the mass of the people now realize that hunger, illiteracy, disease, landlordism and exploitation can all be abolished. They are due in some measure to man's inhumanity to man. This is causing profound unrest among the backward peoples of the earth. They want to set up new governments which will change their status and end their suffering. This is a *political* revolution.

In the third place, there is beginning to be a dim awareness among the mass of the people everywhere that the welfare of *all* the people should always and ever be supreme. The right of any individual is always subservient to the moral right of the people as a whole. This is a *moral* revolution.

Now we in the West have not fully comprehended these three great transformations, certainly we have not always acted on them. If we did we would realize that if there were no Communists anywhere, we would still be living in a period of revolutionary change, a period when the bottom two-thirds of humanity, were demanding their human rights. This group is composed largely of the colored races.

General William F. Dean who commanded the United States expeditionary forces in Korea was a prisoner of the Communists for over three years. What do you suppose was the most valuable fact he uncovered in all this period? *It was precisely the thesis here emphasized.* He writes, "*The most important discovery to me* was that the ordinary Communists who guarded me and lived with me really believed that they were following a route toward a better life for themselves and their children. . . . We can't convince them with fine words"—or, the General implies, by military means. "We cannot convince them at all unless we are willing and able to show them something better. . . . What we need for Korea is something to compare favorably to the Communist promise of a hectare of land without excessive rent, rice without too much millet in it, or a pencil produced in a factory right in his home town."[2]

In contrast to the Western powers, the Communist propaganda rings with appeals against colonialism.

[2] *General Dean's Story*, as told to William L. Worden, Viking. See also book review in N.Y. *Herald Tribune,* May 7, 1954.

The result of all this is that oppressed peoples who are under the yoke of foreign powers feel led to Communism which shows sympathy for them and away from American capitalism which often is bolstering up the military arm of their oppressor.

Just what is the real threat of Communism? Is it not, first, that the Communists have the most powerful war machine in the world today, second only to that of the United States; and, next, that we fear that the people of the world may fall victims to Communist propaganda and infiltration? Now right away, in our hearts, we should know that there is not the slightest danger of America's going Communist. In the entire United States there are only about 35,000 Communists, less than one-fiftieth of one per cent of our population. But there are real dangers that some countries abroad may fall victims to the persuasiveness of its illusions. To understand why this is so, we must recognize the paradox that to overcome the untruth in Communism we must recognize the element of truth which appeals to the oppressed.

Communism is a form of secular religion. It has a faith, a belief in a future utopia, not a Kingdom of God on earth but a sort of Communistic paradise where all goods are distributed "to each according to his need." Instead of the elect of God, Communists believe the proletariat are the rulers of the future. Present dictators are brought to the fore by the dialectic of history and will usher in the new day. So in a way Communism offers an appealing drink of a sweet tasting nectar which disguises the poison which accompanies it. This is tempting to the thirsty and hungry masses.

The Communist theory of the demise of capitalism could be compared to the religious theory of the Last Judgment. Instead of believing in the creation of a Kingdom of God on earth, they believe in the triumph of Communism. It must not be forgotten also that Communism believes the individual should be dedicated to the service of society. The individual must be ready to sacrifice himself for the welfare of the party.

Now while we recognize that Communism is a form of secularized religion we must recognize that its falseness is far greater than its vestiges of truth. For it denies belief in a God and affirms the negation of spiritual values. Furthermore, Communism believes it can usher in a "New Jerusalem" of its own pattern through bloody violence and a tyrannical dictatorship. It unqualifiedly accepts the use of any means to accomplish its ends.

To get the real picture, then, we must recognize that while Communism lifts high a vision of a beautiful new utopia on earth where poverty and ignorance shall be no more, it is actually building a bureaucratic dictatorship and a military state.

The danger of Communism is that it mixes truth with falsehood. If we would understand it, we must separate them. It is true as the Communists state, that poverty, ignorance, injustice and colonialism must be opposed but we must also oppose every negation of democracy, every curtailment of freedom, every vestige of dictatorship, every subservience to political chicanery and every opposition to God and personal spiritual religion. These then are the real forces in Communism which we must combat.

It is not in a myopic utopia of Communist collectivism under a dictator that man will find his salvation, but in dedication to a God of justice and love who kindles kindness and goodwill in all human hearts.

How, then, must we stop Communism? We cannot prevent the spread of Communist ideas by silencing them. In the course of history scientists and religious leaders have been burned at the stake but their ideas continue to spread. Why was this true? Because ideas are contagious when the conditions of life are favorable to their cultivation. In Russia under the Tsar and in China under her old time leaders, ideas spread because of the extreme poverty of the people, because of the injustice and graft which was all about them. The way to oppose Communism is to change the conditions which produce it. We must end poverty, disease, racial discrimination and insecurity. We must oppose prejudice and injustice of all sorts. As Ambassador Chester Bowles says, "We should adopt a clear, convincing and responsible position against vestigial colonialism wherever it remains."[3]

In America our hysteria about Communism has created a fear which is paranoia. Who is a Communist in America? Not the person who wants to live peacefully with the Communists, nor the person who wants to "do business" with Russia. It certainly is not the person who holds liberal political views, who is a reformer and advocates social security, socialized medicine or opposes compulsory military training,

[3] *Foreign Affairs*, Oct., 1954.

because all of these attitudes tend to do away with the very conditions favorable to the growth of Communism.

No, the Communist is the person who wants a government run by the Communist Party and who believes that the only way this will be secured is through a revolution. Many of our liberals, like Owen Lattimore, and religious leaders like Bishop Oxnam, who have been accused of "red" sympathies, are no more Communist than was Abraham Lincoln.

It is simply stupid to say that anyone who favors *anything* the Communists like is a Communist. This is just plain fear psychosis. If one person likes ice cream, and most Communists may like it, this does not make the first person a Communist. Actually there is hardly any social reform that Communists have not advocated at one time or another.

Far more dangerous to America than Communists are the individuals who let Russia call the tune in every action. If Russia is for something they are automatically against it. If Russia supports a government anywhere in the world then they will oppose it. If Communists control some country then they will refuse to let it be represented in the United Nations forgetting that this may be the surest way to perpetuate its Communism.

We must be careful not to be unwitting tools of Communism by giving our names to Communist-controlled organizations but we can be an even greater asset to Communism by opposing freedom and all liberal ideas and so creating what Justice Douglas of the Supreme Court calls, "*The Black Silence of Fear.*"

Let us always remember that the real way to fight Communism is by the pathway Jesus so supremely demonstrated two thousand years ago. Our war must be waged with the weapons of love against hunger, disease, poverty and oppression. We should concede that even China is a part of the real world we live in and should therefore eventually be admitted into the United Nations. We must help the underdeveloped countries achieve material and social equality.

Tyranny cannot long endure anywhere in the world if great nations are permeated with justice and all men are really free. Demonic sin, dictatorship and death have taken on new meaning with Communism, but the Gospel is the same. We must learn to apply it to world problems in their new dimensions.

Prayer

O God, Friend, and Inner Light, we pray for Communists everywhere. We do not want to hurt them, we want to win them to allegiance to Thee and Thy love. Forgive us for having been so often neglectful of the basic needs of the exploited, of the hungry and of subject people that we have ourselves laid the groundwork for Communism by our indifference and neglect.

Drive out of our hearts, fear, hate and passion and make us realize that we have a responsibility to all men everywhere. Burn into our consciences the truth that if the microbe of Communism spreads, it is because we are not following Thee with positive programs of feeding the hungry, healing the sick and ending illiteracy, colonialism and injustice.

May we this day respond to Thee rather than to what man has made of social patterns around us. Grant that we may spread the contagion of love, hope, and mercy to all people near and far. We pray that our love may be so real that it includes a loathing of that which is evil and a bent for that which is good, with always a helping hand to those in need. So, Father, may we always put our confidence in Thee, and in partnership with Thy Spirit of invincible goodwill, help us to win others from materialistic substitutes for Christ's Kingdom of service to faith in the spiritual values of faith, hope and eternal love.

I am inclined to think that if organized Christianity went 'all out' for the religion of Jesus Christ the churches would be a great deal emptier than they are now . . . I fancy most of us still fail to realize that the Christian religion is a terrific, lovely, explosive, world-shattering force, and not an anodyne against life's little or large disturbances. The 'Magnificat' is as much more revolutionary as it is more beautiful than 'The Red Flag.'

R. H. L. SHEPPARD, Late vicar, St. Martin-in-the-Fields, London

The saints may be prophetic. Nay, innumerable times they have proved themselves prophetic. Treating those whom they met, in spite of the past, in spite of all appearances, as worthy, they have stimulated them to be worthy, miraculously transformed them by their radiant example and the challenge of their expectation.

WILLIAM JAMES in *Varieties of Religious Experience*

CHAPTER VIII

Jesus and Social Christianity

WHY is Jesus the greatest personality of which we have any record on this planet? Because he demonstrated more perfectly than ever before or since the powerful fusion of love for God and love for men.

Mankind sees in a mirror darkly. Too often, we see in the Bible what we have been taught to see. In fact we read into that incomparable record other things that are not there. Nearly every Christian tries to make Jesus over into his own idealistic pattern. "Jesus was strongly anti-Communist," "Jesus was the first socialist," "Jesus was a staunch individualist," "Jesus supported the present economic system, note his parable of the talents," and all other manner of rationalizations.

The fact of the matter is that Jesus was so far in advance of us that his ideas as radically outmode our thinking as the hydrogen bomb outmodes the pistol. Emile de Laveleye, a former famous Belgian economist, expressed this in these words, "If Christianity were taught and understood conformably to the spirit of its Founder, the existing social organism wouldn't last a day."[1] James Russell Lowell phrased it this way, "There is dynamite enough in the New Testament, if illegitimately applied, to blow all our existing institutions to atoms."

The heart of Jesus' message was relationship to God and yet it was also relationship to man. One without the other is crippled. Jesus taught that the question of spiritual reality is the way in which we live and move and feel God's love in our lives. The life of selfishness, of getting, of hating is self-defeating. The life of love and solidarity with all men and of inward communion with God is the real spiritual life.

Jesus did not emphasize the cataclysmic. He believed in an evolutionary growth of a new society. The Kingdom of God is within us. We can

[1] *Primitive Property*, XXXI.

start to find the Kingdom here and now. He discarded the ceremonial religious life and insisted on the ethical. Jesus followed the prophetic tradition preparing men for a righteous social order.

If we go through the gospel of Luke testing every action and saying of Jesus, we find that although the individual and the social are inextricably intertwined the social outweighs the individual. Let us test the heart of His gospel by what Jesus said. Right away we find that he would turn the existing social order upside down. He clearly says, ". . . what is exalted among men is an abomination in the sight of God."[2]

Jesus clearly ranged himself on the side of the poor and oppressed. He was continually showing hostility or criticism of the rich. The Sermon on the Mount is a classic example. "Blessed are you poor, for yours is the kingdom of God. Blessed are you that hunger now, for you shall be satisfied. Blessed are you that weep now, for you shall laugh. Blessed are you when men hate you, and when they exclude you and revile you, and cast out your name as evil . . . But woe to you that are rich, for you have received your consolation. Woe to you that are full now, for you shall hunger . . . Love your enemies, do good to those who hate you, bless those who curse you, pray for those who abuse you . . . But love your enemies, and do good, and lend; expecting nothing in return." (Lk. 6:20-35)

If an American leader talked as Jesus did he would be immediately charged with being a fellow traveller. Jesus said, "Blessed are the peacemakers, for they shall be called sons of God." (Matt. 5:9) Supposing someone got up and said, "We must make peace with the Communists, we must love the leaders of Red China, we must stop rearming the Germans," what would he be charged with? If Jesus came as a foreigner from Poland preaching this message, would he be admitted to the United States? No, he would be debarred under the McCarran Act.

The rites, ceremonies and theological beliefs which now divide Christendom were not put there by Christ but by uninformed and denominationally minded men. Our churches should not only be places for spiritual devotion but also places for going back to the inner heart of Jesus' life and teaching.

[2] Luke 16:16.

Jesus was trying to light a candle in the hearts of all who heard him so that men's hearts would glow with the truth of the gospel. He desperately tried to make men avoid the sham of conventional religion. Myth, dogma and rationalizations of all sorts are dead-end streets. Jesus tried to make men combine faith and works.

Jesus warned against the cancerous growths that were eating into society. What were they?

1—The cancerous growth: of possessions, of wealth, of property.

Our American society has mal-distribution of wealth. As far back as 1915, roughly two per cent of the people owned sixty per cent of the wealth and sixty-five per cent owned only five per cent. By 1926 the Federal Trade Commission reported that the concentration had gone on until only one per cent owned sixty per cent of all the wealth. By 1949 there were four million American families earning less than one thousand dollars a year in a period of great prosperity. According to surveys made for the Federal Reserve Board in 1953, as we noted in a previous chapter, over twenty-nine per cent of all families had no savings of any kind.

Jesus blasted wealth all through his ministry, ". . . the deceitfulness of riches, choke the word . . ." (Matt. 13:22) "It is harder for a rich man to enter into the Kingdom of God than it is for a camel to go through a needle's eye." "Take heed and keep yourselves from all covetousness: for a man's life consisteth not in the abundance of the things which he possesseth." (Lk. 12:15)

Jesus tells the parable of the man who tried to accumulate more and more and more, building greater and greater barns. "But God said to him 'Fool! This night your soul is required of you; and the things you have prepared whose will they be?' So is he who lays up treasure for himself and is not rich towards God." (Lk. 12:13–21)

Jesus declared. "He that hath two coats, let him impart to him that hath none; and he that hath food let him do likewise." (Lk. 3:10–12) Again Jesus said, "Do not lay up for yourselves treasures on earth where moth and rust consume and where thieves break in and steal, but lay up for yourselves treasure in heaven, where neither moth nor rust consumes and where thieves do not break in and steal. For where your treasure is there will your heart be also." (Matt. 6:19–21) A little further on he said, "No one can serve two masters; for either he will hate the one and love the other, or he will be devoted to the one and despise the other. You cannot serve God and mammon." (Matt. 6:24)

Jesus tells the parable of the rich man and the beggar who both die. He declares that the beggar immediately goes to heaven but the rich man suffers the tortures of hell as a matter of course. Apparently there are grave dangers to the followers of the Christian ethic in luxurious living.

Property and riches, then, can be a cancer eating into the fibre of men's souls. If this cancerous growth is not cut out, the ultimate end is misery and frustration. If an impartial analysis were made of American society, how many could be said to be living with the goal of accumulation, of wealth, of sumptuous living? If we knew the ratio, we might have a clearer idea of the extent of cancer in our contemporary life.

2—Dangers in present day business practise.

We are not condemning business indiscriminately but in so far as any business is dominated by materialism and does not let God's principles govern the enterprise, it is cancerous and dangerous. In so far as any business exalts property values above human values it stands in danger. To what extent does American business conform to these tests? It would be extremely interesting if an objective study could be made and we could have some idea of the proportion of business firms where God's principles govern. Perhaps any reader can test the concerns he deals with and decide for himself.

It is an open question whether laissez faire capitalism and the profit motive are genuinely in accord with the spirit and teaching of Jesus. You can search the gospels but you will not find Jesus lauding the profit motive. Repeatedly he rather stresses service to the people. One can imagine what he would say to the mass unemployment and recurrent depressions of 1837, 1857, 1873, 1893 and 1929. Most Christians who have thought through the matter of the moral implications of our economic order would state that the consumers cooperative movement far more nearly approaches the Christian ideal.

The profit motive certainly causes cancerous growths in the body of society. For instance, there has been overwhelming proof that cancer of the lungs is partly due to excessive cigarette smoking. In the United States some of the most brilliant and authoritative scientific research has proved this to be true. In England on February 12, 1954, the report of a government committee was made to the House of Commons. This was an exhaustive scientific study of three years duration. The conclusion was: "It must be regarded as established that there is a relationship between smoking and lung cancer." Not only did scientific tests prove this to be true but as more and more people smoked the rate of cancer jumped. Between 1911 and 1919, deaths from this cause were about 250 a year. In 1931 the figure was 1,000. In 1951, there were 11,166 deaths of men alone from lung cancer and 2,081 deaths of women. In 1952, 11,981 men died of lung cancer and 2,237 women. What did the cigarette companies of the United States and Britain do? They immediately began fighting the findings and redoubled their campaign to get everyone to smoke. At American colleges they often gave a pack free to students to get them in the smoking habit.

As we have seen in another chapter, poisoning in our food is notorious and many chemicals are used because they increase profits. The dangers, as well as the benefits, of the patent medicine business have long been recognized. Scores of laws have been passed and inspectors hired to try to protect people. Even military armaments and military waste are accentuated by the profit motive. Thus we have a whole host of evils such as wasting natural resources, promoting scarcity in the field of consumption, monopolizing and restricting products, the adulteration of foods, child labor and the exploitation of women, all because of the profit motive. Jesus insisted that service to God and to one's fellow men should take precedence over profits. The poison of this profit motive is eating into the heart of the American system. Jesus never said, "Whoever would be first among you, let him hold rigidly to the profit motive." Profits which rank ahead of the welfare of the people are inimical to the Christian way of life. Yet our whole economic history has shown many instances of placing profits ahead of human welfare. In 1842 Massachusetts was compelled to pass a law prohibiting the labor of children under twelve years of age for more than twelve hours per day. Fourteen years later Connecticut was forced to pass a similar law prohibiting the labor of children under fourteen for more than twelve hours a day.

If we look with singleness of purpose towards God and his love, can we be sure that even competition is necessarily in accord with the Christian way of love? Through competition a business enterprise endeavors to beat out a rival competitor and too often drives him out of business. The more successful the business man the more he drives out competition, and the end results may be monopoly. In fact, we have had to enact severe anti-trust and anti-monopoly laws. Often these are not adequately enforced. The logical result of the present economic system and its defenders is to say that if a corporation executive violates United States law and is convicted he should be compensated by the corporation. This is exactly what Herbert L. Abrons does say in the *New York Law Journal*,[3] ". . . the fact is that there are certain types of crimes, such as violations of the anti-trust laws, which an individual might commit *only because* he is an officer, director or employee of a corporation, and *only because* he is, or thinks he is, in pursuit of the corporation's best interests . . . Following this line of reasoning to its logical conclusion would lead a corporation to grant a right of reimbursement to its personnel for the defence of criminal actions, *even if they are found guilty* . . ."

The conclusion is inescapable that God would not sanction such actions or such arguments.

3—Another concomitant of the present economic order is the class struggle. But this is hardly in accord with the teachings of Jesus or the prophets. They stood for a classless love. Today some owners of big business stand opposed to organized labor. The Taft-Hartley law is bitterly assailed by labor. Prophetic religion and the teachings of Jesus assert that human rights are always and ever paramount over property rights.

The churches need to get away from extreme emphasis on doctrinal differences and concentrate on applying the moral and spiritual message of Jesus. People should not have the illusion that if they are in the church they are necessarily God's chosen people. The fact is every individual and people must choose God's way of righteousness and truth in their own daily lives. Any church member who proudly maintains that he loves God with all his heart and all his mind and all his spirit while at the same time he does not observe love to *all* his neighbors throughout the world, is betraying Christ. The doctrine of the good neighbor leaves no room for creed, color or race as barriers to fellowship.

[3] Herbert L. Abrons, New York *Law Journal,* Nov. 12, 1953, p. 1062.

The church should be a center where people are brought together to cooperate in doing the social action enumerated in the Sermon on the Mount. Thus the church should be a powerhouse for social action and the practical realization of love for one's neighbor. The church should be a center where social sins can be attacked and met. At present the church tends to have an hour of Sunday School once a week, a sermon on Sunday and a few clubs and meetings besides visitation of members during the week. If in the light of Jesus' social teaching and action such as healing the sick, visiting the poor, and those in prison, the church were to reorganize its practise until it strove to cure every condition in the community, the nation and even the world, it would have to revolutionize present practises. Instead of waiting for a future Kingdom, church members should recognize with Jesus that "the Kingdom of God is in the midst of you." (Lk. 17:21) In the Lord's Prayer Jesus clearly stated "thy will be done on earth as it is in heaven." This means it is the joint responsibility of Christians everywhere to seek its realization *here and now*.

This is the revolutionary concept of religion which must eventually sweep the world. We must strive to transform the world into a friendly society of brotherly men under a Father God. We must strive to love our neighbors, whoever they are,—Negro, Communist, African, Asian, as ourselves. To say that all men are sinners, that because of this our goal is unattainable, does not and cannot prevent our striving to attain as much of the goal of brotherhood and invincible good will as we can.

God is love. His spirit can be seen in history. God is all for us and for us all. The church exists in order to fulfill the love of God in human history. The church should be activated by the Holy Spirit operating in society. The mission of the church is to make the individual have the right relationship to god, it is also to make the individual have the right relationship to his fellows everywhere. God comes to an individual in two ways: by direct personal contact with Him, and as he genuinely helps others. People can find happiness by changing social conditions for the better and so helping their fellow men and they can find happiness in knowing God personally. The highest form of happiness, Jesus taught, was to have both an individual and social relationship to God. Jesus taught that real religion begins by transforming ourselves but then it also means what Jesus proclaimed:

> The Spirit of the Lord is upon me,
> Because he appointed me to preach good tidings to the poor:
> He hath sent me to proclaim release to the captives,
> And recovering of sight to the blind,
> To set at liberty them that are bruised,
> To proclaim the acceptable year of the Lord.

Jesus clearly states that the individual who has been serving human need may be closer to the Kingdom of God than the pious attendant at church services. In the judgment scene the final appraisal was based on *what they had done* to help their neighbors. This was the crucial test, "I was hungry, and ye gave me to eat; I was thirsty, and ye gave me drink; I was a stranger, and ye took me in; naked, and ye clothed me; I was sick, and ye visited me; I was in prison, and ye came unto me." Even when the individual did not realize that he had done this, Jesus said, "Inasmuch as ye did it unto one of these my brethren, even these least, ye did it unto me." (Matt 25:31–46)

Jesus supremely exemplified love in action. We must love all men even our enemies. We must have the power of self-identification with our enemy, of putting ourselves in his place. Love did not ignore sin but it took upon itself the burden of that guilt. It refused to hate but deliberately tried to share suffering. Jesus was a pacifist. How any sane man can reconcile Jesus' statement, "love your enemies" with the deliberate annihilation of millions through the hydrogen bomb is beyond comprehension. Even a theologian like Reinhold Niebuhr admits, "The ethic of Christ is uncompromisingly pacifist." ("Why the Christian Church is not Pacifist," p. 17.) To argue that we must choose the lesser of two evils and thus choose war is nowhere sanctioned in Jesus' life or teaching. On the contrary Jesus demands *complete* surrender to the will of God. If necessary the way of love leads to the cross. Nowhere does it lead to the divinely sanctioned use of hydrogen bombs, bacteriological warfare, and the mass murder of modern warfare. Jesus clearly and unequivocally said, that we must take up our cross and follow him if we are to be *His* disciples. Gandhi saw this clearly when he said, "If you Christians rely on soldiers for your safety, you are denying your own doctrine of the cross." Would Jesus have dropped the bomb on Hiroshima? Would he trust in the power of obliteration bombing? The entire life and teaching of Jesus demonstrated love for all. He could not sanction war.

We know in our highest moments that we are all sinners. We know that we are constantly trying to find our way amid tangled and complex situations freighted with evil. But because this is true does not and cannot mean that we are necessarily forced to choose the pathway of war. God's way is always the way of love, not of hate, of kindness not of the mass obliteration of men, women and children alike. There is no dilemma which can confront us where we may not, if we wish, choose the pathway of Christ. If worse comes to worst we can choose the way of the cross. "Let us take up His cross and follow." Spurious rationalization about the necessity of choosing lesser evils not only denies Christ's teaching about the universality and the validity of the Way of the Cross but it gives us an easy way out from moral heroism and sacrifice. The practical effect is to enable us to lower our standards and to go the way of the crowd. We do not need necessarily to condemn what others do but we ourselves, if we are to follow Christ, must turn away from what we know to be evil. We must ever and always endeavor to practise the way of love.

Jesus' religion is a challenge to every Christian. It means self-discipline, sacrifice, even the way of the cross. No sincere believer can sit by idly while the Negro in South Africa is persecuted and denied elemental rights, he cannot be oblivious to the evils that surround him in his community: gambling, prostitution, the liquor traffic, political corruption, race discrimination and all the rest. He must resist the concentration of the national effort on armaments and the wasting of the national income on militarism in flat denial of Jesus' belief that our strength must rest in moral power and righteousness. Belief can never be divorced from action. We must "live dangerously." There is a crying need for heroes in the moral and spiritual realm *far more* than on the battlefield.

Jesus taught that God's love was the supreme force and power in the universe. Jesus' life illuminated that love and it shines down through all human history ever since. If we have faith in God, we know that God's faithfulness and love are all about us. Can we not join in praying daily, "God's will be done in me?" Let us make sure that the social message of Christianity shines through our lives so that no one can ever say we did not see the vision and respond.

In the following parable of Lowell, he pictures Jesus coming back to see how far Christians today believe in him.

> Have ye founded your thrones and altars, then,
> On the bodies and souls of living men?
> And think ye that building shall endure,
> Which shelters the noble and crushes the poor?
>
> With gates of silver and bars of gold
> Ye have fenced my sheep from their Father's fold;
> I have heard the dropping of their tears
> In heaven these eighteen hundred years.

* * * * *

> Then Christ sought out an artisan,
> A low-browed, stunted, haggard man,
> And a motherless girl, whose fingers thin,
> Pushed from her faintly want and sin.
>
> These set he in the midst of them,
> And as they drew back their garment-hem
> For fear of defilement, "Lo, here," said he,
> "The images ye have made of me."

Prayer

We thank Thee for the example of Jesus, for the light which constantly illumines our pathway when we study His life and teaching. Help us to prove in our actions that we are His disciples. Save us from frittering away our time in fruitless tasks. Guard us when we are tempted to stray away from Thee, protect us from any action which falls short of the love which Jesus so supremely exemplified. Help us to demonstrate by all we do and say that we are really motivated and controlled by His spirit. Ever recognizing our frailty, we ask that Thou wilt help us to unsnarl our thinking and control our speaking. We want to fit our whole lives into Thy plan for us. May our hearts answer Thee in joy that comes from choosing to take our place in a world of work and suffering assured that, if we do, no matter what the trials and disappointments, in the end all things will work together for good. Amen.

Part II

Guide Posts to Progress

When I consider thy heavens, the work of thy fingers,
The moon and the stars, which thou hast ordained;
What is man that thou art mindful of him?
And the son of man, that thou visitest him?
And thou hast made him but little lower than God,
And crownest him with glory and honor.
                              Psalm 8:3–5

The heavens declare the glory of God;
And the firmament showeth his handiwork.
Day unto day uttereth speech,
And night unto night showeth knowledge
There is no speech nor language;
Their voice is not heard.
Their line is gone out through all the earth,
And their words to the end of the world.
                              Psalm 19:1–4

We are such little men when the stars come out,
So small under the open maw of the night,
That we must shout and pound the table and drive wild,
And gather dollars and madly dance and drink deep,
And send the great bird flying, and drop death.
When the stars come out we are such little men
That we must arm ourselves in glare and thunder,
Or cave in on our own dry littleness.
We are such little men when the stars come out!
Ah, God behind the stars, touch with your finger
This mite of meaningless dust and give it substance.
I am so little, under the frown of the night!
Be you my body, you my eyes,
My hands, my feet, my heartbeat and my hunger,
That I may face the infinite spaces, and live:
And stand in quietness, when the stars come out.
         HERMAN HAGEDORN (From *Combat at Midnight*,
    John Day Co.)

We are inhabitants of two worlds, and owe a double, but not divided allegiance. In virtue of our clay, this little ball of earth exacts a certain loyalty of us, while, in our capacity as spirits, we are admitted citizens of an invisible and holier fatherland. There is a patriotism of the soul whose claim absolves us from our other and terrene fealty. Our true country is that ideal realm which we represent to ourselves under the names of religion, duty and the like. Our terrestrial organizations are but far-off approaches to so fair a model, and all they are verily traitors who resist not any attempt to divert them from their original intendment. When, therefore, one would have us to fling up our caps and shout with the multitude, 'Our Country, however bounded,' he demands of us that we sacrifice the larger to the less, the higher to the lower, and that we yield to the imaginary claims of a few acres of soil our duty and privilege as liegemen of Truth.

JAMES RUSSELL LOWELL

CHAPTER IX

Enlarge Your Horizons

WE have just completed an analysis of the present social order and the challenge which it presents to moral and religious principles. We are passing on now in the next six chapters to a consideration of basic guideposts to progress. Each one of these is absolutely essential to every citizen of the Kingdom of God. You who are reading these words must recognize and embody these in your life if you are to be a true follower of the truth of God. If we are to do reverence to God and reverence to life, then, we must: enlarge our horizons; practise equality, justice and freedom; promote economic democracy; recognize the solidarity of mankind; make invincible goodwill a part of the very fibre of our lives and finally, test our character by our actions.

Let us turn to the first principle. Most Christians need to enlarge their horizons. This earth is a mere speck in a limitless expanse of other spheres. There are millions of other planets. God's plans are so far beyond our puny vision that we need a new look, a broadened vision, a horizon which includes the universe.

Few of us keep in our minds how vast is the universe, how infinitesimal our place on the earth. In our own Milky Way there are at least one hundred billion suns, some of them thousands of times larger than our own. When you look at the Milky Way even with a small telescope you can see to a distance of over a thousand light years. Now remember that it takes light only just over a second to travel from the moon to the earth and you get an idea of the vastness of our own galaxy. But the Milky Way is only one out of perhaps one hundred million other galaxies that we can see. As our telescopes get bigger we uncover more and more galaxies.

Our sun and its planets move as a group in an orbit around the center of the Milky Way. The speed is in the neighborhood of 1,000,000 miles an hour. Nevertheless, it takes the sun and its retinue of planets about 200,000,000 years to make a round trip of the Galaxy.[1]

The aborigines in Australia long ago used to think that they were the only beings on earth. They prided themselves on their culture, their gods, their know-how. They were superior to everything in the universe. If some one of the natives ever posed the supposition that there might be human beings elsewhere they were thought to be a bit demented.

Similarly, many human beings on this small earth surrounded by millions of other spheres conceitedly assume that we are the only living personalities anywhere in the universe. The assumption is so fantastic as to be beyond the bounds of reason but many still assume it. Why amidst millions and millions of other spheres the earth should be the only one to have life in an ordered universe is scientifically absurd. *Tattoo this into your mind,* there is life on other planets. Most of the greatest astronomers of our time are united in believing this. For example, Eddington of England comes to the conclusion that this is true. One of the most conservative English astronomers, Royal, states, "We cannot resist the conclusion that life, though rare, is scattered throughout the universe."[2] Professor N. J. Berrill of McGill University declares of course there are many other beings on other planets. He says, "Of this we can be sure: well-placed planets evolve life, and life sooner or later evolves mind." He concludes that the beings on other planets will possess "intelligence and power, deep emotion, beauty in essence, and wisdom grown perhaps far beyond our own."[3]

Today increasing evidence of flying saucers indicates that out of a host of superstition, fantasy and mental mirage, there may possibly be a core of something which we do not yet understand. Hundreds of pictures of some objects of this kind are on file in the War Department. Just what the reality behind these pictures is we do not know.

To cite but one incident, in the summer of 1954 a British plane flying across the ocean towards London was followed by a flying cylindrical object and six smaller craft. It immediately wired for a jet interceptor

---

[1] Fred Hoyle, *The Nature of the Universe,* 1950, p. 56.
[2] *Life On Other Worlds,* Macmillan, 1940.
[3] Maclean's, June 15, 1954.

plane. Just before this arrived the large cylindrical object apparently gathered into itself the six smaller ones and vanished in a burst of fantastic speed. All but one of the crew of the British plane and many of the passengers swore to the incident and stated that they were quite sure the object was not made by man. Capt. P. R. Howard, a veteran of 250 Atlantic crossings, said the object resembled "a large burst of flak and six smaller blobs."[4]

We take no position on whether or not flying saucers are really from another planet or whether they are merely mirages or hallucinations, or what have you. But we believe that it may stimulate our thinking to *imagine* that we are under observation by beings from another planet. We can then ask ourselves what kind of report would they make of our little earth and its inhabitants. To answer this question the author has written the following parable about "flying saucers."

A strange metal box was discovered imbedded in the soil in Montana. It had apparently been dropped by some flying object. It was as hard as steel yet as light as aluminum—a strange combination. Inside there were four sheets of a thin metal-like substance, all covered with beautiful artistic raised hieroglyphics. When these were sent to the foremost linguistic specialists in the world they were said to be a language not known to man. After months of arduous toil the scientists deciphered them. They were observations of beings who came in flying saucers to the earth. Here is what was recorded.

"We have now made forty trips to the Baby Ball (apparently the earth). In spite of its infinitesimal size the Baby Ball is inhabited by a wild, relatively unintelligent species of animals. They fly in slow, air-supported craft and have not learned to conquer gravity. We have deciphered their communication system and apparently they spend most of their time listening to crude love songs and inconsequential stories which are intermingled at all times with extravagant claims for some article which their men of power desire to have purchased. Even music is interrupted by these crude trumpetings.

"Much effort is directed into quarrelling and organized hostility between various coalitions. One large group is continually talking peace while it berates the other group by calling it all kinds of insulting names. For instance, spokesman of a country called 'Chikoslovak' referred to

[4] New York *Herald Tribune*, July 1, 1954.

the actions of the other side as 'hypocritical,' 'imperialists,' 'war mongers,' 'war instigators,' 'massacres of prisoners,' et cetera. They said, 'The United States imperialist interventionists wish to carry on their war of intervention.' They charged that in Germany 'a regime of intervention, of military arbitrariness and dictatorship of the United States imperialists over the German people is being established.'

"The other group calls itself 'the Free World' and condemns another country called Russia in these terms: 'hypocrite,' 'secret preparers of war,' 'diabolical,' 'enslavers of her people,' 'builders of slave labor camps,' 'murderers and slaughterers of her enemies.'

"Nor was this propaganda barrage a matter of mere words. Both sides were using spies and creating trade barriers, both sides were actively fighting each other, and so we went over to observe what these beasts did on the battlefield.

"Apparently one side burrowed into the ground and the other dumped liquid fire, explosive bombs and shot and shell on them. It made no difference, apparently, whether the people killed were fighting or were harmless women and children. The effort seemed to be to destroy as many buildings, even houses, schools and hospitals, of the other side as possible. We flew over the territory and nearly everything had been systematically destroyed.

"Both sides have such a low order of intelligence that they apparently continue to fight, even when they meet for negotiation, instead of stopping all their destruction and settling differences by rational conference.

"We note also that in some countries the peoples are so poor that they are starving and that in others they have so much food that occasionally they even destroy it. The country called 'the United States' produces fifty per cent, of all the so-called 'free world' block, yet uses a large proportion for rearming and fighting.

"We learned from their communication system that one of the countries is spending eighty-five per cent of all their budget for this mass murder which they call 'war, past, present and future.'

"We understand that long ago there was a prophetic mature leader who tried to get the people to practice peace and good-will. This was so inimical to their practices that they killed him.

"Today each side tries to ferret out anyone who opposes the dominant practice of those in power. In the United States they actually have 'an

Un-American Activities Committee' which prepares secret dossiers against many persons who really advocate peace and good-will, or foreign policies contrary to the military machine. They have blasted, for instance, many individuals who seem to have more intelligence and maturity and have proposed more peaceful methods of solving differences, than are currently regarded as sound, by the custodians of the dominant group.

"We carefully considered whether to land and mediate the differences between these two rival groups of power blocs on the Baby Ball but considering the crude and barbaric nature of the animals inhabiting the place we were afraid that they would destroy our flying disk (apparently the flying saucer) and might even kill us. Certainly we do not believe they would tolerate our help for a moment. Indeed if we showed them how to produce more they would probably use it all for mass murder.

"We propose to consult our most mature and learned wise socio-psychists to see if they know any way by which we can genuinely help these creatures to become intelligent and rational beings bent on peace and friendship instead of mass murder."

You say the above report is fantastic but stop and ask yourself what would visitors from another planet be likely to say? Isn't it about time we sink our little differences between East and West and get on with the problem of improving the conditions of all the people on the earth of every color, race, and political belief?

Professor Hoyle of Saint John's College, Cambridge, England, believes, in common with practically all astronomers, that the universe is continually expanding. He fears that in the future our knowledge of astronomy may go backward because of our stupid behavior. He declares, "And in saying this I am not thinking about an atomic war destroying civilization, but about the increasing tendency to rivet scientific inquiry in fetters. Secrecy, nationalism, the Marxist ideology—these are some of the things that are threatening to choke the life out of science."[5]

Instead of feeding our childish fears and prejudices we should rather, in the light of God's great expanding universe, think of the world as just one little earthly family.

[5] *Ibid.*, Fred Hoyle, p. 135.

132   Religion in Action

In the light of this chapter let us assume that His creation and care are far beyond our comprehension, that love is deeper and more poignant than we know, and that we are only in the first faint beginnings of comprehending truth, justice and the love of God which passeth all understanding.

Prayer

O God, forgive us for being so engrossed with our little concerns that we forget the wideness of Thy universe and Thy impartial love for all Thy children. Forgive us our little squabbles here on earth and teach us that all the nations upon this planet belong in one small family. Teach us true humility so that we may rid ourselves of the corrosion of the lust for power. May we search our hearts asking ourselves, are we really Christian or have we inscribed the words of Jesus on our national banners, only too often marching in the opposite direction.

When we are tempted to be inflamed by the passions of a crisis remind us that a thousand years are as a day in Thy sight. Help us to understand that Thou hast been dealing with the wicked since the dawn of history and give us grace to look to Thee before we act. Grant us, O Lord, that we may not be so benumbed by earthly things that we fail to love the eternal things of the spirit. Enlarge our minds and hearts so that we may be dominated with one thought, to love all our brothers as ourselves and to help other nations, not by fighting but by winning them with love, persuasion and example.

Give us faith to believe in Thy mission for us that Thy will may be done among the nations and in our own country rather than that we remain slaves to our own wayward wills. Thus may Thy spirit grow in us and take command of our hearts and our lives.   Amen.

Liberty under the *Constitution* is "liberty in a social organization which requires the protection of law against the evils which menace the health, safety, morals and welfare of the people."
CHIEF JUSTICE CHARLES EVANS HUGHES in 1937.

On Oct. 27, 1553 Michael Servetus was burned at the stake in Geneva because he did not believe the orthodox theology of his day. He refused to accept the doctrines of original sin, the depravity of man and predestination. Jesus he felt was a man whom God had deified. Justice William O. Douglas of the Supreme Court concludes:

"The problem of Servetus was in a sense the problem of this age. Those who speak out against the neurosis that has seized us in the mid-twentieth century risk much. But if they stay silent, they are unworthy of their inheritance. Then they lose the fight for freedom by default. If a few sick minds can transfer their psychosis to the whole community, anyone can readily become a victim of the calumny and lies which the modern hunt for heretics has produced."

If all mankind minus one, were of one opinion, and only one person were of the contrary opinion, mankind would be no more justified in silencing that one person, than he, if he had the power, would be justified in silencing mankind.
JOHN STUART MILL

Nothing could be more remote from socialistic ideals than the competitive scramble of a society like the United States, which pays lip-service to equality, but means by it equal opportunities of being unequal. Our aim should be the opposite. It should be to effect a complete divorce between differences of pecuniary income and differences in respect of health, security, amenity of environment, culture, social status and esteem.
R. H. TAWNEY

CHAPTER X

Equality, Justice, and Freedom

ANY society which practices its religion must insure to its citizens equality, justice, and freedom. We are certain that Communistic countries do not do this. What we forget or ignore are our own deviations from our high standards.

Now equality, justice, and freedom are interdependent; each requires the others. If we do not have equality, if we practise racial discrimination, for instance, we do not have either justice or freedom. On the other hand, if we have racial equality under a dictatorial police state, we do not have either justice or true freedom. No justice can ever be complete unless freedom and equality are added, and no freedom or equality is real unless implemented by justice.

Any one who takes his religion seriously cannot sit idly by while racial discrimination flourishes or economic injustice stabs into the social fabric; or while jingoistic and ruthless politicians destroy any measure of our freedom. Dynamic religion means that we must live "dangerously," if that is necessary to protect equality, justice, and freedom.

Let us consider, first, equality. Perhaps one of the most terrible scourges ever to afflict America has been racial intolerance. The greatest contradiction to our whole theory of democracy was the introduction of slavery in America. This is standing proof of how easy it is for people everywhere to delude themselves when personal advantage complicates their thinking. Even today some have not thrown off the mental shackles which slavery imposed.

The church in America is supposed to include and embody our ideals of what is right and true and just. But segregation within the church is one of the greatest scandals in Christendom. The strong probability is that if we permitted every person to join whatever church he desired, the sincerity and the spiritual power of the membership and the corporate body would really be improved. Actually today in the United States there is segregation in the churches both in the North and in the South. Dr. Benjamin Mays, President of Morehouse College, reports that ministers in northern churches have told him that from sixty to seventy per cent of the membership would walk out if Negroes were accepted.

When the writer was Visiting Professor at the University of Colorado recently, the barbers made the same assertion about their white patrons and used it as an excuse not to serve Negroes. However, the courts stepped in and compelled them to refrain from discrimination. What happened? Actually not a single white patron objected to sitting down in the barber's chair following a Negro.

The World Council of Churches, speaking at Amsterdam in 1948, declared: "The church knows that it must call society away from prejudice based upon race or color, and from the practices of discrimination and segregation as denials of justice and human dignity, but it cannot say a convincing word to society unless it takes steps to eliminate these practices from the Christian community because they contradict all that it believes about God's love for all His children."

In spite of this declaration, the majority of churches in the United States do maintain the barriers of race. This is a great obstacle against the church's taking effective action against discrimination in hotels, restaurants, amusements, and industry. How can the church protest against this evil when it sanctions it in the heart of its own sanctuary? From the best evidence we have, we know that roughly 95% of the Negroes and the whites worship in separate congregations. This is a negation of the brotherhood which was taught by Jesus.

President Benjamin Mays, speaking at Yale University Divinity School, has well said: "Segregation leads to brutality, all kinds of brutality; injustices in the courts, police brutality, bombing and lynching, and it is the origin of prejudice in the child. . . . The truly Christian believer and the truly Christian church can have no part in deliberately seeking to perpetuate this pernicious system."

H. Laurence McNeil, in the *Christian Century,* attacks the church even more severely on its silence when acts of violence against the Negro do break out: "Except in rare instances the leading preachers become as silent as the Sphinx. They go underground. . . . You can do anything to a child of God if he belongs to a minority, without fear."

The whole basis of our Christian faith is equality; yet until the Supreme Court decision in May, 1954, twenty-one states and the District of Columbia permitted or required separate schools for the Negro and the white. Fourteen states require segregation on the railroads and eleven require it on the busses. While only Mississippi and South Carolina require segregation in the hospitals, thirteen states force the segregation of mental patients. The law even restricts what the representatives of the church of God can do: in Georgia it is illegal for a Negro pastor to marry a white couple.

In the hospitals there is often rigid separation of the white and Negro groups. The Southern Conference Educational Fund not long ago sent a questionnaire to the 2,414 medical institutions listed in the American Hospital Directory for eighteen southern and border states and the District of Columbia. Replies were received from roughly 29 per cent, or 711 institutions. Eighteen per cent do not admit Negroes, while 82 per cent or 584 do. But even where Negroes are admitted they are rigidly restricted to a certain proportion of the beds. This means that if there is an emergency and the Negro places are filled a Negro will not be admitted even if it is a matter of life and death. Let us consider a few concrete cases.

George S. Moore, Jr., son of a noted physician, had his back broken in an automobile accident in 1930. At the nearby hospital in Huntsville he was refused admission. There were no ambulance facilities for Negroes, so he was finally taken to Athens, Alabama, in a hearse. During the ride he contracted pneumonia and died before his father could reach him. His father, a distinguished medical authority in his own right, felt that if he had been taken into the first hospital he would have been saved.

In 1931 the Dean of Women of Fisk University together with a Fisk Senior were in a serious automobile accident near Dalton, Georgia. They were refused admission at the publicly supported hospital at Dalton and were taken to Chattanooga, sixty-six miles away. Miss Johnson died that night, the student the next day.

In March, 1937, the wife of the author, W. C. Handy, was taken to Knickerbocker Hospital in New York City. The hospital had promised her physician a private room. However, when the hospital found out that she was colored they made her stay in the ambulance for nearly an hour while they protested taking her. She died a short time later.

In Washington, D.C., in 1945, Sibley Hospital, a church supported institution, refused admission to a Negro woman who was in labor, even to enter the emergency ward. The result was that she had her baby on the sidewalk.

In Chicago in 1949 a writer, Eric Hercules, was hit by an auto. The Woodlawn Hospital refused to receive him and he was taken, after an hour and forty-five minutes, to the Cook County Hospital. He died three hours later.

In August, 1950, three cases from an automobile accident were denied beds in the Breckinridge County Hospital, Hardinsburg, Kentucky, because they had "no facilities for colored people." They were left untended on the floor of the emergency room for three hours and all that was given them was morphine. One man died on the floor and the others were finally taken to Louisville, where they recovered.

In 1951 an eighteen year old boy suffering from diabetes died after being refused admission to the City Hospital in Akron. There was an empty bed but it was in a room occupied by a white man.

In spite of the cases cited, discrimination in the hospitals is getting less and less. Recently the Kentucky State Senate, for instance, unanimously passed a bill prohibiting any licensed medical institution from refusing care to any person on the basis of color.

In other words, progress is being made faster in the hospitals than it is in the churches. Yet all the evidence from the Bible is against racial segregation. Lines are drawn, to be sure, in the Bible between the Jews and others, but it is drawn on religious not on racial lines.

Jesus proclaimed a God who was Father of all mankind. He emphasized again and again the fatherhood of God and the brotherhood of man. Again and again Jesus pictured some one from another race as being closer to God than those who considered themselves "chosen." He did this in the story of the Good Samaritan. And Jesus declared that the Roman Centurian had greater faith than he had found "in all Israel." President Mays has pointed out that non-Jews could be admitted to a local Jewish church if they accepted the conditions of conformity laid down for them. But, he says: "In our time where segregation is based on race or color there is nothing one can do to qualify. He cannot qualify even when he accepts the same creed, practises the same ritual, prays to the same God, and partakes of the same culture. Segregation based on color or race makes it impossible for the Christian of color to qualify; for one cannot change his color and he cannot change his race. And this restriction is tantamount to penalizing one for being what God made him and tantamount to saying to God, 'You made a mistake, God, when you made peoples of different races and colors.' "[1]

It has been conclusively proved that there was no racial discrimination in the early church nor even in the Middle Ages. It seems clear that the color or racial bar in the church did not emerge until the seventeenth century; it is a relatively modern phenomenon. In fact, it was only after the imperialism of the West against primitive native people that the church began to practice racial discrimination. It is quite clear, then, that since there is no theological basis for racial discrimination in the church, it is an evil thing which is in direct contradiction to the life and teachings of Jesus.

In so far as segregation is practised in the churches of the United States we do not have equality. There is no question that the practise of racial discrimination scars the soul of all those who practise it. Not only does it prevent equality, justice, and freedom, but at the same time it prevents us from being Christian. Those who practise this segregation in the sanctuary of God are to that extent denying the Lordship of Jesus Christ. They are erecting prison bars around their own souls.

Slowly Negro segregation is breaking down in our schools, our hospitals, our amusements, and in many, many phases of the community life. But as President Mays has so aptly stated: "It will be a sad commentary on our life and time if future historians can write that the last bulwark of segregation based on race and color in the United States and South Africa was God's church."

At this point it is worth pointing out that the North should not take too much pride in its record. For the problem of race and caste is a national problem and areas are not too different. In the North there is residential segregation and this buys school segregation. Actually the basic principle of separate but equal schools was first established in Boston.

[1] Address before the World Council of Churches, Evanston, 1954.

There is no simple solution to prejudice. The decision of the Supreme Court does not solve the problem; we must implement it. To be sure, it is a tremendous advance because equality is now the supreme law of the land.

Even Supreme Court decisions do not come by magic. They come out of long years of struggle. To prepare the recent Supreme Court case on segregation $40,000 had to be raised. Without compensation, one hundred and forty-nine lawyers participated in preparing the brief. Sociologists and scientists contributed their services. The proponents of segregation were unable to secure a single scientist of note to support their contention. Practically all the scientists agreed that the mere fact of segregation hurts the Negro.

It is amusing to note that some six weeks after the United States Supreme Court decision in this case, the Soviet Union announced that the decision was not important because it would not be implemented. In this one respect, Governor Talmadge of Georgia seems to be following the Communist line!

It is not only what is done today; it is what has been done in the past, since the foundation of our Republic, which bears fruit. Let me give an illustration of what one girl did in the town of Canterbury, Connecticut, long before the Civil War. In those days there were few public high schools, and Prudence Crandall was conducting a school for girls. Some Negro girls asked to be taken in. They had studied with all the other children in the grammar grades and she admitted them. Immediately the wealthy and "respectable" families withdrew their children. Prudence Crandall then decided that if the white children could not come she would invite Negro children from all over New England to enroll in her school. This greatly shocked the Town Fathers and they immediately passed a resolution that no Negro school could operate in the town. Prudence appealed the case to the courts. The case dragged on interminably and finally a mob was organized in the town, which completely wrecked her school. But look what this mere slip of a girl had accomplished! Her brother gave up his own legal career to devote himself to the cause of equal rights and ever since that time Connecticut has taken an advanced stand in the matter of racial equality.

What Prudence Crandall did so many years ago all of us must do here and now—act fearlessly for equality, for justice, and for freedom.

The curious fact is that reports of segregation have been hurting the United States of America around the world. Everywhere it is strengthening Communistic propaganda and causing the United States untold damage. Yet we continue to violate the law of God and the teachings of Jesus in perpetuating it. Conversely, it is probable that the Supreme Court decision on segregation has been of immense help to our country.

It is time for all Christians who really wish to be genuine followers of Jesus to speak out against all forms of racial discrimination and to do their best to put an end to it in the United States and anywhere that it rears its diabolical head.

Besides equality, religion demands justice for the individual and for *all* individuals. This means economic justice for the native in South Africa, it means justice for the native in Kenya, and it means justice for the poor share cropper in the United States.

We now have the know-how to provide a comfortable living for all persons on the planet. Harrison Brown, Professor of Geochemistry at the California Institute of Technology, puts it this way: "When we look at the situation solely from the point of view of technological and energetic feasibility, we must conclude that the resources available to man permit him, in principle, to provide adequately for a very large population for a very long time." He goes on to say that from the social point of view we may not have enough intelligence to do it. "Our vaunted industrial economy which makes this population possible, in India as well as in England, is in such a precarious balance that we can easily visualize its destruction in a series of wars, or possibly even in only one more great war. Mankind would then probably revert to an agrarian existence."

The Scandinavian countries have done better in creating a balanced economy and justice to all than most of the other countries. They have kept out of the devastating world wars. It seems probable that the standard of living of the bottom sixth of the population is far higher than the corresponding segment in the United States. The reason for this is that they have a planned domestic economy, wherever it is vital to the consumer. It is neither capitalism exclusively nor socialism nor cooperation alone, but it has some of the best features of all three.

For example, the state is in business. It operates nearly one-fourth of the forests. It derives considerable profit from about one-third of the mines. The state owns the railroads, the telegraph, the telephone, and the radio. The result is that broadcasting has no advertising and each radio owner pays $2.50 a year to maintain the service. The government also maintains a monopoly in tobacco and the distribution of liquor. It restricts the amount of liquor which any one person can buy. The local municipalities own the water works, gas plants, and electric light services. Usually electricity is distributed through local consumers cooperative associations. As a result three out of four farm houses are electrified. Sweden also has a cooperative movement which we will consider in the next chapter.

Sweden has a good deal of social legislation. For example, the old age pension law of 1936 fixes pensions according to the cost of living. In medicine the people have free pre-natal advice, practically free hospitalization in the lying-in wards, and payments to mothers both before and after childbirth. In addition there are free health centers for children, free dental care in the schools, and support of children if the father dies.

Besides this, Sweden has more freedom from fear than we in the United States. The hysteria and fear which grip the States is absent there. Individuals may even be Communists without causing hysteria. Communists are opposed in the give-and-take of free debate and then have little real power. Sweden is no Utopia. The average income is not high, but it is much more equalized than in the United States and big business is not so dominant as in many other countries.

As we said at the start of this chapter, we believe that equality requires justice, and justice necessitates freedom. The absence of a single one of these basic principles negates all three.

In the United States recently some have been saying that the external danger of Communism is so great that we are justified in whittling away our liberty by denying visas to distinguished foreign visitors, discharging teachers who take refuge in the Fifth Amendment and refuse to testify, and denying passports to many United States citizens to go abroad. We believe that to the extent we negate equality, justice, and freedom, to that extent we make a climate more favorable to Communism rather than less.

The price of liberty is eternal vigilance and each one of us has the responsibility to do our bit for freedom.

Equality, Justice, and Freedom 145

The condition of civil liberties is an index of our observance of the Constitution which we venerate. Probably at no time in American history has there been more undermining of civil liberties. Long ago the founders of our American Republic introduced the idea into our Constitution that certain human relations were to be outside the control of the government. In the Bill of Rights the government was forbidden to do certain things: "Congress shall make no law respecting an establishment of religion, or prohibiting the free exercise thereof; or abridging the freedom of speech, or of the press, or the right of the people peaceably to assemble, and to petition the government for a redress of grievances."

But there are those who would undermine our civil liberties. Any one who is operating a "racket" or who is getting huge profits at government expense will try to prevent freedom for any one who would expose him.

Unfortunately today we are all living in a society where views are obscured by the mists of prejudice. Bias is a disease which not only obscures but distorts our vision. Emerson once remarked that he had gained a good deal of inspiration from the Hindu Scriptures. Immediately one of his hearers spoke up and said he also had read them but found nothing at all in them. Emerson turned to him and replied, "That only goes to show, my friend, how very narrowly you have read them." This narrowness in viewing our world today is a common malady.

Gradually our freedoms have been whittled away. In 1912 the writer travelled all over Europe without a passport. Today many Americans can no longer travel abroad because it is a penal offense to go without a passport and the arbiters of the Passport Division may or may not grant them. Even wives are not allowed to visit their husbands who are detained in distant China. Restrictions are placed on trade and export to countries behind the "Iron Curtain." The individual who has unorthodox ideas may no longer express them and be certain he will remain free. An hysteria of fear is stifling our heritage of freedom.[2] De Tocqueville long ago declared, "I know of no country in which there

---

[2] See *America's Need: A New Birth of Freedom*, American Civil Liberties Union.

is so little true independence of mind and freedom of discussion as in America." Let us guard against this being true in our time.

We are all in danger of becoming the victims of complexes. We become so biased and prejudiced that we are chained to false ideas. We are sometimes incapable of seeing *any* good in certain other groups or nations. When this is true we are victims of a complex.

Some respectable citizens are so prejudiced that they would outlaw almost *all* suggestions for change. Minorities like the Communist Party, which today protest against encroachments on liberty for themselves, would, if they should come into power, outlaw the other group.

Those who oppose freedom today maintain that while they approve of the safeguards of the Constitution these were not intended to shield the expression of Communistic ideas. In this way civil liberties are always being broken down by well-meaning citizens who profess all along to be their loyal supporters. They maintain that nowadays such "dangerous communist thoughts" are being propagated that we need to be protected from contact with foreign radical ideas. The result is that some very distinguished citizens are being persecuted.

Take as a concrete case Dr. John Punnett Peters, senior professor of medicine at Yale University. Because of his eminence in the field of medical science he served in a more or less voluntary capacity with the Surgeon General of the United States. On January 7, 1949, Dr. Peters received a questionnaire from the Board of Inquiry on Employee Loyalty of the Federal Security Agency, which raised questions as to his loyalty. After his reply the Agency Board wrote that it was entirely satisfied. It should be borne in mind that at no time did Dr. Peters have access to confidential or strategic information.

On December 7, 1951, Dr. Peters was advised that the Agency Board would hold hearings on specific charges against him. Hearings were held in March 1952, by a panel of the Agency Board and Dr. Peters was cleared and advised that no reasonable doubt existed as to his loyalty.

On April 6, 1953, Dr. Peters received a letter from Mr. Hiram Bingham, Chairman of the Loyalty Review Board, saying that they declined to accept the decision of the previous Board and that new hearings would be held. On May 12, 1953, a panel of the Review Board held new hearings. At the hearings numerous eminent persons, including

Charles Seymour, former President of Yale University, Charles E. Clark, Judge of the United States Circuit Court of Appeals, Allan Gregg, Vice President of the Rockefeller Foundation, C. N. H. Lang, Dean of the Yale School of Medicine, and others testified to their complete confidence in the integrity of Dr. Peters and his loyalty to his country. In spite of all this favorable testimony, the Review Board decided that there was a reasonable doubt as to Dr. Peters' loyalty, so he was removed from his position with the Public Health Service.

At all hearings Dr. Peters testified under oath that he had never been a member or supporter of the Communist Party and that he was opposed to all forms of totalitarianism. The net result is that after three and one-half years and three investigations, two of which resulted in clearance, on the strength of the vague, unsworn testimony of *a few unidentified persons* Dr. Peters' privilege of serving his government was terminated. Eventually the Supreme Court was to rule in favor of Dr. Peters but still his case is a good example of the damage that bias, prejudice, and hysteria can do in our time.[3]

This is but one case out of hundreds[4] that might be cited to show how liberty is being undermined at the present time and how our government is losing the services of eminent men in many fields.

To combat this hysteria and to promote liberty, equality, and justice every citizen must stand resolutely against redbaiting, racial prejudice, and injustice. At present redbaiting is one of the greatest political weapons in the arsenal of unprincipled politicians. The American Civil Liberties Union issued a report, *In the Shadow of Fear*, which declared that today we are afflicted with "an unprecedented array of barriers to free association, of forced declarations of loyalty, of blacklists and purges" and that we are in danger of creating for the first time in our history "a secret police system with its array of informers and under-cover agents."

Americans everywhere must get back to the basic principles of liberty for all, even the ideas we hate, as Thomas Jefferson stated, *as long as there is freedom to combat them.* We must not become

[3] See "Petition for Writ of Certiorare." In the Supreme Court of the United States. John P. Peters, Petitioner.

[4] For the case of Dr J. Robert Oppenheimer see Alsop, J. & S., *We Accuse,* 1955.

neurotic and view the world as a network of conspirators and patriots, of devils and angels. Let us again place our faith in the Gospel of Jesus and the prophets.

One and only one test of the actuality of the religious life of a country is, how far it really has equality, justice, and freedom. If every reader would test this in his own community and then get the churches and synagogues to act, America would make progress. Stop and ask yourself these questions:

(1) Are Negroes permitted to join all the churches in my community? Can they stay at any hotel? Are they eligible to join the Rotary Club, for instance? Do they in fact belong to it?

(2) Do the poorest tenth of the population live in homes in slum areas? Are they congested in one-room or two-room homes?

(3) How many unemployed are there? During a depression? At the present time?

(4) Do you have a consumers' cooperative store in your community? if not, why not?

(5) Does the community have newspapers owned by different groups?

(6) Are people afraid to speak the truth as they see it?

(7) Are workers in the factories well organized into trade unions of their own choosing?

These and many other questions should be asked if you wish to find out whether your community is implementing EQUALITY, JUSTICE, AND FREEDOM into the community life.

Prayer

Lord, not for light in darkness do we pray,
Not that the veil be lifted from our eyes,
Nor that the slow ascension of our day
    Be otherwise.

Not for a clearer vision of the things
Whereof the fashioning shall make us great,
Not for the remission of the peril and stings
    Of time and fate.

Grant us the will to fashion as we feel,
Grant us the strength to labour as we know,
Grant us the purpose, ribbed and edged with steel,
    To strike the blow.

Knowledge we ask not—knowledge Thou hast lent,
But, Lord, the will—there lies our bitter need,
Give us to build above the deep intent
    The deed, the deed.

JOHN DRINKWATER.

Materialism has brought about a decline in the influence of religion upon American life. Confusion in our thinking and a sort of paralysis of the national will have been the inevitable results of this decline. Here then we have the source of that weakness which is causing so much concern to men of good-will. . . . Materialism is the real enemy, at home and abroad. In its varieties, there is little difference of kind; the difference is largely one of degree. Both are deadly for America.
>
> THE ROMAN CATHOLIC BISHOPS of the United States, Nov. 20, 1954.

Woe to those who stint the measure:
Who when they take from others, exact the full;
But when they mete to them or weigh to them, minish—
Have they no thought that they shall be raised again
For a great day,
A day when mankind shall stand before the Lord of the Worlds?
>
> From *The Koran*

Earnestness is the path of Nirvana, thoughtlessness the path of death. Those who are earnest do not die, those who are thoughtless are as if dead already.
>
> DHAMMAPADA PROVERB

Civilization must be judged and prized, not by the amount of power it has developed, but by how much it has evolved and given expression to, by its laws and institutions, the love of humanity.
>
> RABINDRANATH TAGORE

Moving out of the Neolithic age may be the world's most difficult problem . . . It is the retention by Atom Age man of the Neolithic point of view that says, "If your sheep eat our grass we will kill you. We may kill you anyhow to get all the grass for our sheep. Anyone who tries to make us change our ways is a witch and we will kill him."
>
> CARLETON S. COON in *The Story of Man*

This [one man one vote] has constituted the democratic strength of the co-operative movement. Whether a co-operative commonwealth will displace the present mixture of political democracy and economic plutocracy, we do not know. But judging from the experience of such nations as Denmark and Sweden, it may be safely asserted that a wide extension of this highly democratic form of economic enterprise will not only be good in itself, but will be a powerful check upon many of the abuses of our present capitalistic system.

H. A. OVERSTREET in *Our Free Minds*, p. 199

CHAPTER XI

Economic Democracy

THE United States is often severely condemned for inequities in the economic area but no matter what is said it must be recognized that on the whole we have more wealth than any other country in the world. We produce more automobiles, for instance, than any other land; we have more television sets, whether or not this is an asset, and our standard of living is high.

We believe in community responsibility for social welfare. Each year Community Chests and Councils of Social Agencies raise money for social work. We have had social work. We have had social security and public relief funds for over a quarter of a century. Medical care is usually available for the poor and for people of moderate means there is health insurance. We have had some form of compensation for industrial injury for perhaps 40 years. We abolished the 12-hour day in steel in 1923 and today the 40-hour week is general. We have considerable public housing.

We have effective control of railroad rates since 1906 and Public Service Corporation regulation, beginning in Wisconsin in 1907, is now universal. Theoretically we made monopoly illegal in 1890 even though it is not adequately enforced. All of which goes to show that we do not really have *laissez-faire* capitalism in the United States.

However, we are still vigorously opposed to government ownership of production. We do accept government ownership of the Post Office, of the schools, the highways, the sewers, and the water supply.

To a considerable extent American Business is highly competitive and strongly opposes dividing markets and fixing prices. In spite of all this we have serious flaws in our economic order. Concentration of ownership continues and inflation keeps increasing the price of consumers goods to the people.[1] Now some businessmen believe that our economic system is reasonably in conformity with Christian principles. Others strongly disagree. When we consider the conflicts among owners, managers, workers, not to mention exploiters of all sorts we realize we are still far from perfection.[2]

Long ago the sainted Walter Rauschenbusch whose *Prayers of the Social Awakening* have reverberated around the world, wrote as follows, "Capitalism has generated a spirit of its own which is antagonistic to the spirit of Christianity; a spirit of hardness and cruelty that neutralizes the Christian spirit of love; a spirit that sets material goods above spiritual possessions. To set Things above Men is the really dangerous practical materialism. To set Mammon before God is the only idolatry against which Jesus warned us."[3]

We all know there is nothing sacrosanct about any contemporary structure of society. At present we have democracy in the economic field in the sense that anyone can go out and try to make a million dollars for himself. We have sketched some of our lines of progress but we must not forget the tendency of man to get used to any economic environment in which he is immersed. We see evils in the Soviet Union. Roger Baldwin reports that Russia is ruthlessly using forced labor in the countries it dominates. We do not always see that big business monopoly and cartels may threaten democracy here at home.

Benjamin Franklin maintained, "God grant that not only the Love of Liberty, but a thorough knowledge of the Rights of Man, may pervade all the nations of the earth so that a philosopher may set his foot anywhere on its surface and say: This is my country."

In the Second World War President Roosevelt proclaimed his Four Freedoms:

Freedom of Speech, Freedom of Religion, Freedom from Want, and Freedom from Fear.

The United Nations unanimously approved the Universal Declaration of Human Rights in 1948. The first article declares that "all

---

[1] See Lynch, David, *The Concentration of Economic Power*, Columbia University Press, 1946.
[2] Buchanan, Scott, *Essays in Politics*.
[3] Rauschenbusch, Walter, *Christianizing the Social Order*, p. 315.

human beings are born free and equal in dignity and in rights." Article II states, Everyone is "presumed innocent until proved guilty." Article 12 states, "No one shall be subjected to arbitrary interference with his privacy, family, home, or correspondence, nor to attacks upon his honor or reputation." Article 13 states, "Everyone has the right to leave any country, including his own, and to return to his country." Article 23 states, "Everyone has the right to work . . . and to protection against unemployment." Other articles uphold the right to join a trade union. Although this was adopted unanimously in the United Nations, the United States has not observed all its provisions, Article 13, for instance.

Recently we have been going through a second industrial revolution called *automation*. This is the regulation of the production process by self-operating, mechanical, hydraulic, pneumatic, chemical, electrical or electronic devices. This has resulted in tremendous changes. For example, in the automatic engine plant of the Ford Motor Company, twice as many engines are turned out, with one-tenth the man power, as formerly.

In a radio assembly line which produces 1,000 radios a day and used to employ 200 workers, now only two workers are used to run the line.

In the face of these changes, if we are to secure economic democracy and prevent needless unemployment it would seem that we should have a guaranteed annual wage for all workers. The C.I.O. has been advocating this for years. Why should not workers have the benefit of this system just as much as business executives, teachers, or ministers?

If we are to secure freedom from want then controls on prices must be maintained. At present controls have been taken off basic foods and prices have been skyrocketing.

As far back as 1951 the annual report of Philip Murray, President of the C.I.O., stated, "Abundant evidence has been accumulated by Congress during the last year which indicates that the concentration of economic power in the hands of a comparatively few big business corporations is progressing at an alarming rate."

Communism offers men bread if they will give up their freedom. American reactionaries say if you want to have bread you must let us control the economic life. It is just possible that the American reactionaries and the Communists may both be wrong. The great problem before the world is to harness the technological resources of the world and translate them into the good life for everyone. This struggle means that we must have both freedom and economic justice. One third of the world is living on less than one dollar a week. Two thirds of humanity live in poverty, hunger, disease, starvation, illiteracy and face premature death.

Now just what are some of the principles that might be adopted to meet the challenge of automation, if we are genuinely to achieve economic democracy.

1. In general, more of our economy should be owned by those who use it.
2. It should be democratically controlled.
3. It should be efficiently run at the lowest possible cost.
4. It should provide subsistence to all.
5. It should provide equality of opportunity for all.
6. It should prevent monopoly.

Now it seems established that the cooperative movement in the by and large follows all these fundamental principles.

We should recognize that there are three forms of ownership, private profit, cooperative, and public ownership. It is all right to have private ownership but at all times an alternative should be available, if and when private industry fails.

Sweden has demonstrated what can be done in this regard. The Swedish cooperative movement fights high prices wherever they believe monopoly has taken an unfair advantage of the people. For instance, when margarine was outrageously high, the cooperatives started a small factory and within two months the price had dropped ten cents a pound. To break the high price of flour the cooperatives purchased a large mill. As a result, the price of the best quality flour dropped by almost one dollar a bag. Rubbers used to be controlled by a rapacious trust. After the cooperatives started their factory the price of rubbers dropped nearly a dollar a pair. Today the cooperatives make nearly seventy per cent of the tires in Sweden.

The International Electric Light Combine used to keep the price of electric light bulbs extremely high. After the cooperatives started their manufacture, the price dropped ten cents a bulb.

Similarly by starting factories making cash registers, soap, washing material and proprietary articles such as tooth paste, prices fell. The saving to the public on cash registers alone ran to over a million dollars a year. To prevent high rentals, the co-ops built housing units. In 1953 alone, 4,760 flats were completed.

In the United States Americans were encouraged to purchase Liberty Bonds from the government due in ten years. They were paid 3.9% interest. Yet inflation has been so severe that when the individual received his money after a decade, he had lost in actual purchasing power some ten per cent of all he had invested counting the interest he had been paid. In Sweden the cooperatives issued cost of living bonds which at maturity are paid in purchasing power as of the time the money was invested. This means that if inflation had doubled the cost of goods the owner would be paid back double what he put in.

Thus the cooperative movement in Sweden has provided a real measure of economic democracy because the cooperatives are controlled democratically by the people who use them.

In the United States, the cooperatives have been gradually expanding. In 1955, over eleven million families used the cooperatives to help themselves to better health, more buying power, greater income from the farm, credit at lower interest rates and other benefits. This is almost double the number of individuals who are stockholders of all the major corporations listed on the New York Stock Exchange. The Credit Union cooperatives alone had 9 million members in the Western hemisphere and 7 million in the United States. Assets of these credit unions are now over 2 billion dollars. Mutual insurance companies had 4,500,000 members; rural electric cooperatives had 3,500,000. The consumers' cooperatives, both urban and rural, were alone doing more than a billion dollar business. In addition farmer cooperative associations including both the purchasing and marketing co-ops did a business of over 7 billion.[4]

In 1950, the twenty-two cooperative wholesale societies which were members of National Cooperatives, Inc., owned and operated 158 factories, refineries or other productive units. The member societies belonging to these wholesale organizations did a business even in 1946 of roughly 700 million dollars.

Before cooperatives were formed in gas and oil some of the largest

[4] Figures for 1954.

companies in the United States refused to sell oil to the cooperative organizations. The only answer they could make was to go into the business as cooperatives. Today they are doing a business of over 366 millions annually or twenty-two per cent of the total in this field in the rural areas of America.

The largest group of distributive cooperatives in the United States is the farmers' organizations. They are engaged chiefly in marketing farm products for their members but they also supply them with various services and commodities needed for farm and household use. Today there are over ten thousand active farmers' cooperative societies.

In 1937 there was only one cooperative hospital, the one founded by Dr. Shadid in Elk City, Oklahoma. By 1948 there were six cooperative hospitals operating successfully. In 1955 there were 184 cooperative health associations. These include about a dozen cooperative hospitals and clinics. The health cooperatives serve 750,000 members. This is not counting some of the large labor health plans which are primarily cooperative in character and which would boost this total to something over 4 million.

In Saskatchewan, Canada, they have a system of municipal hospitals. The individual can pay fifteen dollars a year and it then costs nothing to go to the public ward of the hospital and he can stay as long as he is sick.

By 1953 there were some 673 cooperative housing projects in the United States with 82,855 dwelling units valued at over $788 millions.

In the colleges and universities there are now so many cooperatives that a national organization, the North American Students' Cooperative League, has been formed.

In the chaos and hunger following World War II in Europe, the government turned to the consumers' cooperative movement to arrange for the sending of food packages abroad. Thus came into being CARE, the Cooperative for American Remittances *Everywhere*. Murray D. Lincoln, president of the Cooperative League and president of the Farm Bureau Insurance Companies, was elected president. CARE's member organizations—cooperatives, farm, labor, religious and relief organizations—put up three-quarters of a million dollars of their own capital. They secured long-range credit from the U.S. government to handle the 10-in-1 food packages which had been packed for use of the

Army, but were not needed after the close of the war. These packages got CARE started on its food crusade, but lasted less than a year. CARE has since packed its own food and has shipped $175 million worth of food, clothing, books, tools and medical supplies to 40 countries throughout the world.

During the World War when 110,000 Japanese were removed from the Pacific Coast, all the business enterprises in the relocation camps were organized on a co-op basis. The Government had provided four million dollars for these stores, but the Consumers' Cooperatives were set up so efficiently that they did not need to touch a dollar of the Government's money. At the end of the war when the Japanese were freed, they had received over a million dollars in patronage dividends alone from these cooperatives.

Anyone who studies the cooperative movement will see that it conforms to the highest standards for economic democracy. Its fundamental principles are:

1. One member, one vote. This insures democracy. No matter how much stock a person may hold he has only one vote.
2. Legal rate of interest, only, on capital.
3. Surplus after fund for interest on capital stock, reserve and education, is returned to members in proportion to patronage. In other words the organization is conducted on the basis of service for all its members, not for profits to the few.
4. Unrestricted membership, although there is a nominal fee for joining. If a member has no money he can join and his membership fee will be deducted from the surplus which would otherwise be returned to him.
5. Cash sales at the market.
6. Constant education in the principles and aims of cooperation.
7. Federation as soon as possible with the nearest cooperative societies with the ultimate purpose of national and world cooperation.

What is our country now doing in the rural areas? It tries to reduce the amount of food produced and actually has paid farmers for non-production; or we have been keeping the price of butter so high by government purchases that few people can afford to buy it. What we really should be doing is to try and get every person to have the maximum amount of food at the lowest possible price.

We seem to have arrived at an era of plenty and have more food than our own citizens will use. So we let the government pay for the surplus. We then store away millions and millions of pounds of butter until it spoils, we jam our warehouses with wheat and fill caves with cheese.

At the end of 1953 there were 7,159,000 agricultural workers against 55,083,000 others. It might be said that perhaps forty per cent of the workers of the United States are either employed on the farms or producing for them. The prosperity of the nation thus depends on the farms and our food supply comes from them.

What do the farmers purchase? They use fertilizers, chemicals, steel, oil and electric power. We are no longer in a period of pure individualism. Each of these great industries is getting handouts from the government, so also are the farmers and the workers. Manufacturers have their tariff protection, their fair trade laws, their tax depletion and their tax write-offs. Actually tax write-offs have covered some 61 per cent of all new defence facilities. Labor in its turn has a guaranteed minimum wage and unemployment insurance while farmers have price supports and production controls. No wonder some of the people call this "creeping socialism." But the point is, all those who are getting special favors, whether steel corporations or farmers, want them continued.

If special favors, for example, in producing butter, make it more profitable for the farmer to produce unneeded goods for the warehouse and a government bounty, than for a crop really needed by the consumer, is this not dangerous to our economy?

Much more sensible than our present system would be a production payment plan for perishables. This would be a bonus to farmers direct. This would mean that prices would seek their natural level. The more that was produced, the lower the price to the consumer.

Another way to get a sound rural economy is through the cooperative movement. By 1951, three million farmers had invested over a billion dollars in their cooperative businesses. If we include the 900 rural electric cooperatives, over three-fourths of the farmers belong to some type of cooperative.

When the farmers began to buy the Welch Grape Juice Company they received $95 a ton for their grapes and $55.53 in allocation certificates or over twice as much as they would have received in the open market. The farmers can probably buy complete control within five years.

Mr. Murray Lincoln, one of the great leaders of the cooperative movement in the United States, estimates that the farmers could buy out the National Dairy Products Corporation within three and one half years through a similar program and could buy up Bordens in perhaps a year longer.

The cooperative movement could cut the costs to all the American people in the following two ways among others.

First, the cooperatives could furnish the farmers with the goods and services they need for farming at a far lower cost than they now have.

Second, the cooperatives could provide distribution machinery to deliver goods to the consumers at prices below what they are now paying. This would prevent the necessity of storing most of our unused foods thus saving half a million dollars a day, which is the present cost to the nation for this waste.

Some may argue that the cooperatives are free from taxes and thus have an unfair advantage. Let us examine the facts.

In the 1920's the Congress provided certain types of tax exemption for agricultural cooperatives as an aid to American agriculture. These exemptions were helpful to the farmers, but by 1950 less than half of the farm-owned cooperatives which were eligible for exemption were taking advantage of it. In 1951 the Congress removed this exemption completely. The consumer cooperatives in the cities have never had any tax exemption of any kind. Cooperatives as a whole now have no tax exemption. They pay federal income tax on any monies which are actually held in the cooperative and not paid out in cash or allocated to the members. This is the same as in any other business. The cooperatives do not pay taxes on money which is paid out to the cooperative members. No other business would have to pay taxes on any of the money it paid back to customers either. Actually, cooperatives do not have a preferred status or tax exemption when this is taken into consideration. The Congress and the courts have always held that where there is no income there is no income tax required. Cooperatives are subject to 24 or 25 other kinds of taxes just as are other types of business enterprise. In many communities the cooperatives are the largest taxpayers.

Actually it was not the cooperatives which received a 16.8 billion dollar gift from the government in the form of fast write-offs after Korea. It is the corporation not the cooperative which gets most of the benefits from tariffs, depletion allowances and fair trade laws.

For the first time in history we know how to raise all the food that is needed to supply the population of the world. Arnold Toynbee says that ours is "the first age since the dawn of civilization, in which people dared to think it practicable to make the benefits of civilization available for the whole human race."

The American economy should be based primarily on consumption rather than production. A healthy economy will have full employment and high consumer spending. Since population is constantly increasing, we shall certainly need 25 per cent more farm production in the next decade.

We should have a program of cooperative rather than exploitative investments abroad. This may involve barter agreements under which we would trade foods for raw materials or minerals.

We ought to cut down the distribution costs so as to reduce drastically the spread between the farmer and the household purchaser of food. The consumer cooperative movement could easily reduce this spread and benefit all the people.

In order to stimulate the cooperative movement why should they not be given the same opportunity for fast tax write-offs that capitalistic groups have?

Why should not CARE be given the opportunity to give to the world's starving millions the food stores that are now in danger of spoiling in warehouses? This in a small way is beginning to be done.

It is apparent from the record of the cooperatives around the world that the movement is in line with many of the principles of Christianity and that it also is a powerful force making for economic democracy. Do we care enough to try to move forward towards liberty, equality and fraternity in the economic areas of life?

Prayer

Grant us light, upon the society in which we live that we may throw our lives against the currents going in the wrong direction. We thank Thee for the privilege of hard work, for the satisfaction that comes with a good deed done and for the chance to place our time, our energy and our influence towards new and better things. Create within our hearts the spirit of invincible goodwill and help us to see clearly those positive, constructive ways of life which will contribute to the establishment of the Kingdom of God on earth.

Grant us the satisfaction that comes from being co-workers with Thee in building fairer and happier communities for all men to live in.

Help us to feel men's brotherhood so perfectly that wherever others are in need, we must act. Help us never to be discouraged, no matter what the obstacles. Help us not to be overcome by evil but to overcome evil with good, and thus in the end may we be true sons of Thine. Amen.

Prayer

Cast Thy light upon the society in which we live that we may know our own against the currents going in the wrong direction. If we thank Thee for the privilege of hard work, for the satisfaction that comes with a deed well done and for the chance to place our time, our energy and our intelligence towards new and better things. Create within our hearts, the spirit of invincible goodwill and help us to see clearly those behaviour patterns and ways of life which will contribute to the establishment of the Kingdom of God on earth.

Grant us the satisfaction that comes from being co-workers with Thee in building larger and happier communities for all men to live in. Help us to feel more a brotherhood so perfectly that wherever there is weakness we must act. Help us never to be discouraged, no matter what the obstacles. Help us not to be overcome by evil but to overcome evil with good and thus in the end may we be true sons of Thine.

Amen.

"If any one says, 'I love God,' and yet hates his brother, he is a liar; for whosoever does not love his brother whom he hath seen cannot love God whom he hath not seen."

I John 4, 20.

"Ever since the world's far-off lands were discovered, what has been the conduct of the white people to the colored ones? What is the meaning of the simple fact that some of the primitive groups are dying out, and that the condition of others is getting worse and worse as a result of their discovery by men who professed to be followers of Jesus? Who can describe the injustice and the cruelties that in the course of centuries they have suffered at the hands of Europeans? Who can measure the misery produced among them by the fiery drinks and hideous diseases that we have taken to them? If a record could be compiled of all that has happened between the white and the coloured races, it would make a book—which the reader would have to turn over unread, because its content would be too horrible.

"We and our civilization are burdened, really, with a great debt. We are not free to confer benefits on these men, or not, as we please: it is our duty. Anything we give them is not benevolence but atonement. For every one who scattered injury some one ought to go out to take help, and when we have done all that is in our power, we shall not have atoned for the thousandth part of our guilt. That is the foundation from which all deliberations about 'works of mercy' out here must begin."

ALBERT SCHWEITZER, medical missionary and author, from *On the Edge of the Primeval Forest*

CHAPTER XII

The Solidarity of Mankind

How easy it is for an individual in one nation to condemn another group which it hates. When our forefathers pioneered to establish a new nation on the North American continent, one of the most distinguished British writers of his day, Dr. Samuel Johnson, declared of Americans, "They are a race of convicts and ought to be thankful for anything we allow them short of hanging." Now when we have become powerful how easy it is for us to use similar blasts against Communists revolting from a Tsar's tyranny, for instance. Just because of these human weaknesses we should be mature enough to recognize a vital principle—*the solidarity of mankind*.

We are built one of another. Every civilization has contributed something to the sum total of human wisdom. Even the follies of people have helped to teach us what to avoid. Old habit patterns of thought are now being eroded by swiftly moving changes. We must have tolerance and more tolerance for the behaviour of other individuals and groups. We must recognize that had we been born in a different social setting, a different cultural pattern, had we had a different life experience, we might now be behaving as is the group we despise and hate. Therefore we must try to understand not only what are the characteristics and behavior of our brothers everywhere but, and more important, *why* they are doing it. How did they get that way? When we finally reach this maturity, perhaps we shall be in a better position to appraise, evaluate, even change our behaviour. This involves getting rid of vested habit patterns of thought. We should try to assume in our enemies the highest motives that would explain their actions, rather than the lowest. This is not easy, but it must be attempted if we are really to recognize the principle of the solidarity of mankind.

By this time most of us should recognize that we are living on an interdependent globe which in point of time is shrinking by the minute. We should be concerned with the genuine welfare of all the 2,400,000,000 human beings on this planet. We should certainly strive for *equality of opportunity* for every child to develop his capacities and capabilities and for the end of privilege in any form which impairs this equality.

Education should be available for every child in the world, and yet it should be a process in which the child is taught that every generation must improve over the past. So we should give freedom for new ideas. But what about the Communist infection?

All ideas should have the right to be expounded but those that are considered wrong should be controverted at the bar of public opinion. In any country where all ideas are free and where the condition of the people is good, false ideas tend to die, just as germs die when they are exposed to the sunlight.

At present we do not practise the basic principle of the solidarity of all mankind intelligently. As we have previously shown, to guard the whole world by military might is impossible. The United States comprises only about one-sixteenth of the human race, yet today Pentagon and State Department officials talk about "our" defence line as stretching around the world. It takes in the islands of the Pacific, Korea, Japan, Formosa, the Elbe; it runs from Gibraltar to the Suez. Our bombing bases ring the Soviet Union. Indeed, the *U.S. News and World Report* as far back as April 1, 1949, headlined: "U.S. Defence Zone: the World."

The late Senator Taft in May, 1950, declared: "If we go out to put modern invasion airplanes in every country surrounding Russia then we become an aggressor. What I object to is undertaking by contract to arm about twenty nations all around the world, all around Russia, obviously an aggressive move."

On August 25, 1950, Francis P. Adams, the then Secretary of the Navy, apparently declared for a war of aggression. This policy would, he claimed, "cast us in a character new to a true democracy—an initiator of a war of aggression—it would win for us a proud and popular title —we would become the first aggressors for peace."[1]

[1] New York *Times,* Aug. 26, 1950.

The Solidarity of Mankind   169

If Russia ever tries to get a foothold in some small country in South America, we invoke the Monroe Doctrine and drive them out. But if China, which was promised Formosa at the end of World War II by the United States, believes our navy should not now prevent her taking it, we are outraged. This in spite of the fact that Formosa is just off the coast of China and thousands of miles from the United States.

For years France fought to keep French Indo-China under her imperialistic control. The United States participated by sending in arms and ammunition. It was broadcast all over the United States that the rebels were Communists, under the control of red China. In spite of all that France could do, she failed to win and against some United States pressure she made peace. The French commander, Brigadier General Christian de Castries, the "hero of Dienbienphu," then stated, for all the world to hear, that the Vietminh rebels were made up largely of *genuine Nationalists,* and *not* dominated by Communist China.[2] This left the United States in the embarrassing position of having been contradicted by the very general whom they had been supporting!

Since 1950 we have maintained a perpetual war economy. F. J. P. Veale maintains that it is now possible to keep the average man "for long periods in a condition of emotional frenzy, paralyzing his reasoning faculties and rendering black indistinguishable by him from white."[3] Professor Harry Elmer Barnes maintains regarding the Korean conflict as follows:

A foreign nation or nations are an enemy only in formal fiction. The real enemy is forces and factors within the boundaries of the nation—partisan competition and economic depression. In such a war, the President and his party were winning a victory every day, even when our forces were being routed temporarily. So long as Democratic tenure seemed assured and the depression was postponed, 'victory' was constantly at hand. The worst possible defeat would have been a quick and decisive military victory over the North Koreans and the Chinese. This would have ended the emergency, weakened the Democrats and threatened us with abysmal depression.[4]

[2] *World Interpreter,* Oct. 8, 1954, p. 7.
[3] Veale, *Advance to Barbarism,* p. 270.
[4] *Advance to Barbarism, op. cit.,* p. 277.

Now if mankind is one small group of brothers we must repudiate the whole cold-war concept of "perpetual war for perpetual peace" and get back to trying to help our brothers, *all our brothers*.

We have already called attention to our policy of storing millions and millions of pounds of butter which we cannot use and yet refuse to sell to Russia who needs it. Is this the highest and best Christian way to end the cold war?

We live in one little world. The so-called division between "the free world" and the Communist world is partly a fiction of the mind, even though we recognize the evils under Communism. In the first place, much of the so-called "free" world is not free. Think of the dictatorships in South America, of the imperialism practised in countries which we support, of the tyranny over the racial majority practised in South Africa. In the second place, whether we want it or not, we are all brothers one of another.

The Russians are sincerely scared of us just as we are sincerely scared of them. The following is a speech by a woman collective worker in Russia. Of course she has been propagandized by the Communist control of the press, but she really believes what she says.

> I am 62 years of age. I well remember the terribly harsh conditions of life under the Tsar's regime. From sunrise to sunset we toiled in the fields. Everywhere was poverty, illiteracy and suffering. Our life has completely changed under the Soviets. In our collective today almost all work is mechanized. Every year the collective members live better.
>
> While the Soviet people were busy building a new world the imperialists were preparing a new world war. Unnumbered millions died and others suffered, mothers lost millions of sons.
>
> I am the mother of five sons. Two sons died in the world war. Together with all women and mothers I register a protest from the bottom of my heart against the imperialists who are preparing to unleash a new war. The Soviet people stand firmly on the side of peace. With us are all the people of the world. Let this never be forgotten by the war mongers.

Now since the world is one, if we are to win against Communism we must be true to our ideas of freedom, justice, and equality all around the world. But what does Justice William O. Douglas of the United States Supreme Court say?

The Solidarity of Mankind

America, proud of her standards of freedom and justice at home, has in recent years been too often associated not with the forces of liberation, but with the forces of repression. . . . The truth is that Asia (and Africa too) is seething with ideas that are not orthodox. If we are congenial only to the orthodox, if we are afraid to explore ideas to the periphery, if we do not encourage experimental attitudes, then we will be alarmed, confused, and bewildered abroad. Then every socialist, every rebel, every unorthodox political leader in Asia will look like a dangerous undercover man for the Kremlin.[5]

America, if she is to be true to the Declaration of Independence, which was our charter of freedom, must be true to these same ideas all over the world. But Stringfellow Barr says we are acting on five false assumptions:

1. "That Russia is all that stands between mankind and a stable peace."
2. "That American 'know-how' and American money can rebuild the world economy, or at least enough of it to stop Russia."
3. "That 'free enterprise' can do the job even better than the government."
4. "That, even if we allow the United Nations to do a small fraction of the job, it can best do it on small yearly appropriations.
5. "That America can best preserve freedom by backing any anti-Communists she can find anywhere, including reactionaries and even fascists."[6]

In fact, is it not true that if all the Russians should die tomorrow, the great majority of mankind, who live in poverty, hunger, sickness, and ignorance, would still go on revolting?

What the world needs is an International Development Authority under the United Nations to help the undeveloped countries. This would do for them what the Tennessee Valley Authority did in our own country.

Actually the United States voted with Russia to kill the idea in the United Nations. Before that, the United States killed UNRRA, which was a great international relief organization under the United Nations. Prior to that, our own President killed Lend-Lease, although he now admits that he made a mistake in doing so.

[5] Introduction to *Citizens of the World,* Stringfellow Barr, p. 12.
[6] *Ibid.,* p. 62.

World War II cost the United States alone more than three hundred billion dollars. Yet when the late Senator Brian McMahon proposed that the United States spend ten billion dollars a year for five years to eradicate human misery around the globe, a Senate Committee proposed only ten millions, a sum less than New York City spends to clean its streets and dispose of garbage. Walter Reuther, head of the C.I.O., urges that we spend thirteen billions a year for a hundred years to stop human misery, but thus far the United States has preferred to spend her money largely for armaments.

The great majority of men and women on the globe are determined to put an end to their hunger, poverty, sickness, and ignorance. They believe that it is possible to usher in an era of plenty for all. Force will not stop this revolution, destroying Communism will not stop it, bombing all the Communists in the world will not stop it. The only way is to prove to the masses of the world that we can give them the conditions of life which they long for. In fact, when we attack Communists there is always a danger that the hungry people of the world will believe that we are trying to prevent them from solving the problems of wholesome living which the Communists have promised subject people around the world.

It will be interesting to see what happens in Guatemala. We have been sympathetic to the overthrow of a radical regime there. Will we now ameliorate the conditions of the masses and bring in a new era of prosperity and happiness? If we do, we may win the people; if we do not, in the long run we are bound to lose. We must keep up an unending effort to build the foundation of freedom everywhere.

Science and technical advances have made the entire world a small neighborhood, where we are all bound together. Stringfellow Barr has well stated that:

> By urging that the United Nations apply to a reeling world economy the measures we Americans pioneered in the Tennessee Valley, our neighbors are actually showing us an exit from a rat race that has already cost us more than one hundred thousand casualties, billions of dollars, soaring taxes, inflation, and a kind of wartime hysteria that has endangered our civil rights as they have not been endangered for decades.[7]

[7] Stringfellow Barr, *op. cit.*, p. 124.

The Solidarity of Mankind

It is highly dangerous if not suicidal to go on attacking ideas of our brothers around the globe while we refuse to help the great mass of mankind in Asia and Africa to a better life.

St. Paul has well said: "He hath made of one blood all nations for to dwell on the face of the earth."

Modern science has achieved one small world for all humanity. Economically, the one world has arrived. In point of time we are already in it. We shall either recognize this one world and rebuild it together through voluntary cooperation and tolerance or we shall destroy it through war.

If we should establish a world development authority, thus providing adequate food for all the peoples of the world, we would ultimately reduce disease, spread education, and the natives of Asia, Africa, and Latin America would become in time the equals of the white man.

If the two great rivals in the cold war would give up trying to destroy capitalism on the one side and communism on the other, and join together in a war on human misery, the one world of tomorrow would be achieved. There is little doubt that if the United States would genuinely offer to back an International Development Authority through the United Nations and would agree to give them ten per cent of the money now being spent on armaments, provided the other countries would do the same, we could go forward to undreamed of progress.

Lord Boyd Orr, former Director General of the Food and Agricultural Organization, believes that the only alternative to the decline and fall of Western civilization is such an International Development Authority. Says he:

The Western Powers are faced with the rising waves of revolt of Asia, Africa, and Latin America against poverty. They can try to resist it by force or buy it off by the offer of technical assistance and trifling loans with political strings attached to them, which will break on the first strain. In that case they will ultimately be destroyed or submerged. On the other hand, either with or without cooperation of the U.S.S.R., they could recognize the inevitable and use their overwhelming industrial superiority to create a new world of plenty.[8]

[8]Orr, John Boyd, *The White Man's Dilemma,* London, 1953, p. 102.

We should take the lead in a war on human misery. We should pool our capital with that of other nations and take part in a great crusade to help people everywhere have food, health, and the abundance which they crave. If we would do this instead of concentrating our spending on the weapons of mass destruction, we would be following the principle of the Golden Rule. If we did this we could win against the Communists because we would be genuinely helping our brothers and sisters around the world. The alternative policy of containment through military power will in the long run be disastrous. It does not spell out the solidarity of mankind.

Prayer

Teach us, our Father, how to look at the things we see, and to look at them without bias or predjudice. We may not know how much of our troubles are caused by refusing to look at the facts or by viewing them so differently.

We are all too familiar with "dirty looks," "scornful looks," "unbelieving looks," "black looks." Give to us discerning and understanding looks. With the truth waiting to be looked at, discovered and applied, forgive us when we refuse to look at it or to welcome it. If Thou wilt help us to cast the mote of prejudice and pride out of our eyes, then shall we see clearly.

We pray for good sight and good sense, in the name of Jesus Christ. Amen.

THE REV. PETER MARSHALL, D.D., in the Senate of the United States

Prayer

Teach us, our Father, how to look at the things we say, and to look at them without bias or prejudice. We may not know how much of our troubles are caused by refusing to look at the facts, or by wishing them to different.

We are all too familiar with guilty looks, "downfall looks," "unbelieving looks," "black looks." Give us an discerning and understanding look. With the truth compare us be looked at, discovered and applied, forgive us when we refuse to look at it, or to welcome it. If Thou wilt help us to take the smoke of pride out of our eyes, then shall we see clearly.

We pray for good sight and good sense, in the name of Jesus Christ. Amen.

The Rev. Peter Marshall, D.D., in the Senate of the United States.

God of Justice, save the people from the war of race and creed,
From the strife of class and faction—make our nation free indeed;
Keep her faith in simple manhood, stern as when life began
Till it find its full fruition in the brotherhood of man.
WILLIAM P. MERRILL

The general adoption of the scientific attitude in human affairs would mean nothing less than a revolution in morals, religion, politics and industry. The fact that we have limited its use so largely to technical matters is not a reproach to science, but to the human beings who use it for private ends and who strive to defeat its social application for fear of destructive effects upon their power and profit. A vision of a day in which the natural sciences and the technologies that flow from them are used as servants of a humane life constitutes the imagination that is relative to our own times.
JOHN DEWEY

Blessed is the servant who loves his brother as much when he is sick and useless as when he is well and can be of service to him. And blessed is he who loves his brother as well when he is afar off as when he is by his side; and who would say nothing behind his back he might not, in love, say before his face.
SAINT FRANCIS OF ASSISI

We must learn above all, the first lesson that all the earth needs to know: that Christianity, democracy, and sanity, all three; center in love and brotherhood, in a sharing of a common humanity, in making room on this earth for all to live on it in human dignity and with self-esteem; in making room in our own hearts for understanding, love, and simple decency.
LILLIAN SMITH

Civilization must be judged and prized, not by the amount of power it has developed, but by how much it has evolved and given expression to, by its laws and institutions, the love of humanity.
TAGORE

CHAPTER XIII

Invincible Goodwill

An individual in relation to society is something like the diagram of an atom in nuclear physics. He is being influenced by hosts of other individuals and by other groups. There is constant interaction and response. This may be a conscious or an unconscious process. It is hard for the individual even if he wishes to overcome the effect of the cultural milieux in which he is immersed, to rise above the powerful forces which are playing upon him. This is why too often the prophet in any age is despised and rejected in his own lifetime only to be revered and honored in the next generation.

We have been considering certain "guide posts to progress." These include the enlargement of our horizon so that we will not be too limited by all the passions and phobias of our own societal sphere. We must build into the foundations of our living, certain basic principles. These include equality, justice, and freedom which are necessities if we are to create the good life. If we genuinely and wholeheartedly believe in democracy we should recognize that political democracy is not enough. Just as a monopoly for one political party destroys freedom, so political democracy may be undermined if we permit economic autocracy. Democracy must have its roots in every aspect of our life or it may be stifled by the fast-growing weeds of privilege, power and economic dictatorships of all sorts and descriptions. Nor can we have genuine liberty and democracy in one country while we condone or approve exploitation or colonialism in another. This corrodes our own freedom while negating theirs. We must recognize the *solidarity of the human family*. Corrosion anywhere corrodes us.

We come now to another principle which is basic. It is the quality of invincible goodwill. If we would make progress both as individuals and as groups we must cultivate a spirit of goodwill which is impervious to all barbs from without. This is indeed difficult but the supreme leaders of the human race have had this quality. Even towards those who were arresting him or trying him unjustly, Jesus showed no anger but rather a deep understanding. How annoyed and cross we get even towards those against whom we have but a minor grievance, not to speak of nations against whom we are violently antagonistic.

A mortal danger to us all is self-centeredness. The more people that an individual can genuinely help the happier will he become. When Christ takes bitterness and prejudice from one's heart, then the potential effectiveness of the individual is increased many times over.

Often individuals in their relations with others try to dominate, to use the other person or group for their ends or they fear them or fight them when they ought instead to use the spirit of invincible goodwill.

This, like music, charms and disarms others, even when they do not understand it. We have heard of the reaction of even deadly snakes to the right music. Human "devils" often respond to invincible goodwill when almost nothing else will win them.

Again and again in missionary work in China and South Africa the leader who tried to win the natives by goodwill came in the end to be beloved by all. A careful study of missionaries in all countries of the world proves that in the by and large they come to love the people they work with. One reason for this is that we all tend to like the people *we know*. On the other hand it is easy to fear and distrust those afar off. We do not understand their background or their outlook.

Colonel Raymond Robins starting as a miner, toiling at fifty cents a day, amassed a fortune in the Klondike digging out gold with his own hands. Later he became a great social worker and champion of labor in Chicago. But in 1917 he was appointed a member of the Red Cross Mission to Russia. While the world attacked the Bolsheviks and condemned and hated Lenin, Robins got acquainted with him and before long became convinced that here was a powerful leader who was bringing his people out of degradation and ignorance of the world. While the West of that epoch was convinced that Communism, weak and revolutionary, would pass from the scene in a decade because of its evils, Robins declared that on the contrary, Russia would become one of the great powers of the world. It was because he had the spirit of invincible goodwill and refused to let himself be blinded by the falsehoods and propaganda of hate, that today history records he was far nearer right than were the leading diplomats of his day.

Benjamin Lay, a Quaker who lived in the early days of the American Republic, was outraged that Quakers could reconcile slavery with their professions of Christianity. He spoke against it, he even dramatized his opposition by stabbing a sword into a make-believe Bible which he had filled with red juice to show what slavery was doing to the heart of the gospel. He predicted the day would come when it would be illegal, and discrimination would be abolished. He was laughed at and persecuted but he was right. The spirit of invincible goodwill had taken command of his life and it brought results.

Consider another example, Baiko San, the widow of a Japanese priest who served the villagers in the shrine which her husband had formerly administered. One night her home was entered by a robber who threatened her with a sword unless she would give up the money belonging to the shrine.

"Young man," said Baiko San, showing real kindness in her voice, "you *can* kill me with that sword of yours. But if you do use that sword, it will only be a kindness to me. For a long time now I have prayed the goddess of mercy to let me leave my body. I am ready. I want to go. That sword may quite possibly be the means of release I desire. But, young man, how about yourself? Suppose you kill me. Will it be well with *you*? What will happen to your soul? As for your body, you'll be caught if you kill me. And then, what? However, that is not my concern. It's your choice not mine. As for the money, I have some saved from what the people have given me. It's in the recess over there, back of the altar. Help yourself to it. I haven't any knowledge about the other money. And now I'm going back to sleep. Good night!"[1]

In the morning when she woke up she found that invincible goodwill had worked, her apartment and her money were undisturbed.

Today, there are many forces working directly against the spirit of invincible goodwill. Let us cite just one illustration. Some of the media of mass communication build hatred instead of goodwill. We do not now refer to the "hate campaigns" against certain countries whipped up in our press.

[1] Hunter, Allan A., *Courage in Both Hands,* 1952.

Let us rather revert to the comics in America and their dangerous effects. Recently Dr. Frederic Wertham has written a devastating study of the "comics" showing their contribution to juvenile delinquency. He calls this quite appropriately "The Seduction of the Innocent." (Published by Rinehart, 1954.) Unfortunately these comics are not only highly injurious to our own youth but they are exported around the world to damage our prestige abroad and harm the youth of other nations as well. Some sixteen years ago the crime comics were only being sold to the tune of ten million copies a month. Today they have a circulation of some ninety million copies a month and it is estimated that they bring in around 100 million dollars a year. They systematically inculcate hate, greed, passion and crime. The damage to the rising generation is incalculable. Dr. Wertham maintains that the "chronic stimulation, temptation, and seduction [provided] by comic books . . . are contributing factors to many children's maladjustments." He clearly proves that the "comics" establish false standards of ethics and conduct and contribute to juvenile delinquency. What do these books teach the young: burglary, cruelty in bewildering detail, deceit in all its forms, mayhem, robbery, theft, murder, racial discrimination, sex and violence. Dr. Wertham concludes, "They suggest the forms a delinquent impulse may take and supply details of the technique." He believes it is "primarily the normal child who is affected" . . . "by reading of sex, sadism, violence and other crimes."

Dr. Wertham's book was so important that it was chosen by the *Book-of-the-Month-Club* as an alternate choice. After an advertisement of this book had already been prepared announcing this choice, the *Club* became fearful of a possible libel suit from a few of the comic-book publishers and dropped the book entirely, never even mentioning it. Up to date no libel action has been brought against author or publisher which shows the danger was apparently not too great. However, as far as the *Book-of-the-Month Club* was concerned their subscribers were kept in complete ignorance of its publication.

In the Senate Judiciary Subcommittee on Juvenile Delinquency hearings, William M. Gaines, President of the Entertaining Comics Group which publishes seven so-called horror books with a monthly circulation of over a million and a half, admitted that these publications don't "do kids a bit of good" but he maintained the children aren't really harmed.

Invincible Goodwill 183

When asked by the Senatorial Committee whether he had any limits to what he would publish, he declared he was limited by "good taste." Senator Kefauver then pointed out a cover of one of his publications depicting a man with a bloody axe in one hand and the head of a woman in the other. Senator Kefauver then wanted to know if that was good taste what bad taste would be. Mr. Gaines replied, "It would be bad taste if the head were held a little higher with blood dripping out." Exhibits were then submitted from Mr. Gaines' concern and other publishers showing scenes of bloodshed, crime, murder, sadism, torture and violence. The advertising in these comics alone proves that all this has its effect, for weapons of all kinds are advertised by mail.[2]

Senator Kefauver accused the Child Study Association of America of "fraud and deceit of the public" for not divulging "that staff members who advised parents on comic books for their children were in the pay of a comic book publisher." He said that Miss Josette Frank, the association's educational associate and Dr. Loretta Bender, senior psychiatrist in charge of the children's ward at Bellevue Hospital, the two principal people the Child Study Association was using to evaluate comic books, were also in the pay of the comic book industry. Later Dr. Bender took the stand declaring that she received $150 a month from the comic books' publisher to serve on the editorial advisory board although she admitted they had not met in six months. After the comics were published she distributed them in Bellevue to gauge the reactions of the children!

The manager of Marvel Comic Book Company which has a total monthly sale of about ten million copies said he was in business "for the profit motive" and "cannot change the reading taste of the public." He said they tried putting out "Bible Tales" in comic form with the help of the Yale University Divinity School and lost $29,000 on the venture.

William Richter, counsel to the News Dealer Association of Greater New York which represents more than a thousand outlets for magazines said crime and horror comics were included in bundles even when not ordered and that if the retailer "returned an unreasonable amount he can be cut off completely." (*Herald Tribune,* April 23, 1954)

No wonder that the Federal Bureau of Investigation reported that

[2] See New York *Herald Tribune,* April 22, 1954.

major crimes in the United States are at an all time high and are climbing four times faster than the population. The crime rate has jumped twenty per cent since 1950. It estimated that in 1953, 2,159,080 major crimes were committed. This includes only murder, manslaughter, rape, robbery, serious assault, burglary, larceny and theft. This *does not* include such major crimes as: arson, embezzlement, carrying concealed weapons and all sex crimes other than rape.

The report said youths under twenty-one were responsible for 50.6 per cent of all crimes against property. The value of all property stolen in 1953 was estimated at over $400,000,000.

This then indicates that not only do we not have enough invincible goodwill in our relationship to youth but that we are manufacturing crime, hatred and immoral disease through our comics. The cold war and the reaction of the press is still another spot where we are manufacturing fear and hatred instead of goodwill in the international world.

Now if invincible goodwill is absolutely essential to our moral health it is high time that we begin to take steps to see that both on the domestic scene and in international relations we build friendship rather than hate.

John Ferguson, of Kings College, England, tells us that "though the witness of the Early Church was not universally pacifist there was wide recognition of the fact that conscientious objection to military service was the only way for the Christian, and wide testimony from the most acute writers that war and Christianity were wholly incompatible." (*The Enthronement of Love,* London, 1951, p. 38)

An Egyptian Church Order of the Fourth Century declares in Statute 28 that no soldier shall be received into the church but if one is a member and is "commanded to kill he shall not do it." The Canons of Hippolytus in Italy reads, "A man who has accepted the power of killing, or a soldier, may never be received into the church at all."

13 (Riedel) "Persons who possess authority to kill, or soldiers, should not kill at all, even when commanded." Justin Martyr who was put to death by Marcus Aurelius in 165 A.D. declared that rather than go to war he would gladly die.

Clement of Alexandria states that Christians reject war and cleave to peace. Origen, the outstanding scholar of the early church declared, "For we no longer take sword against a nation, nor do we learn any more to make War, having become sons of peace for the sake of Jesus who is our leader."

The Synod of Ratisbon, 742 A.D. stated, "We absolutely and in all circumstances forbid all God's servants to carry arms, to fight and to march against an army or an enemy."

Christians have come a long way since those days of the early church when men were being martyred, but it is doubtful if in refusing to outlaw atomic weapons we have come nearer to God's will. We should practise invincible good will to all, not mass slaughter and destruction. Even when a nation wins a war, as we did in World War II, it is doubtful if we are led to practise more invincible good will. When we had Germany completely at our mercy, in surrender, what did we do? We soon began the trials in Nuremberg. Were they really demonstrative of the best in our civilization? They were based on the assumption of aggression and perhaps even more on crimes against the laws of war and against humanity. But since none of the victorious allied militarists who had committed similar violations were ever placed on trial and only the enemy, to some degree the trials were punishment for losing the war.

Professor William Ernest Hocking, the chairman of the Department of Philosophy at Harvard says "that, of all comparable civilized nations, we of the United States have by far the worst criminal record."[3] It is doubtful whether we should take the lead in punishing generals of an opposing army which has been defeated. We do not yet know enough to be able to punish nations through programs of scientific penology.

It is a demonstrated fact that nations do change their habit patterns. The United States has not always been so belligerent as she is today. Russia has not always been Communist. The character of any nation is the character of its people. We often go through the questionable political somersault of saying that the Chinese are a people of fine character but that their Communist rulers are devils. The reality of the matter is that the present Chinese rulers may be of a higher caliber on the average than the people. In speaking of the treatment of enemy nations, Professor Hocking goes on to say, "The most effective method . . . is promptly including the new state in the United Nations, with the obligations entailed requiring the peaceful settlement of disputes

[3] *Christianity Takes a Stand,* Penguin, 1946, p. 45.

with other nations. Ostracism from the organization under law is a tacit invitation to the excluded nation to ignore legal responsibility." (*Ibid.* p. 55)

Now in treating a country like Germany which was defeated in the last World War what steps should we take? It would seem that any solution should give reasonable guarantees to the Czechs, the people of France, Poland and Russia that they will not be attacked. It must also be a proposal that will win the support of the majority of the German people. This would involve restoring their unity, enabling them to have freedom, and letting them build a peaceful prosperous economy.

If Germany is rearmed the conditions set forth above cannot be maintained, for all the surrounding people will fear that a strong Germany might be a war-like Germany. Thus it would seem reasonable to propose that Germany should be demilitarized for a period of ten years to see if a system of disarmament and collective security cannot be achieved. A United Nations Commission should continuously inspect to see that Germany is not rearmed. History will record the verdict on the methods we are now using to rearm Germany but they involve dangerous risks.

It would probably be possible to get Russia to agree to free elections in both parts of Germany if all foreign troops were withdrawn and India were to supervise the elections. If some such agreement as this were reached, Germany might become a neutral buffer state in the conflict between East and West. This then is the kind of proposal in the international arena which might spell out invincible goodwill if done in time.

At present the world is building suspicion, hatred and ill-will far faster than it is counteracting these evil forces. The only solution is to turn back to the teachings of the prophets and of Christ.

John Wollman, a Quaker born in 1720 in West Jersey, in his *Journal*, writing in 1761, brings out clearly that social reforms begin with ourselves. He writes,

Wealth is attended with power, by which bargains and proceedings contrary to universal righteousness are supported; and here oppression, carried on with worldly policy and order, clothes itself with the name of justice and becomes like a seed of discord in the soil. And as this spirit which wanders from the pure habitation, prevails, so the seed of war swells and sprouts and grows and becomes strong, till much fruit are ripened.

Thus cometh the harvest spoken of by the prophet, which " is a heap, in the day of grief and of desperate sorrow."

He goes on to say that we must ask in our inner hearts, do we have any secret cause to promote other than pure universal love? If so we must change ourselves.

Is this what the United States or the Soviet Union does today? The reader can answer for himself. That nation which first begins to exemplify invincible goodwill in action will the sooner achieve the peace and goodwill which we all need.

This suggestion is not new. All down through the ages it has been said. Epictetus, the Greek philosopher, for instance, declares,

Cleanse your own heart, cast out from your mind pain, fear, envy, ill-will, avarice, cowardice, passion uncontrolled. These things you cannot cast out unless you look to God alone; on him alone set your thoughts, and consecrate yourself to his commands. If you wish for anything else, with groaning and sorrow you will follow what is stronger than you, ever seeking peace outside you, and never able to be at peace; for you seek it where it is not, and refuse to seek it where it is.

How perfectly the last sentence applies to our seeking the righteousness of power, military might, to solve the complex problems of the world, rather than the power of righteousness.

Again take the statement of the German scholar, Meister Johannes Eckhart, who lived in the Thirteenth Century:

I have often said that a person who wishes to begin a good life should be like a man who draws a circle. Let him get the center in the right place and keep it so and the circumference will be good. In other words, let a man first learn to fix his heart on God and then his good deeds will have virtue; but if man's heart is unsteady, even the great things he does will be of small advantage.

In other words, invincible good-will is the only road to solving our problems both individually and internationally. Today we blame Russia as a devil who is forcing us to rearm and to fight. The Soviet Union in her turn blames us. Is it not time that we try the weapon of *invincible goodwill*? Should we not be grateful that Red China wants to come into the United Nations? Should we not welcome her instead of threatening, as Senator Knowland, the Republican leader in the Senate, does,

188 *Religion in Action*

to withdraw from the United Nations if China is admitted? Here is our opportunity to exert direct influence upon representatives of China in the councils of the nations. Just as invincible goodwill is irresistible in the community, and the individual who practises it is revered and admired, so in the family of nations it is the practise of invincible goodwill which wins the victory.

If it is said that invincible goodwill sometimes fails in dealing with a bandit, for example, or with selfish men, one can only retort that in the long run if fully practiced, it always wins. Jesus, crucified on the cross still utters the words, "Father forgive them for they know not what they do." The final result is that he won the allegiance of more men than anyone in all history and is still winning them.

Prayer

Forgive, O God, the selfishness, the narrowness, the blindness, the suspicions and misunderstandings which have sometimes shut out friendship from our hearts. Purify our lives and activate them with Thy invincible goodwill. May we reflect each day and in every relation of life, the will of God. Help us to build human friendship regardless of race, color or creed. Deepen our efforts to understand those whose way of life is at variance with our own, that we may transcend our differences.

O God, teach us how to love one another as Thou hast loved us. Teach us to see beneath the outward forms of men to the inner core of the best that lies treasured in their hearts. Make us realize that when we love enough, we care even for those who have not yet found the way to Thee and who may be living in ignorance and sin. To those who have suffered moral defeat, help us to show understanding love even as we would have Thee view our own shortcomings. May we ever have patience, sympathy and goodwill towards those whom we are prone to misjudge.

May we make a part of our lives Thy radiant and friendly spirit that something may pass from Thee through us to them.

We come to Thee again that our selfishness, our callous disregard of some whom we dislike, may be transmuted into unfailing love for all humanity. Thus may our coldness and harshness be melted by Thy love until we are transformed into new creatures who share the invincible goodwill of Jesus in every action of life.   Amen.

Our civilization cannot survive materially unless it can be redeemed spiritually. It can be saved only by becoming permeated by the spirit of Christ and being made free and happy by the practise which springs out of this spirit.
>President Woodrow Wilson

True Godliness does not turn men out of the world, but enables them to live better in it, and excites their endeavor to mend it.
>William Penn

God offers to every mind its choice between the truth and repose. Take which you please—you can never have both.... He in whom the love of repose dominates ... gets rest, commodity and reputation; but he shuts the door to truth.
>Ralph Waldo Emerson

As life is action and passion, it is required of a man that he should share the passion and action of his time at peril of being judged not to have lived.
>Justice Oliver Wendell Holmes, Jr.,
>Memorial Day speech, 1884.

CHAPTER XIV

The Test of Action

NEARLY all those who are religious believe in translating their faith into action—at least in theory. The difficulty is that it is so much easier to slide along in our accustomed grooves. We don't always recognize that all our professional or life work should be dedicated to God. We get used to a certain standard of living and we don't want to change it. Actually our whole life is a demonstration of how we do or do not translate our religion into action.

What are some of the guide posts which we can use in testing our pattern of behavior, to see if we really are exemplifying our faith? The answer to that question would require an entire book, but let us consider just a few suggestions out of many which might be made.

1. We must fear God, not men. This means that we must have such faith in God that we can be fearless. William Lloyd Garrison is one of the greatest examples of this aspect of the test of action. Early in his teens he became convinced of the evil of slavery. When he was only twenty-one, in 1826, he was already attacking it. In that year he wrote: "Nothing but death shall prevent us from denouncing a crime which has no parallel in human depravity." As editor of the *Liberator* he spoke out with crusading zeal against slavery and for freedom. The state of Georgia quickly retaliated by putting a price of $5,000 on his head. In Baltimore, in 1829, he was sent to jail for "denouncing slavery in a free country," so he described it. Later he was seized by a mob outside his office and with a rope about his waist he was dragged towards the city hall in Boston. The police finally wrested him from his captors and put him in jail for safety. In spite of his reputation as a flaming radical, Garrison remained a strict Christian pacifist all his life. Leo Tolstoy, the great writer, was deeply impressed by Garrison and declared that

the latter was the first clearly to state that no man has the right to take away the liberty of another for any reason whatsoever. Tolstoy concluded, "Therefore Garrison will forever remain one of the greatest reformers and promoters of true human progress."

Another leader who demonstrated this principle was John Woolman, a great Quaker who lived in the eighteenth century. In quietness and power he opposed the evils of greed, poverty, slavery, and war and was frequently cast into jail. But his *Journal,* in which he records his profound religious belief and his adventures for God, will live as long as men have faith and courage.

2. We must endeavor not to preach to others a doctrine which we ourselves do not practise. For when we do, however beautiful our words, they wither on our lips. Wendell Phillips was a man who practised his faith. Brought up in a cultured environment, a graduate of Harvard, a brilliant young lawyer, he believed wholeheartedly in his country as the supreme embodiment of good. But on October 24, 1835, as he was sitting in his law offices, he heard the sound of a mob outside. On the street he saw a man being dragged thru the streets. He was told that it was William Lloyd Garrison, "the damned Abolitionist." This incident changed Wendell Phillips' entire life. He gave up his law practise and spent his life in championing social justice. He even defended the Nihilists in Russia after they had killed Czar Alexander II. Said he, "In Russia there is no press, no debate, no explanation of what the Government does, no remonstrance allowed, no agitation of public issues. . . . In such a land dynamite and the dagger are the necessary and proper substitutes for Faneuil Hall and the *Daily Advertiser*." One does not need to agree with everything that Phillips said still to recognize that he was one of the greatest champions of the Bill of Rights in all our history, and that he lived his faith.

3. We must endeavor to use the intelligence that God gave us. Albert Einstein was a living example of this. Not only did he become one of the greatest scientists of all time but he applied his great intelligence to the social issues of the day in such a way that the whole world is indebted to him.

4. Patience, humility, and cheerfulness are essential. If we try to live our religion we shall inevitably come in conflict with the vested interests of our time. To overcome every obstacle and to endure, these

three qualities, so easy to say and so difficult to achieve, are great aids. Good humor, humility, and especially patience will overcome every barrier and every trial.

Countless individuals in history have exemplified these traits. Helen Keller who, though blind, has made a notable contribution to the world, is one. Pelagius, who lived about the fifth century, is another. He was so shocked at the lax morals of conventional Christians that he raised his voice demanding that men equate their actions with their God. Many of his teachings were then vigorously opposed by the Synods of the day and even by the Pope. Henry George, the great crusader for economic justice, should stimulate us to action. Early in his married life he was so desperately poor that they came near starving, and at one time, in the 1860's, he declared that if he had not secured a job to print a few cards which enabled him to buy a little corn meal he might have died. A month later we find a notation in his diary: "Am in desperate plight. Courage." But this very experience combined with his patience, humility, and cheerfulness made his entire life a passionate concern for the welfare of humanity and led John Dewey to sum up his life in these words: "It is the thorough fusion of insight into actual facts and forces, with recognition of their bearing upon what makes human life worth living, that constitutes Henry George one of the world's great social philosophers."

5. If we live our religion we must strive desperately to love every one. This is a particularly hard saying for most Christians today. Perhaps they hate and despise the Russian Communists, and if they are liberals they may be bitterly hostile to Senator McCarthy or whoever represents the antithesis of their own political beliefs.

Dr. Henry Hodgkin, the great missionary statesman who gave his life in China, has this to say of his own life practise:[1]

I will always seek to discover the best and strongest points in my brother's behavior.

I will give him credit for sincerity.

I will try to avoid classifying him, and assuming that he has all the characteristics of the class to which he is supposed to belong.

I will emphasize our agreements.

When others criticize, I will try to bring out favorable points.

[1] Kirby Page, *Living Joyously*, p. 336.

When there is misunderstanding, either I of him, or he of me, I will go to him direct.

I will seek opportunities to pray together.

I will try to remember that I may be mistaken and that God's truth is too big for any one mind.

I will pray for those from whom I differ.

What a different world it would be if we all practised these rules!

David Livingstone, who lived from 1813 to 1873, is a good example of the practise of good-will towards all men everywhere. He was born in Scotland, worked in a cotton factory, and decided to give his life to the natives of Africa. He was one of the pioneer explorers of that continent, but while he was doing this he healed the sick, taught the natives, and practised love and good-will to all with whom he came in contact. He died among the natives whom he loved, in 1873.

6. We must also strive to be generous in spirit. Jesus once said, "If a man forces you to go one mile, go with him two." Most of us find this principle a difficult one to follow. When the writer used to be arrested by Communist police when he was a war correspondent for the American press in World War II, he had this problem. He found that if he complimented the policemen, telling them it was war time and they were right in being scrupulously careful, and again when he reached the police station, if he thanked the officer in charge for his loyalty and his caution, the result was that he would be released in short order. Correspondents who followed the opposite strategy of condemning and abusing their captors were usually detained far longer.

Finally, if we really wish to live our religion we must strive to make every hour of our day—in fact our entire lives—dedicated to the service of God. We must check all that we do to see how much of it is in His service. Stop and ask yourself: "Is everything I do, in the family, in my work, and in my community, consecrated and dedicated to the will of God for me? If not, what can I change?" Jesus was one of the few souls in all human history who stand out as perfect examples of this principle.

Many other criteria might be enumerated here but we have perhaps cited enough to start our thought processes revolving, each in his own way. But the test of action applies also to *social institutions* and to the *national state,* as well as to individuals.

If we stop to think, we know that nearly every significant aspect of life is tested by its results in action. A political administration may make great promises, but in the end we judge it by *what it does*. A business may have prospects of high success, but the final test is the balance sheet of performance, not the glowing promises of the prospectus. The United States may boast that it supports democracy and is against tyranny, but it will be judged in history by deeds, not words. If it supports with arms a succession of dictators, whether in South America or in Spain, it can hardly be said to be completely democratic in that respect.

The United States refused to sell arms to the liberal government of Guatemala. Later they gave aid to the rebels. Consequently, the military Junta won against the regularly elected officials of the government. Late in 1954 the military dictatorship held its elections. The election rolls had been purged and, just to be sure, voters had *no secret ballot*. They were forced to declare their choices to the dictator's election officials. It was a Hitler type of election, and a new constitution perpetuating the dictatorship was adopted. Any government must be judged by its *actions,* not by its professions of democracy. There seems to be a moral principle at work in history. Men simply cannot, in the long run, go against the moral grain of the universe and not get splinters. The United States has received some splinters along with her successes since the end of World War II, and it is now generally recognized that our reservoir of goodwill abroad has become less.

Why were the prophets revered? It is because of their action. They opposed human oppression but acted in kindness, for justice and human brotherhood. The reason why they are remembered and honored down to this day is that they acted. Amos denounced luxury and social injustice. Isaiah spoke in oracles against the evils of his time. Habakkuk made his generation think, through terrible taunt-songs. All of them acted. Jesus demonstrated a life of active goodness. "Not every one that saith unto me, Lord, Lord, shall enter into the Kingdom of Heaven; but he that *doeth* the will of my Father."

Action, too, can change men's lives even when the individual is not led forward directly by religious faith. To illustrate this point let me take an ancient example[2] from the Far East.

[2] From *General History of Chinese Empire* (in Chinese), reprinted by The Commercial Press, Shanghai, 1935.

In the period of the East Tsin Dynasty 317–420 A.D., a notorious bandit by the name of Chou Ch'u lived in one of the villages. He was a man of tremendous strength but of bad character. He was successful in robbing and terrorizing the entire area in which he lived. Bribes were regularly paid by those with property who feared him. Now it so happened in a nearby thickly wooded mountain, there lived a tiger which preyed upon the inhabitants. He would lie in wait for a child and then pounce on it.

There was also a river in this region where the women went to wash clothes and the people went bathing. But in this same river there were crocodiles which the villagers called dragons. These "dragons" would often lie submerged in the water and then grab a man, woman, boy or girl, pull the body under water and finally devour it.

One year when there had been an unusually good harvest Chou Ch'u suddenly began to realize that the people were still unhappy. He could not understand this so out of curiosity he asked one of the old men:

"Why in such a good harvest year, is every one so worried and unhappy?"

"Why, how could we be happy when we are facing three great dangers day and night?"

"Oh, what do you mean, what are they?"

"Well there is the tiger in the South Mountain," said the old man, "and the 'dragon' in the river, and finally there is you."

Chou Ch'u was astounded. He thought the matter over and finally went out alone and killed the tiger. Next he turned his attention to the "dragon" in the river and although it took him several days he finally disposed of him too.

During the absence of Chou Ch'u every one in the village was happy. In fact he was gone so long that the people thought he had been killed and held a celebration. When he returned and found what the people had been doing he realized for the first time how much they hated him.

By actually doing something to help the people the "dirty glass" of his mind had been cleansed and he saw himself in a truer light. He wanted to change his ways. He went to the famous Chinese poet, Lou Jung, and told about his predicament. The poet replied, "The spirit of man is to have a will and action to do good and you must not be so much disturbed about the consequences of your action if it was really ethical and good."

Chou Ch'u decided that from that time forth he would make the rule of his life to do good and demonstrate kindness in action. He became a Magistrate and succeeded in finally disposing equitably of cases which had piled up over a thirty year period. Because of his merits he was finally appointed Governor of Hunan. He educated the people, rehabilitated the community and came to be loved and revered by all. Chou Ch'u had learned, that the fun of life is in giving not getting. In the end Chou Ch'u even sacrificed his life for the people.

Unselfish action for humanity thus builds bridges of kindness within the life of any man. These may lead to goodness and to God. On the other hand, we believe that if the individual has a vital faith in God, his deeds of service will probably be far more effective since they will be geared to His power and His plan.

In India long ago a group of human beings were discriminated against somewhat as the Negroes in South Africa or in some Southern states in America. In India they were called "untouchables." In the village of Vykom, South India, many roads were prohibited to the untouchables. Many residents of India did not believe in this discrimination but did nothing.

Finally, a courageous Christian Indian took action. He walked down the road with an untouchable. The Brahmins beat them up. The next day they tried it again and were arrested. The protest spread. So the police placed a blockade across the street. Gandhi's followers met this by placing a picket line just opposite the police. They were to stand in prayer before the police. Night and day they did this in six hour shifts, exhibiting no violence but testifying to the power of truth. For months this struggle went on. The Gandhi followers even built huts by the side of the road so that they could conduct this unique protest more effectively.

In the end this Christian action won. It had taken a year and four months of disciplined action. The untouchables were finally allowed to use the road and nearly all other roads in the province were thrown open to them.

Fei-Yen, a Chinese Christian girl, had to act when her village was captured by the Japanese. She got a farmer to give her some old clothes and big boots. She cut off her hair, donned the old clothes, and disguised as a boy worked in the medical clinic helping the Japanese. By night she helped the wounded Chinese guerrillas and by day the suffering Japanese. Months later, when the Japanese had taken the whole area, she operated the American missionary station although all the Americans had fled. How did she get permission? She merely said she was working for the missionaries who couldn't speak Japanese. Said she, "And they still think there's a missionary somewhere about, but you see I take all the messages." Every day she conducted a worship service in a room packed with Chinese and she ended her prayer with these words: "O God, please help us to root out of our hearts all hate and pride and fear and anger because we know they are the things that make wars like this possible." Fei-Yen acted instead of saying that it was hopeless to do anything.

Ned Richards was a conscientious objector in the United States in 1917. He decided to try to go to the most dangerous spot in the world, wherever he could do something constructive. He was told that West Persia, with its cholera, dysentery, typhus, smallpox, and ruthless Kurds was the spot. Off he went and began caring for 500 orphans. When the Kurd tribesmen came he merely handed them everything he had and tried to help them to good food. Instead of the destruction and death which would have followed had he used force and arms, the Kurds took only some money, some shoes, two or three overcoats, and a medical case. Otherwise no damage was done. Ned Richards had acted.

Frank Laubach could have been discouraged when he thought of the 1,200,000,000 illiterates on this planet. Instead, he took off his coat and went to work. He has been travelling around the world ever since, helping people to learn to read and write. The result is that millions of people now are able to read who otherwise would have remained illiterate. His slogan is "Each-One Teach-One," and the movement continues to spread because Frank Laubach acted.

Allan A. Hunter tells of a Russian who showed great generosity to his greatest enemy. It was in World War II. The Germans had been invading Russia, slaughtering as they marched. They were at the gates of Stalingrad. This is his story:[3]

---

[3] Hunter, Allan A., *Courage in Both Hands*, p. 68.

The Test of Action

A young German corporal who had just been sent up to the front as a replacement was lying on the ground seriously wounded in the head. Suddenly to his terror he saw a Russian soldier stooping over him. The Russian put out his hand. But there was no revolver in it! No knife! Only compassion. In a few moments the Russian had finished his job and the German's wound was bandaged. To his amazement the German was allowed to go back to his unit. After the doctor had examined the dressing of the head wound he said it had been done perfectly.

Here is a case where a Russian had acted in a friendly way to his bitterest enemy.

The test of all our pretensions is, in the last analysis, *what we do*. If we all really *act* on our highest faith, may not those words become a reality in a far off future?

Part III

Changing the Social Order

"These things shall be,—a loftier race
    Than e'er the world hath known shall rise
With flame of freedom in their souls.
    And light of knowledge in their eyes.
They shall be gentle, brave and strong
    To spill no drop of blood, but dare
All that may plant man's lordship firm
    On earth, and fire and sea and air.
Nation with nation, land with land,
    Unarmed shall live as comrades free;
In every heart and brain shall throb
    The pulse of one fraternity."
          JOHN ADDINGTON SYMONDS, 1840–1893

    Holy Spirit, Love divine,
      Glow within this heart of mine;
      Kindle every high desire;
      Perish self in thy pure fire.
      Holy Spirit, Power divine,
      Fill and nerve this will of mine;
      By thee may I strongly live,
      Bravely bear, and nobly strive.

                        S. LONGFELLOW

An Indian sage says, "As a mother watches over her only child, as she tends it, protects and brings it up: so, Everyman, should you raise up and train and protect in yourself that which is dearest of all in the world: Love toward men and all that lives" ... As a candle only shines when the wax of which it is made is being spent, so life is only real when it is being spent for others.

     LEO TOLSTOY, taken from *Unity*, Chicago, Ill.

I am your friend, and my love for you goes deep.
  There is nothing I can give you which you have not got;
But there is much, very much, that, while I cannot give it,
  You can take.

No heaven can come to us unless our hearts
  Find rest in today. Take Heaven!
No peace lies in the future which is not hidden
  In this present little instant. Take Peace!

The gloom of the world is but a shadow.
  Behind it, yet within our reach, is Joy.
There is radiance and glory in the darkness,
  Could we but see, and to see, we have only to look.
I beseech you to look.

Life is so generous a giver, but we,
  Judging its gifts by their covering,
Cast them away as ugly, or heavy, or hard.
  Remove the covering, and you will find beneath it
A living splendor, woven of love, by wisdom, with power.

Welcome it, grasp it, and you touch the
  Angel's hand that brings it to you.
Everything we call a trial, or sorrow, or a duty,
  Believe me, that Angel's hand is there; the gift is there,
And the wonder of an overshadowing Presence.
  Our joys too; be not content with them as joys.
They, too, conceal Diviner gifts.

Life is so full of meaning and purpose.
　　So full of Beauty—beneath its covering—
That you will find earth but cloaks your heaven.
Courage then to claim it: that is all!
　　But courage you have; and the knowledge that we
Are pilgrims together,
　　Wending through unknown country, home.

And so, at this time, I greet you.
　　Not quite as the world sends greetings,
But with profound esteem and with the prayer
　　That for you now and forever,
The day breaks, and the shadows flee away.

FRA GIOVANNI—1513 A.D.

CHAPTER XV

Beginning in the Family

Now let us turn our attention to certain concrete problems confronting every social order, which vitally concern each one of us. First, let us consider the home, the basic foundation unit of every society. Second, we should all be vitally tied into some religious organization both to give us inspiration and a share in their action program. Again, we will consider the problem of the criminal and all those unfortunates confined in penal institutions. Another chapter deals with our responsibility towards organized labor and still another discusses the question of a world organization and the United Nations. These, then, are the issues which we shall be considering in the next six chapters. We cannot be patriotic citizens, not to mention religious believers, and ignore them.

As to the home, we start from the premise that it should train children to be servants of God and this means serving the common good. Home is a place for *growing,* growing into a wholeness of personality and character, from infancy through old age. A child that is trained with understanding at home for such growing will not remain self-centered. He will learn to look outside himself and find happiness in helping others. He will increasingly find satisfaction not in getting but in giving, but this kind of growth depends on a rare home environment. How far does the average American family attain this ideal? We have no statistics but it is a difficult goal.

Few will dispute that the family is the most important influence in the life of the child. The human infant is helpless. A turtle can lay eggs in the sand and then abandon them. When the young hatch out they will find the pond and from that time on make their own way and get their own food. This is not true of human offspring who need long continued care.

But the pioneer pattern of the family is changing. Many now live in cities and sometimes both parents work. The family is no longer a close-knit unit. Commercialized recreation has often superseded other entertainment. With the coming of television even recreation within the house often comes from outside and is not subject to real control on the part of the parents. Relatives may not live near-by as they once did but live in other states. A brother, once he has left home, may be lucky if he sees his sister once in a year.

Nevertheless the opportunity of the home to build character is enormous. It can teach the child the values of goodwill, honesty, perseverance and unselfishness. The language the family speaks becomes his mother tongue. If the family is friendly and tolerant to all groups the child may grow up without racial prejudice; if they are industrious, he may learn the value and fun of work. If the family is religious, the child will tend to accept religion and make kindness and sincerity a part of his own life.

Because this is true the face to face association groups are probably the most important in trying to change the social order. But it must always be remembered that the ideals of the family may in large measure be negated by the neighborhood, the school or the community life. The child born into a family which does not believe in race segregation, may nevertheless imbibe strong racial prejudices and phobias if living in the South.

In a certain sense it might be maintained that there are no stable primary face to face groups today for we are all part of a dynamic changing society. The whole structure of society is in flux and our older institutions are under terrific stresses and strains. Our culture is subjected to pressures of all sorts and to the bombardment of ideas from all around the world. No one knows just where the world-stirring events of our time will take us. The family, along with all other institutions, is affected by the inter-play of these forces.

It is not our purpose to discuss the family exhaustively but rather to raise certain questions to stimulate our thinking. One cannot, of course, discuss the home without bringing in the school which is bound up so closely with the life of the child.

At the outset we should make clear that the family is moulded by the groups of which it is a part and there is a constant interaction going on between the various institutions in society and the individuals which make up the social structure.

It is probably true that the ideal family supplemented by the ideal school and the ideal church or synagogue could raise children dedicated to serving society rather than their own selfish desires. But unfortunately no institution or individual is perfect and we have all been refracted by the culture in which we are immersed. In a Communist society children tend to be infected with the Communist virus, in a capitalistic society they tend to be warped in the direction of capitalistic values.

The school tries to transmit and preserve the social heritage while at the same time it endeavors to train the mind of the child and teach it not what to think but how to think. Too often, in actuality, the school tends to pass on an uncritical acceptance of the major patterns of values in the society in which it is immersed. What then are some of the values that the American school transmits:

1. Personal achievement, with marked attention on business and financial success. Love of money, power and bigness are ingrained into the minds of children. Rarely is economic success questioned on a moral base.
2. Activity and work. We must be doing something, whether the end result is useful socially and ethically is not always analyzed.
3. Ethical judgments of good or bad. We are trained to be on "the good side" but this often means we equate goodness with our way of life or we learn to be cynical and say the ideal is impossible.
4. Efficiency and practicality. Whatever we do, we must get things done.
5. Progress. We are taught to believe in progress but in *our* terms not with open minds towards "foreign" practices.
6. Material comfort and democracy.

The schools often end by producing prejudiced persons, loaded with preconceived ideas.

Professor William E. Hocking recently analyzed our efforts to educate Germany away from Naziism after its defeat. He labels our attempt, "American knight-errantry in education."[1] He declares that the educational pattern we tried to foist on Germany was some fifty

[1] Hocking, W. E., *Experiment in Education*, 1954.

years out of date. What we should have tried to do was to lead Germany to teach herself through an "appeal to ethical first principles."

Can we learn the lesson from our faulty efforts in Germany to see that much needs to be done to improve our education at home? Professor Hocking believes "that there are ethical first principles, affording firm ground for the judgment of political behaviour, national and international, our own and others." Now all of this training should begin down in the grades and extend up through the university.

If we are to change the social order we must make sure that the schools are the best that it is possible to build. Our teachers should be free. They should not be subject to Loyalty Oaths and pressures for conformity. They should be able to follow truth as they see it. The family has a responsibility towards the schools, for what they teach will make a vast difference to the rising generation. Every parent should take an active part in the parent-teacher organization of his community. In all that has been said we do not mean to imply that our primary and secondary schools are not doing good work. Of course, they are but they can be made even better if they have more appropriations, better salaries and even more cooperation and understanding from the homes of the people.

It is obvious that if we want to change society for the better, the family is one of the most important key places to begin our efforts. But here then is the rub, the family as a social institution is part of the total complex of the society in which it is immersed. All parents have been moulded by the social milieux in which *they* grew up. Furthermore, the economic status of families varies. Can a particular family meet the needs of all its members? If it is unemployed and living in a slum area that places one type of strain on the home, if both parents are forced to work and leave the children alone, that places another danger on the children.

It is also true that divorce has been gradually climbing in the United States. In 1890 the rate was only one half of one per cent but by 1946 it had climbed to four and six-tenths per cent. This means that there was over one divorce for every four marriages during 1946. Yet it is obvious that a broken home is not the ideal place to bring up children.

Besides this the home is no longer the self-contained unit it once was. Since the Industrial Revolution, many economic ties have been removed from the home such as baking, spinning and weaving that once made for family cooperation. Now increasingly the wife and mother is employed outside the home, which often leaves the children to be cared for by others. As the rights of women have increased with respect to ownership of property, voting, control of children, divorce and the like, the old traditional family bonds have been loosened. As a result of these and other factors, the home does not have the unity and stability it once had.

Today all the major institutions of society operate in the direction of emphasizing individualism of family members at the expense of family-mindedness, weakening to this extent the capacity of the family to influence its own members.

For example, at a very early age the radio comes into the home. Children tend to tune in what they like to hear. When the television is part of the environment children are profoundly affected by whatever programs, good or bad, they see and hear. If the children read comics, these too come from outside the home. At the Cleveland airport in 1954 a fifteen year old boy forced his way into a passenger plane and demanded at the point of a gun that he be taken to Mexico City. He was shot to death by the pilot. Actually his gun was not loaded, he was merely having fun as in the comics.

At an early age the children go to school; then begin the multiple group contacts outside the home which pull the children in all directions. Members are more and more likely to view the family as existing for them and not them for the family.

In spite of all this the family is the primary place for the building of character and social responsibility. If the parents desire it, they can begin to train the children to have an incentive to devote their lives to the common good rather than for selfish aggrandizement. They can see to it that the children have books and periodicals which stimulate in this direction.[2] But the children will not be fooled by mere moral precepts. They will be influenced largely by living examples. What are the moral ideals which the parents *really* represent? A family which lives in luxury will unconsciously affect the thinking of the children towards material values.

The family can restrict harmful outside influences to some degree.

[2] See for example, *Sharing is Fun,* Koinonia Foundation, Baltimore, 1953.

But if their friends are materialistically minded their effect on the children may not be inconsiderable. It is an open question whether to install television because the children can waste so much time looking and because there are so many injurious if not downright bad programs.

To mould children in the home for the highest values, parents must be absolutely dedicated themselves. Their lives must be consecrated to God and the common welfare in all that they do and say. Unless their occupation, their motivation and their entire lives are so dedicated, children will be so affected by what they see their parents *do* that the child minds will not be fooled by mere moral assertions.

If a family wants to mould its children for the better, it can have family devotions each day with readings from adventurous leaders such as Grenfell, Schweitzer and others. The movies can be studied and reports secured from sources which can be trusted about each one before children go to them. The Consumers Union is one such source but friends who have seen the pictures can also make reports.

Parents who really want to mould their children can see that they have selected influences brought to bear upon them at different ages. Summer camps can be chosen after the most careful study to be certain that their children will have challenging speakers and leaders who promote unselfish service for the common good. In the later stages of high school they can even be taken to Europe to enlarge their horizons about foreign peoples. Each summer's activity should be worked out in advance so that the children get the maximum of wholesome work experience in jobs which will be helpful. If it seems best during college, a student can be encouraged to take an entire year of work in some university abroad.

We have observed families where out of six children five went into the ministry and into foreign missionary work. This is a tremendous achievement. But at best the task is difficult. Take smoking, for instance. There is increasing evidence that this contributes to the incidence of cancer in later years. Even supposing the parents do not smoke, can they prevent the children from doing so? This is possible but extremely difficult. The pressures of social conformity act on the child until sooner or later he yields and begins to smoke. This seems to him a mark of maturity. If he could only be made to realize that in his lifetime this will cost him thousands of dollars and may also take away his life through cancer, he might be able to stand out against it. Some parents challenge the child by offering him a real inducement not to smoke. For example, one gave the child a second hand automobile provided he refrained from smoking until he was twenty-one. Whether this is wise or not depends upon the child, his aptitudes and his associations.

It is obvious that next to the family, the schools are perhaps the most important influence which moulds the child. American schools which are training our children, incomparably our most important treasure and resource, have been allowed to deteriorate while we have concentrated our attention and our money on automobiles, television and military preparations. At the very least we should double the ten billion dollars that we are now spending annually on our schools. At present school buildings, teachers, libraries and salaries are all short and inadequate.

It is generally recognized that our public schools should not have more than thirty students in one classroom yet at the present time over half the classes in the country are larger than this maximum and many teachers have to try to handle sixty students at once.

School buildings are, too often, antiquated, inconvenient, makeshift. Over a million and a half children are forced to get their education in barracks, churches, rented garages, stores and other defective places. In 1955 the U.S. Senate Labor and Public Welfare Committee heard testimony regarding the woefully inadequate school buildings. One high school student, Tim Branham from Jones Creek, Kentucky told the Senators that in his school there were only four small rooms with 265 students. Whenever they have an "assembly" the principal tried to speak into all four rooms at once.[3]

The Engineering Man Power Commission of the Engineers Joint Council[4] reported that today the Soviet Union is turning out two-and-a-half times as many engineering graduates each year as the United States. The report also declared that in the Soviet Union there were 175 *university*-level technical schools with combined enrollment of

[3] N.Y. *Herald Tribune,* Jan. 29, 1955, p. 4.
[4] Composed of representatives of the American Society of Mechanical Engineers, the American Society of Civil Engineers and the American Chemical Society.

300,000 while the United States has a similar combined enrollment of only 150,000.[5]

Besides these deficiencies there is some danger that our education will develop a "herd" mentality, that the schools will try to secure uniformity of minds and standardization of product. If teachers are afraid to say what they think and do not have freedom to dissent then we may, in our own way, be approaching a controlled mentality such as the Soviet Union has. What we must try to do is to welcome originality in the child and protect the rights of minorities. This is the only road to true freedom. Besides training the mind our schools should be developing character, and Parent-Teachers Associations can do a great deal to encourage teachers to demonstrate morality in action.

It becomes, therefore, of vital importance that we have patriotic, forward-looking teachers who will stimulate a student to have idealism, unselfishness and creative enthusiasm to change and improve society through his life. Christians do not always see to it that the public school teachers have adequate salaries. In the past in certain localities teachers have been paid less than the collectors of garbage.

The church can aid in all this process by doing more for the family as a whole. Each church should have stimulating classes for parents on how to teach and train their children, for they often forget that rearing children is a full time job and the physical part is only half.

Possibly the parents can be encouraged to influence their children in the home through informal projects, crafts and daily creative tasks. If we were advanced in our social religious practises, each church would have teachers who could act as family specialists to help parents through advice and gatherings in the home itself. In addition the church should have special meetings for different age groups for informal discussion of live topics in which the children would be interested.

As the children get older they should be taken to the various institutions of the social order: the jail, the prison, the factories, the slaughterhouse, the reformatory, the slums, even the saloons where they could see the drunks and what they were doing. In certain cases it might be worth taking the children to see a trial in a court room and observe the procedures of the law.

[5] From reports given at a Conference at Columbia University Club, Jan. 28, 1955.

By seeing the worst as well as the best children would grow up knowing what to avoid as well as what to seek. In every society there are sincere, dedicated souls who are striving with *all* their lives to change the social order for the better and to follow truth, justice and liberty for all. In some way children must be brought into contact with these rare personalities and every now and then they will catch the contagion of their lives of service.

In some way children must get the concept while they are in the home that every individual has a responsibility to change his community and the entire social order for the better. Children can hardly be expected to get this ideal unless their parents are actually *doing something* in this area. Therefore the home can only be a training ground for a moral social consciousness if the parents are exemplifying the ideals which they are trying to instill in the rising generation.

It must always be remembered, however, that we are living in a complex society and that as long as selfishness, materialism, and pagan values hold sway anywhere there is the danger that they will corrode the moral fibre. The family will be more effective in changing society if society itself is open to change.

Every family in the United States needs to take to heart the words of the late President Franklin D. Roosevelt. "Too many of those who prate about saving democracy are really only interested in saving things as they were. Democracy should concern itself also with things as they ought to be."

Hints for Parents

1. Love your child and let him know it.
2. Try to put yourself in the place of the child. What are his major interests, what things seem important to him, how can you help him in those things which concern him most.
3. Treat your children as you would your closest friends.
4. Remember the house belongs to the children too. They may not have been consulted but the place is partly theirs and they have some rights to do what they want in it.
5. Take as a guiding principle that if your child reacts badly to your treatment of him you have done or are doing something wrong.

6. Have fun with your children in ways which they like, this may be on picnics, parties, or going to a good movie.
7. Ask yourself, what would I respond to best if I were in his place. Don't inflict your fears, your worries, your admonitions on him. Be positive in your attitudes and actions.
8. See if you can guide your child by placing him in situations where he himself will want to do the thing that is best for him.
9. Be sure to arrange with the neighbors for decent places where the children can play, and swim if it is summer time. There should be adequate places where the children can have fun without troubling the neighborhood.
10. Welcome the children of your vicinity into your yard, and into your home. They need comradeship just as we all do.
11. See to it that there is a community council looking out for the welfare of all the children. It will be responsible for the welfare and the organizations for children. It will keep careful track of child delinquency and what is causing it.
12. See to it that the schools in your community are the best that can be secured, the equal of any schools in America. Make sure that the teachers and administrators are paid good salaries. Be sure that the number of schools and classrooms are adequate, and that the parent-teachers' organization is functioning well.
13. Where possible have children represented on planning councils for their welfare so that they can be partners with the adults.
14. Finally, see to it that the churches of the community are playing their part in the welfare of the children.

Prayer

Sear from our hearts, O God, indifference, complacency and the willingness to be content with things as they are. Grant unto us that the fire of Thy love may burn up the dross within us and make us more completely dedicated to Thy service here and now. Help us to realize the great importance of our family, its welfare and the future of our children. But, O God, guard us from deadening our hearts by stopping at our own fireside. Make us realize that the welfare of every other family is just as important in Thy sight. Give us a sense of responsibility for every family in our community regardless of race, creed or condition. Help us to recall the words of the Master, "Suffer the little children to come unto me," that we will tolerate in our communities only those conditions of spiritual, mental and physical health that are worthy of Thee.

Grant, O Lord, that there may be within us a deeply dedicated affection for all children everywhere, may we be patient when we are sorely tried by them, and give us spiritual strength to see and overcome our own weaknesses.

Above all, give to us such a clear vision of Thy love that no unworthy affection may move us away from righteousness; give us the strength of heart which no adversity can impair, and a consecration that will not yield to temptation no matter how subtle.

May we wish for every family in the world the finest and best things that we desire for our own, and do our part in working with others and with Thee to realize this goal—thus may we be genuine children of Thine in the family of God.   Amen.

Instead of being baffled by any difficulties that we may feel about church membership we need to ask ourselves quite seriously where else may we turn. What organized institution is there, apart from the church, that has as its major purpose the fostering of Justice, Mercy, and Truth and the freedom that they jointly make possible? Bad and divided as the church may be, it is the only organization really working at the job of affecting men's lives in the deep way in which they must be affected if what we prize is to survive. . . .

If faith is to be effective in undergirding civilized society, it must be given some concrete embodiment. . . . What is needed is something that can set men's souls on fire. . . . What, in historical experience, has most often been able to do this? It is that hypocritical, bickering organization that we call the church. Without it we might long ago have been submerged.

D. ELTON TRUEBLOOD in *The Predicament of Modern Man*

THE LITTLE GATE TO GOD

In the castle of my soul
Is a little postern gate,
Whereat, when I enter,
I am in the presence of God.
In a moment, in the turning of a thought,
I am where God is,
This is a fact.
When I enter into God,
All life has a meaning,
Without asking I know;

My desires are even now fulfilled,
My fever is gone
In the great quiet of God.
My troubles are but pebbles on the road,
My joys are like everlasting hills.

So it is when my soul steps through the postern gate
Into the presence of God.
Big things become small, and small things become great.
The near becomes far, and the future is near.
The lowly and despised is shot through with glory.
God is the substance of all revolutions;
When I am in Him, I am in the Kingdom of God
And in the Fatherland of my Soul.
                    WALTER RAUSCHENBUSCH.

CHAPTER XVI

Church and Synagogue Are Indispensable

The United States is dotted with churches, synagogues, and chapels. Many of these no doubt have their shortcomings. They tend to take on the attitudinal pattern of the people who make up the membership. Nevertheless, it is difficult to overestimate the effect of all these power centers for righteousness. Their mere presence is a reminder of God, however interpreted. Have you ever considered a community, a city, or a nation without such a focus for right living?

Near Denver a wealthy atheist, militantly opposed to the church, once long ago tried to establish a community in which the church was barred. What was the result? To this community gradually gravitated the agnostics, the atheists, and the criminal elements. In the city as a whole, even families which were not too religious wanted a church or synagogue nearby to which they could turn, if only for the sake of the children. They liked some of the social activities of church life, if nothing else, and they wished to have the privilege of attending on Easter or when in trouble or sorrow.

To be sure, the prostitutes and some citizens of questionable repute were quite willing to live in this churchless center; perhaps they were grateful that the church was not there to plague them. Soon, in response to the demand of these residents, saloons and gambling places established themselves in the neighborhood. This still further antagonized any respectable people who, because of the housing shortage, did try living there. They gradually moved away. Alarmed by all this, the wealthy real estate owner finally decided, even though he did not believe in God, that he simply must have a church or synagogue in the community if he wished to sell his lots advantageously. So in the end he donated land for a church.

Defective as our society may be, it would be far worse did it not have the moral and spiritual leadership which church and synagogue provide. Every loyal American should thank God for these great institutions and should help support them. But because all this is true we should not blind ourselves to the difficulties confronting religious leadership in this country. Can we escape a narcotic religion?

We might as well face it. We are living in a semi-pagan society which calls itself Christian or religious. Many of those who make up the membership of our churches and synagogues are only faintly religious. Too often they represent merely a ceremonial ratification of prevailing morality.

In the history of the church we find countless illustrations. For example, in the railroad strike of 1877 such a well-known religious leader as Henry Ward Beecher opposed the strikers and asked why they should not be able to live on one dollar a day. Said he, "a man who cannot live on bread is not fit to live."

In Rev. Russell Conway's popular lecture, "Acres of Diamonds," which he delivered over six thousand times, he said: "I say, get rich, get rich . . . 98 out of 100 of the rich men of America are honest. That is why they are rich." On the other hand, he believed that the majority of those who were poor were "being punished for their sins."

In 1892 the *Christian Advocate* opposed the theory that a company had any obligation to confer with its workmen.

In opposition to such supporters of conventional morality, great leaders like Walter Rauschenbusch declared, "The kingdom of God breeds prophets; the church breeds priests and theologians." Rauschenbusch devoted his efforts toward building the Kingdom of God on earth, studying and interpreting the social application of the Gospel.

The church today recognizes the deadly peril of self-interest and pride within all of us; nevertheless it should also recognize its social responsibility to try to correct social evils. Most of its leaders do now recognize in their hearts that the *status quo* is not ordained of God, but they do not always implement this in their sermons.

Recently Dr. Joseph D. Huntley in the Broadway Tabernacle

Church in New York City said that part of the responsibility for the rise of Communism must be blamed on the church. It has a tendency to treat Christianity as an intellectual exercise instead of practising its prophetic ministry. He went on to say: "Had the church proclaimed to the world the revolutionary character of the teachings of Jesus Christ, Asians as well as others might have bowed the head and bent the knee to this Christ rather than to Lenin or Stalin. The sad but honest truth is this: We were afraid that the social teachings of Jesus might upset our own preconceived ideas of the comfortable society, and because of this fear the so-called social gospel was put in our hip pocket."

Defective as the church often is, conditioned by the social standards of its time, often controlled by the "successful" business leaders in any community, it nevertheless always has the ideal of Jesus and the prophets as its professed goal. Nearly all ministers are men who have at one time or another dedicated their lives to God and His service. They genuinely want to give their lives in service.

The National Council of Churches, in a resolution adopted at Denver in 1952, declared that the Christian churches "have a prophetic role to play within the national life. It is their duty so to sensitize the conscience of the nation and of all classes and institutions within it that no group of citizens shall arrogate to itself perpetual rights and privileges which it denies to others."

Actually the church should be helping every individual to a God-centered heart and life and at the same time it should be trying to create a new and better social environment. Both the individual and the social are facets of the religious task.

Church and synagogue can never afford to turn their backs on the social and economic causes of sin and suffering. If they do, their spiritual leadership is spurious, not following God as proclaimed by the prophets or by Jesus.

We are living in the wealthiest country in the world. Will the owners of wealth in a democracy dominate the lives of others, or will our productive mechanism become the servant of all? Will religion dedicate part of its resources to seeing that all of God's children have a more equitable distribution of food, clothing, and shelter, so that with a fair standard of living they can develop their innate gifts and potentialities? Thus far, too often the church has acquiesced in racial discrimination, isolating the Negro and the white into separate institutions to worship the same God. Will we overcome these shameful sins? On both sides we must learn to understand and appreciate. Can the industrial economy bring worker and owner together in a bond of friendship and mutual service? Seldom in Rotary, Kiwanis and other service clubs do we find that the trade unions are represented. Ministers and rabbis belong to these service clubs—why should they not take the lead in bringing in representative men from organized labor? They are essential to our common life.

Any spiritual leader has a truncated concept if he does not act to end injustice.

One of the greatest evils in American life is the acquisitive spirit and its consequences. How can it be brought into captivity to the will of God?

Increasingly we find wealthy men among those who commit suicide. One man of wealth, of whom the writer knew, during the depression saw his fortune fade in those trying days from *five* to *three* million dollars. This so preyed upon his mind that he died. We are finding that more and more of our population need mental care, other hundreds of thousands have become alcoholics. All of these people could be redeemed if religion could grip their lives. If serving God and society had come ahead of serving self, these derelicts would have found real happiness in life.

Zaccheus on his conversion said, "Behold, Lord, the half of my goods I give to the poor; and if I have taken anything from any man by false accusation, I restore him fourfold" (Luke 19:8). From that moment he was a saved man, although the dedication of the whole man, all his wealth and activities, would have been a greater challenge. How many of the wealthy class in our religious institutions have given even half of their money to worthy causes?

In any society the inheriting of wealth poses problems. The writer had an uncle who was owner of the Encyclopedia Britannica Company. He believed in giving his children everything they needed while they were in school and college, but once they were out they were on their own and he declared that he would not leave them anything when he died. He used to say, "If the children are any good they won't need help, and if they are no good it would be wrong to leave them money."

How can the church change the attitude of men towards the social sins of our time? Is not the most potent way to awaken the sleeping conscience of the people always to be alert to proclaim the social sins of our age, of our leaders, of our community? Jesus said, "First cast out the beam out of thine own eye, then thou canst see clearly to cast the splinter out of thy neighbor's." We must keep from becoming spiritually anemic, and the church must continually be injecting the vitamins of social and spiritual responsibility for *all* the evils of our neighborhood and our world. We cannot ignore these and remain Christian. It is up to the church to bring moral judgment not only against individual but against social sins.

In any age there exists the danger that religion as practised will be subservient to the contemporary respectable powers that rule in the orbit where the church functions. Do not some visitors even wonder in seeing an American flag in the pulpit whether our primary loyalty is to our nation or to our God? Certainly we must beware of a captive religion, captive to the spirit of the culture and the epoch of which it is a part. Religion must never be pushed to one side, confined within a beautiful church compartment, isolated from life. Too often conventional Christian morality is considered to mean attendance at church as well as generous financial support for its program. Rarely does the church ask each member to make an accounting for *all* he does in his individual work. In our higher reflective moments we know there tends to be a conflict between the inner spirit of Christ and the outer world we live in. We become acclimated to the beauty surrounding religious observance but not to the task of transforming the community itself into a reflection of God's purposes in human life. The church should really contain a light which shines out into the community and this must be the light of God.

The official report of the Third World Conference on Faith and Order has this to say, "Churches too much at home in the world will hear themselves called out of the world. Churches too wrapped up in their own piety or their own survival will see again Him who identified Himself with the deprived and the oppressed."

Every church should have fellowship circles of prayer. These are cells of the spirit which enormously increase the dynamic power of God. Neighborhood groups are organized which meet regularly for Bible study, meditation and fellowship. Some churches hold spiritual retreats several times each year. This is getting back to the dynamic which early religious groups generated and which made them ready to suffer and die for their faith.

In some way every Christian must see the opportunity to serve God in his vocation. He knows in his heart that he is called to faith and service; worship and consecrated work. He must be led to see the consequences of his actions in daily life. Gradually the atomic scientists have realized their moral responsibility for the A- and H-bombs. The captains of industry and finance should similarly be led to examine and analyze in social values what they are doing. Every business man must recognize that at the end of the road, as well as now, he will be judged by his life and his work. Will he hear the words, "Well done, good and faithful servant?"

Too often the business man feels that if he takes a prominent part in the church that automatically makes him a devoted Christian. Prayerful consideration should make him feel that in reality he should be an Ambassador of Christ to the community. The Gospel must be translated into his daily work or his Christian calling is spurious.

The church must be free of entangling organizational and institutional impedimenta for they may isolate her from the market place and the life of the community.

In some way the church must make every member ask himself: "Is the work I am doing worthy of Christ? Is the social effect of it beneficial or harmful judged by Christ's standards?"

God's calling demands commitment, in the work men do in the world. Any religion which separates religious faith from work is fallacious. Too often the gospel of work in America is a secularized one. One of the deacons in a prominent church told the writer that when he went into his office on Monday morning he gave himself completely to the making of profits. If an employee was inefficient or made an error, it would be wrong to practise the Golden Rule and keep him. After all, the deacon said, his first responsibility was to the stockholders' demand that profits come first, last and all the time.

This highlights the fact that the church should endeavor to bring men's work as well as their membership into the fellowship of God. Every Christian must have a *working* loyalty to God carrying Him into every area of the business life. The job or profession which every man has must thus be brought into the orbit of the Kingdom of God.

Now in order to do this effectively some churches have organized specialized groups within the church to discuss what Christian vocation means in their line of work. Among the groups organized are: bankers, dentists and doctors, lawyers, real estate operators and a general group composed of miscellaneous business men. Each group meets by itself to decide how it can make its own work more Christian. As a result of one such meeting a business man decided to employ a Negro girl in his firm. He felt that his office should be a center to demonstrate racial equality.

In these ways and many others the church must teach all its members that religion is man's total response to God's call for him. His religion is determined by all his life which includes *all* his activities. He must be led to "put on the whole armour of God."

The Christian-in-politics is a calling of which we hear too little these days. In some way the widespread apathy of the average citizen must be shocked, and inspired by the judgment and will of God proclaimed from the pulpit. Seventy-five years ago the average voter was much more alive to governmental problems than he is today. In 1880, for example, 87% of those eligible voted, while in 1948 the number had fallen to 51%. In the Congressional elections of 1950 the proportion was even smaller—only four out of every ten eligible voters cast their ballots. Senator Margaret Chase Smith hits the nail on the head: "Failing to vote is indicative of something far more dangerous than non-voting itself. Such failure reveals a state of mind and an attitude that is basically un-American. It is basically un-American because it is a form of refusal to fight for and protect the American way of life, the American home, and the American family."

As far as education is concerned, few citizens take enough responsibility. When the writer asks parents from the comfortable or upper class group whether they can tell the name of the teacher of their child, only about one out of ten can do so. When one continues to ask if they have ever invited a teacher home for a meal, seldom is there an affirmative answer.

In one great university the writer asked a professor whether he sent his children to the public school or not. "Oh no," he replied, "I send them to the best private schools." "Why don't you get behind a movement to improve the standards in the public schools?" I inquired. He retorted: "I carefully estimated how much time and money it would take really to effect any adequate change in the public schools and I decided it was cheaper for me to pay the colossal expense of sending my children to private institutions." Apparently his conscience had not been awakened by church or pulpit to see that his solution was neither the fully Christian nor the democratic way.

Now church and synagogue have a responsibility for both good government and good schools. If they dodge this responsibility they are evading the moral basis of the religion they profess and are denying that all of life belongs to God.

What is true of the government and the schools is true in large measure about the treatment of the criminals in our jails, about hospital facilities, about the unemployed and the poverty-stricken.

In view of the fact that the United States Government can spend billions and billions of dollars on a program to develop the atom and hydrogen bombs, which can slaughter millions of the human race, why should not the religious forces of the nation spend money for research on what religion should and can do?

If we were wise enough, and Christian enough, or prophetic enough, we would set competent and consecrated people to making a test survey of what all the churches and synagogues of a certain city or community are doing in the social field.[1] This would also involve knowing exactly what conditions exist in the community, in order to locate any situations where the religious forces are failing to meet the need. Among problems which would have to be surveyed and reported on would be the following:

1. Civil liberties
   Minority groups should have complete freedom to express their sincere beliefs.
2. Medical care
   Are there adequate hospital facilities for all?
3. Industrial relations
   Are the industries organized into trade unions which function adequately?

[1] See also Goldstein, Sidney E. *The Synagogue and Social Welfare.*

4. Housing
   Are there slums? Can the poor get decent homes at reasonable cost?
5. Recreational facilities
   Are they adequate to keep young people occupied in wholesome activities in their leisure time?
6. Crime
   Is the rate higher or lower in other communities? Is the jail helping its inmates to change their lives through an adequate organized program?
7. Education
   How many in the high school drop out before graduation? Why?
8. The accident rate
   How do traffic fatalities compare with other communities?
9. Racial discrimination
   To what extent is this evil present in your community?
10. Promoting peace

At the conclusion of such a survey the church would be challenged as never before to change the conditions which need remedying. This might even necessitate a paid worker under the religious forces of the community, to galvanize the community and secure united action.

Later, after two or three years had passed, a new survey would again have to be made to discover the results. Such questions as these could be raised: Has the percentage who vote in the elections gone up? Has the disease rate gone down? What has happened in the area of racial discrimination? In a word, to what extent has the community become more moral and social in every area? If not, how can the situation be improved?

It is the considered opinion of the writer that the churches could vastly improve our communities, not only by making individuals more deeply spiritual but in reforming our social order by reducing crime, poverty, disease, and other social evils which still plague us.

It would not be surprising to find that in any community which attempts to do this, not only would church membership rise but the number of consecrated, devoted followers of God who are giving their entire lives to His service would increase. It is not implied that this program would be easy. But is it any more difficult than developing the atom and hydrogen bomb, for instance?

The church has its outreach around the world. What about the foreign missionary movement? Could it exert an even more profound influence on international affairs than it now does?

Missionaries must, of course, demonstrate in their lives just what a Christlike life really is. Ralph Keithan, one of the great Christian missionaries in India, has been trying to do just this. He admits that the missionary may have his faults, but "let it be known that that sinner is a pilgrim on the path of truth, not a coward sitting in the rocking chair of Western civilization. India wants to know today what Jesus Christ may mean to her. We missionaries face the naked, the hungry and exploited around us. Unless our living has vital relationship to this dire world of need our witness will be a scandal."[1]

He goes on to say: "Perhaps the missionary's greatest sin is bringing to India and other nations a church that is not a church. Here in India we see a caste—and class-ridden church—when this new nation is striving for a 'casteless, classless society.' We see this church tending to be an urban or bourgeois church and not a church of the needy, of the people in the slum and village."

A foreign missionary should never take part in politics. This is the responsibility of the native Christian layman. The Nationalist Christian Congregation of St. Paul's Hindustani Church in Bombay, India, recognized this when it passed the following resolution:

We are fully convinced of the fact that the action taken by the Government of India against certain foreign missionaries, whose activities were embarrassing to the Government, was mainly on political considerations and that the general attitude of our Government in regard to the future of the foreign missionaries in India is based on their fair policy of strict adherence to the principle of full religious tolerance.

It went on to oppose "the denationalizing influence of the age-old alien system of church administration which came to India along with her foreign rulers in its sectarian forms, so much so that each denomination brought, and still brings, along with it the name, culture and outlook of the particular corner of Europe or America in which it originated."[2]

It is obvious that foreign missionary activity should scrupulously

---

[1] *Christian Century*, Feb. 17, 1954.
[2] *The Hindu Weekly*, July 12, 1954, p. 16.

avoid seeking to *control* the native church in any country. The natives should run their own church. Christian missions should demonstrate the possibility of giving aid to native religious leaders without dictating terms. Furthermore, great care should be exercised that the church which is set up in a native land does not become so dependent that it is reduced to perpetual dependence.

The fact that Christianity seems to the natives of another land like a foreign religion and often gives the impression of "foreign imperialism" should lead missions to allow the native peoples to use their own forms and to clothe Christianity not in our forms but in theirs.

We must make Christianity indigenous in every land. It must actually take root in the soil of the country in which it is located.

Denominationalism is the curse of foreign missions. We should build a unified movement and have one mission board for all denominations, and if possible an international board. It must be a missionary movement which does not ignore the vital social and economic problems which confront native peoples.

Future missionaries should be educated for "the whole man," for they should go where the need is greatest. In India this means the poverty-stricken villages and slums. Probably, as Keithan has demonstrated, this often means being "married to Lady Poverty."

Too often, while missionaries render medical service and establish medical schools, the graduates of these institutions do not go to the villages. Furthermore, missionary doctors in India say the people need food rather than pills and injections.

The missionary movement must stand resolutely against exploitation in all its forms, against class and caste and against imperialism even when it is supported by their own home land. This means that the missionary movement can begin to bridge the chasms between East and West which threaten the world today with "perpetual war for perpetual peace."

It goes without saying that the missionary movement must have prayer at its center and in the heart of every disciple.

Of course, the Western church must share its wealth with the churches of Africa, China, and India. But this must be done not as governments give their wealth, on condition that certain "military" steps are taken. The Western church must make the churches of every nation it helps indigenous. They must build faith in the midst of their own culture and in ways best calculated to win their own people.

All of this may be difficult, but, as Keithan has well put it, "We must be ready to leave the walls of our mission compounds, to leap over denominational fences, to sally forth from our cramping theological ghettos, and breathe the cleansing air of reality. If we find the world we emerge into a world of darkness, we know that He who goes with us is the Light of light. With Him we can venture into the slum and the village where need cries out."[3]

If the church would follow this program in its missionary effort, the chances of World War III would be visibly diminished.

Now, in conclusion, to return to the broad problem of religion in our own native land, what must we do to be saved?

We should pause and ask ourselves whether we cannot change our habit patterns in the churches to make religion more vital, more dynamic, more real. Just as we have made material progress which has given us the automobile, the airplane, the electric refrigerator, and a host of comforts in the material realm, so we cannot escape the analogy that psychology and the social sciences can contribute needed improved techniques in applying our religion to the changed cultural pattern of our time. When the church begins to do this in a new and active way we will not have overcome sin. We shall always need the grace of God and the forgiveness of God for our sins. Pride, power, and selfishness will still remain. But at least we shall have begun to meet the social problems confronting us with more spiritual and moral power. In emphasizing the social side of religion let us make clear that this never works permanently without a vital personal religion, a reliance on the guidance and strength of God. We must ever strive to deepen our inner spiritual life. But the reverse is also true. "He who doth not love his brother whom he hath seen, how can he love God whom he hath not seen?"

[3] *Christian Century*, Feb. 17, 1954.

Prayer

Help us, our Father, to show other nations an America to imitate—not the America of loud jazz music, self-seeking indulgence, and love of money, but the America that loves fair play, honest dealing, straight talk, real freedom, and faith in God.

Make us see that it cannot be done as long as we are content to be coupon clippers on the original investment made by our forefathers. Give us faith in God and love for our fellow men, that we may have something to deposit on which the young people of today can draw interest tomorrow.

By Thy grace, let us this day increase the moral capital of this country. Amen.

In the Senate of the United States, June 11, 1938
REV. PETER MARSHALL, CHAPLAIN

May we help forward the coming of social justice! Our place ought always to be beside the poor and the humble, those who labor and perish.

ROMAIN ROLLAND

If work is to find its right place in the world, it is the duty of the Church to see to it that the work serves God, and the worker serves the work.

DOROTHY L. SAYERS

Two boys were guilty of immorality in the Ashram of Gandhi so he fasted seven days. Then he said to the boys:
"There were three ways open to me: (1) Punishment . . . I know by experience it is futile, even harmful. (2) Indifference. I could have left you to your fate . . . (3) The method of love. Your character is to me a sacred trust. I must therefore try to enter into your lives, your innermost thoughts, your desires, and your impulses, and help you to eradicate impurities, if any . . . Being the chief among the teachers, I had to take the punishment on myself in the form of fasting . . . If I am to identify myself with the grief of the least in India, aye, if I have the power, the least in the world, let me identify myself with the sins of the little ones who are under my care. And so doing in all humility, I hope some day to see God—Truth—face to face.

MAHATMA GANDHI

CHAPTER XVII

"I Was in Prison and You Came to Me"

IF anyone visits jails throughout the United States and abroad he will be shocked at what he finds. Too often the record is one of neglect, incompetence or just plain incarceration, nothing else. Often in the United States there may be some kind of religious service in the institution on Sunday but otherwise society is rather indifferent to the fate of these children of God.

Take as an example the jail in a Southern state visited in 1954. Each day the men went out on the roads to work when the weather was good. When it rained they were confined to their cells. The place was overrun with bedbugs and vermin. Many of the beds had no blankets and the prisoners complained because they had no access to medical help. One man believed he had broken a rib but he was not permitted to see a doctor. There was no reading matter or recreation of any kind. Yes, they had a religious service on Sunday but the minister did nothing to help change the jail itself.

The result is that in this particular institution it is probable that the jail served largely as a breeding ground for crime. There was no study of each inmate to see how he could be helped, there was no rehabilitation work at all. The prisoners simply stayed their allotted time and then were pushed out into a hostile world where nine times out of ten they would continue in a career of crime.

Remember, all of us have faults. Nearly everyone is a potential criminal. Most citizens break the law at some time or other, if only by automobile speeding or through illegal parking. Most criminals who are apprehended are usually taken first to the local jail. So this is where most first offenders find themselves. Now, if anyone studies the history of the treatment of criminals in the United States, it has been a sorry record of man's inhumanity to man. We have used all sorts of stupid punishments. There may be floggings, the stretcher, the sweatbox, the strait jacket, the iron yoke, the thumb screw and the water cure. In recent years, many of these have been abolished. Some of them still are used. In one great modern sepulchre of iron and steel cells, they use a new form of punishment which the warden says he learned in World War II. A prisoner to be punished is placed in a special cell, then they turn on the laughing gas!

Long ago, we were even more brutal. In medieval times, prisoners were sometimes burned at the stake or stoned to death. The death penalty was given for a great many crimes. Later on in the Twentieth Century, society began building so-called "model" institutions. It is true the steel structure had many mechanical improvements with toilets in every cell, for instance, but even here people were often kept in solitary confinement. Usually, we dumped all kinds and varieties of prisoners into one institution—the young and the old, the professional bank robber with the chronic alcoholic, the psychotic, the homosexual, the feeble-minded, the epileptic, along with first offenders and even those who were innocent.

Now if we really wanted to be mature and creative in our handling of the offender, what should we do? We should probably consider that criminals should be treated somewhat the way we treat people in hospitals. There, when a patient comes in, we do not just shut him into a room and treat him identically as we treat all the other inmates, we try to find out what is wrong with him, what is causing his physical difficulty. This is exactly what we should do in the jails, but we have hardly begun to think in these terms.

Some time ago the author was appointed chairman of the Legislative Commission on Jails for the State of Connecticut. Later, we received $50,000 of Federal Government money to investigate all the jail prisoners. We employed doctors, case workers, psychiatrists, and social workers to make studies covering the physical, psychological, psychiatric and social conditions of the jail population. We wanted to find out what kind of treatment they really needed to restore them to normal citizenship.

What do you suppose our findings were? We learned that some 45.4 per cent of the population primarily needed *"Situational"* treatment. That is, the cause and treatment of the delinquent depended in whole or in part upon adjusting the environment; the home, the school, conditions of employment, his companions, in short the major stimuli surrounding the individual. Now, in order that you may understand what we mean by a situational case, let me give you a concrete illustration. Here is a man who is married and the family has one baby. They are living in Waterbury, Connecticut. The man is employed in a factory. He is an excellent worker. In fact, the employer has never had anything against him and has periodically increased his pay. The factory begins to have to lay off workers, but this man is not worried for he is one of the most skilled in the entire plant. But the time comes when, due to the depression, the whole factory is closed down. Now this star worker has lost his job. Still he does not worry, he has $5,000 in the bank. The family continued to live quite comfortably. Suddenly a tragic thing happened. It was a period of depression and the bank failed. Society has now taken away the man's job and it has taken away all his money in the bank. In those days, there were few relief agencies. The man did not know how to get food. For two days, they went without eating. Water was put in the baby's milk bottle. Finally, the baby cried all night long. The next morning, in desperation, the man went down and stole a woman's purse and bought some milk and food for his wife and baby. That night at last the baby slept. But the next day the father was apprehended. He was tried, convicted and sent up for seven months in the local jail. There he was kept in idleness in a cell. This we believe was treating the man not for what is wrong with him but simply to punish him. Take an analogy from the field of health. Supposing a man has scrupulously guarded his physical well-being but when he goes abroad he is careless and eats food that is not properly washed. Would it be sensible to send him to jail for six months to teach him to be careful or would it not be better to cure his dysentery and let him be free? We believe that if the jail were an institution like the hospital, what would be done for this man would be to find him a job, that is what he needed, that is what he wanted.

Now let me give you another case. We will call the name of this man, John Smith. His father was an immigrant and they lived in Hartford, Connecticut. He was on the football team in college, was a pre-medic student and his grades were above the average. So far as we know from records at the college this boy had never indulged in drinking. However, it was New Year's Eve and before the night was over the group got tipsy, quarrelled and exchanged blows. The result was that two of the boys were hurt. In the end, Smith was arrested for his part in the fracas and given a six months' sentence. He was at fault, they had been drinking and he should never have been involved in fighting. Nevertheless, from a scientific standpoint the question is what kind of treatment would be most likely to create a good future? We believe it might have been better to permit him to go back to college on probation. If he was confined in jail at all he should have been allowed to concentrate on college subjects. Perhaps, since he was intent on a medical career he could have done routine duties in the hospital. Medical books should have been at his disposal. None of these things were done for him. When he did get out, he was debarred from his college. It took a long effort on our part finally to get him into another institution, and today he is a successful practicing physician. If the current jail practise alone had been followed and nothing positive done he might now be a hardened criminal, a liability and a charge on society. We believe that all treatment of delinquents should depend upon what is wrong with them and what they need, to be restored to health.

Let us now consider another group. We found that three per cent of all our prisoners primarily needed medical treatment. If they were given the right medical program, they would not need to be in an institution at all. Here is a man who had tuberculosis. Of course, he didn't know he had the disease, he was working in a factory at a lathe, all day long. When he came home to his family, his wife tried to have him scrub the kitchen floor. Naturally, he didn't like this, but he did it nevertheless. The next day he toiled eight hours at his lathe and came home dead tired, for unknown to himself, he had tuberculosis. This time his wife met him at the door and said she had been kept so busy by the children, that she'd had no time to wash the dishes and she would appreciate his doing it. The man began to wash the dishes and then to quarrel with his wife. This culminated in his throwing a plate at her.

She called the police and he was taken to jail. Now all that was really necessary to help this man was to cure his tuberculosis. When he was no longer ill he was not so tired and cross when he came home. He had no difficulty with his wife. He didn't need the jail, he needed health.

Still another group of inmates, 17.1 percent of the total, needed the services of a clinical psychologist. They greatly needed personality attention. Let me give you a concrete case. Here's a man who goes into a dentist's office saying he has a terrible toothache. The doctor is filling the tooth of a young woman and he is asked to wait until the doctor finishes his case. A few minutes later, the outer door banged and the dentist ran out to see the man going down the steps. He said, "What's the matter, couldn't you wait?" The man said, "The pain in my jaw is so terrible, that I'm going out to get a drink." Later, when the dentist finished work on the woman patient, she found that her purse had been stolen from her coat in the waiting room. An alarm was sent out to the police and the next day the man was caught trying to sell the empty pocketbook to a policeman! Now this same man had a long record of other offenses. He had passed fraudulent checks. One time he had invited three friends to a good restaurant. They had had a delicious meal. When it came time to pay, he simply wrote a fraudulent check. However, it was accepted at the restaurant. He then got into a taxi and drove around town for two hours and finally told the taxi driver to take him to the center of the town, whereupon he got out without paying his bill. The driver said, "Aren't you going to pay me?" and the man said "No," and walked off, whereupon the driver called the policeman. Now, it's obvious that here is a psychiatric case. Any man who would rob a patient and then try to sell the empty pocketbook to a policeman, needs psychiatric attention. A man who would pass a fraudulent check and then immediately get into a taxicab and drive all around town and refuse to pay the bill is also a mental problem case. To turn this person loose without any treatment, will in all probability result in further criminal activity and loss to society. This man was forty years of age. He had a chance of being cured if properly treated. Society, itself, is responsible for his further criminal behavior if it fails to take every precaution to see that he is released only under proper supervision. It is possible that this case might need *prolonged* institutional care.

Now there is another group of about eight and five-tenths per cent of all the prisoners who had a definite anti-social philosophy. While they were in the jail being punished for one crime, they were planning the next. They believed that it was all right to steal. Sometimes they felt that society was a grand racket anyway and that they were just as much entitled to get what they could illegally as others were to get huge profits. Some of them would make it a habit to rob stores. They tried to claim that they were really more considerate than some of the big corporations for they did not take money from the poor, only from those who could afford to lose it. Now obviously, the people with a definite anti-social philosophy, men who are bound and determined to commit crime as a career should not be released unless and until their attitudes can be changed. These men need to have the services of educators, clergymen and psychiatrists who can help to change their philosophy. But what do we do at present? We merely put them in a jail or prison and leave them there for a specified period and then turn them loose again. What is the net result? One of the men we studied had committed 47 offenses and just for good measure he married a woman who had a record of 50 offenses. Is it intelligent just to lock up an individual of this kind for a short time and then let him loose to commit more crimes?

Finally, we found that 26 per cent of the jail prisoners really needed permanent custodial treatment and eight per cent needed temporary custodial care. Why was this true? Well many of them were mental defectives. Here, for instance, is a man whom we will call George Lee. He is 59 years of age and has had a long record of offenses. He has a very low I.Q. He is a chronic alcoholic; he has been arrested 63 times for drunkenness and once was hospitalized for a fractured skull. He has also had syphilis. With an I.Q. of about 59, he had completed only nine grades in school. In occupational skills, he shows little mechanical ability. Now, if a person of this kind is just placed in jail, kept for a few months and then released, he goes back into the same habit channels and the same associations as before. He commits another crime. Society must protect him in an environment where the temptations will not be so strong. This means custodial treatment. But again this is precisely the treatment we do not provide at the present time. We merely lock him up in jail for a few months and turn him loose to commit another crime.

All the individuals in our jails should be studied scientifically, after physical, psychiatric and case studies have been made; then they should be treated for *exactly what is wrong with them*. What is the real cause of their difficulty? It is absurd to give identical treatment no matter what their condition. How violently we would protest if a hospital should do this. But the jail should also be a center where men and women receive scientific diagnostic treatment for their particular ailment. A man whose real need is to be cured of tuberculosis should not be treated the same as a mental defective.

Now let us consider for a moment, the kind of institutions which we should have in the United States for treating these people. When the author started work in the jail at New Haven, Connecticut, the first person we sent to the Penitentiary was the jailer. He had been stealing from the state and, worse than that, had been hiring the prisoners to forge the books, so they got a complete course in forgery while they were in the institution. Thus many men sent to the New Haven jail were getting training for crime, not being cured of their ailments! Unfortunately, there are almost no jails in the United States where the best scientific treatment is now being given each inmate. It is not only the loss and disaster to each individual implicit in our present jail system, but the loss to society which is incalculable. It is just the same as though we should permit patients with smallpox or leprosy to mingle with all the other people in cities, towns and villages, thus causing epidemics all over the nation. Consider a concrete example, a true case of the heavy cost of the present system. A young man and woman went to a church social in Bridgeport, Conn. Afterwards they had to take the streetcar home. As they were waiting on the platform in the center of the street for the trolley an automobile drew up; suddenly the rear door opened and the girl was seized. The driver put his foot on the gas and the car went off at great speed leaving the male escort standing yelling for them to stop. Three hours later, the girl was dumped out on the street. Naturally she didn't want to testify in open court so when the culprits were caught, they pleaded to a lesser offense and were sent up for only a few months. While in the institution they were plotting their next crime. Our system of giving no clinical treatment, of not finding out the causes, results in further crimes against society, again, and again, and again.

Now by way of contrast let us visit an institution in Copenhagen, Denmark where they are trying scientifically to treat inmates to cure their ailments. In this institution, the warden who is a psychiatrist writes to all the other prisons in Denmark asking them to send him the worst prisoners they have, and he gets them. What does the doctor try to do with these men? First, he studies them scientifically to find out precisely what is wrong with each one. He secures a case history of their past, their occupational record, their criminal record, and any other facts which can be secured. He has the power to release them on probation at any time. They do not have a fixed sentence. He always tries to win their friendship and tells each man, "I want to get you out of here, let's work together, so that you can be free at the earliest possible moment." The result is he usually wins their cooperation. Some of them enter classes provided in the prison. All have their physical ailments, if any, scientifically attended to but all of them also are getting the kind of treatment that will help them to take their place once more in society. When they do leave, they are on probation, they have to report back to the warden.

The writer attended a clinic where some of those who had left the institution were reporting back. One case was that of a married man, a former inmate. He returned for his regular check-up together with his wife. After a short visit the wife turned to the Warden and said, "Don't you think it's possible for you to take my husband off parole now and let him live as any other citizen does. After all he has made good." The warden turned to her and said, "I would like very much to do this, but look at the employment record of your husband. Every time he is only employed for a short time before he changes his work so he has skipped from one job to another, never staying as long as six months with one firm. I think he ought to keep coming back until he has really become fully adjusted and stays in one organization and in one work job on a more or less fixed basis. Until that time he might need my help but as soon as he finds a permanent position I will take him off parole."

Because of its treatment this prison is really changing the lives of its inmates. This institution doesn't always succeed any more than a hospital does in the United States. Some patients with cancer die. But in a very large proportion of cases, this Danish institution is successful in changing the whole pattern of life of the individual, who is then able to take his place as a self-respecting citizen of society. This is what needs to be done everywhere with so-called "criminals." This in many ways is what Jesus tried to do. You remember, He refused to condemn even the woman taken in adultery. When the people wanted to stone her to death according to the law of the land, Jesus said, "He that is without sin among you, cast the first stone." As a result, without going to prison or being killed she was cured by His wisdom and kindness.

Let us begin clinically to treat criminals, especially first offenders. Let us discover what has caused them to commit their offense, and then let us change them by applying scientifically proved methods. When society genuinely reaches this stage, we will have advanced far in maturity and intelligence. Potential criminals will be transformed into self-respecting useful citizens in a society of adults. It is probable that delinquency results from an interplay of biological, psychological and cultural factors. Some of these are hard to change, but some factors are much more easily susceptible of modification. We should endeavor to change those factors that can be modified, and help redeem the man who has been in difficulty. The responsibility for the condition of any jail rests on every church member, every citizen. Have you visited your local jail and have you done all in your power to make the jail as effective in its way as is the school?

The Ministerial Association in every city in the United States should have a standing committee on the jail. It should be the duty of this committee to see to it not only that the prisoners have a religious service each Sunday but, far more important, that the inmates have a chance to be cured of whatever ails them. While in the institution they should have access to all the worth while books in the public library. Classes should be arranged for those who will study and some work for every able bodied man which will help him. On release they should be given genuine aid so that they can take their place as self-respecting citizens of the community.

Only when we have made our jails as curative as our hospitals can we really meet the test of Jesus. Then in truth He can say of us, of our churches and synagogues, "I was in prison and you came to me."

Prayer

God of Truth and Justice, who unveilest Thyself not so much in words as in spirit and in action and has taught us to do justly, to love mercy, and to walk humbly with Thee; grant us to remember the words and examples of Jesus. We thank Thee for Him and for his life, for his many deeds which did help the poor, the ignorant and the downtrodden. Especially keep us from forgetting His words about coming to those who are in prison. Help us to step out of our own self-centeredness. Grant that we may see the problems of our community with great clearness, what is good and what is evil, how they mingle, guard us from being caught in the interplay of one with another. May the light from Thee shine through our lives into all those whom we meet and so may we be instruments of Thy love. Guard us from having alibis as to why we cannot do more. May each of us help to make better institutions in our own communities; better hospitals, better jails, better rehabilitation centers. May we all be kept from cheap and shoddy patterns of action and instead genuinely build character both in ourselves and others and so bring men nearer to Thee.

Always keep your eye on yourself first; and admonish yourself first before you admonish your dearest friends.

If you conquer yourself perfectly, you will easily conquer all things beside.

Perfect triumph is the triumph over self.

He is truly great who is great in the love of God.

He is truly great who is little in his own estimation, and counts the highest honors as nothing.

When a man humbly acknowledges his own faults, he easily appeases others, and quickly conciliates those who are angry with him.

Blessed are the eyes which are closed to the outward things, and open to the inward things.

 From *The Imitation of Christ*, by THOMAS A KEMPIS.

Spiritual regeneration, to develop goodwill, faith and understanding among nations is the most important factor of peace.
> GENERAL GEORGE C. MARSHALL, former United States Secretary of State, upon receiving the 1953 Nobel Peace Award.

Our Share

And we ourselves? Are our hands clean?
Are our souls free from blame
For this world-tragedy?
Nay then! Like all the rest,
We had relaxed our hold on higher things,
And satisfied ourselves with smaller.
Ease, pleasure, greed of gold,—
Laxed morals even in these,—
We suffered them, as unaware
Of their soul-cankerings.
We had slipped back along the sloping way,
No longer holding First things First,
But throning gods emasculate,—
Idols of our own fashioning,
Heads of sham gold and feet of crumbling clay
If we must build anew, and build to stay,
We must find God again.
And go His Way.

JOHN OXENHAM from *All's Well*, Doran, 1916, p. 65.

CHAPTER XVIII

Overcoming the Criminal in Us

In the last analysis, social change rests back on the individual. If a society is to have real moral power, it must be made up of moral individuals. There are people who are largely interested in their own material success, in what they can do to advance their own selfish pleasures. Then there are those who see beyond themselves to what is intricate and far reaching; in a word, who find their happiness in the happiness of others.

Let us not blink the fact that it is easy for all of us to be self-centered. If our family, our clique, is well off we may shut our minds from the lot of the less fortunate. Even those who use the inventive power of their minds may do so for personal aggrandizement. The invention we make, the book we write, the business we run may really be all for *our* pride and privilege.

There is another subtle danger, to let the routine of daily life overwhelm us, to do the same thing over and over again, without trying to improve it. To guard against this disguised form of hardening of the arteries, we must always endeavor to improve our environment, to remedy some situation which causes difficulty for others. This may mean helping to get a library for our community, or a co-operative store, or even a working aid for the wife. For if we imprison ourselves in the environment that society has thus far been able to build, we are truly becoming as criminals in a self-built prison enclosure.

Again, if we are intolerant of others we are letting the criminal in us hold sway. The only way we can have true liberty is to let others who differ from us have complete freedom. Because we see one course of action as just and true, and another person wishes something so different that we think it is wrong and terrible, does not give us the right to prohibit him from expressing his opinions. If we do that, the criminal in us is ruling again. Genuine believers in liberty believe in free and open discussion for all men everywhere. To become quickly and passionately "against" something is a dangerous vice. There is probably some truth and justice on the other side and we ought to try to recognize it.

Then there are those smug, self-satisfied people who are supremely content with themselves. They have "hardening of the brain." They are conceited, cocksure, dogmatic, and unyielding. Most of us have a little of this criminal trait at times.

The criminal tends to justify his action, no matter how selfish. We all have this characteristic. What *we* did is right, of course; what the other fellow did is wrong. We keep stamping our own image on the work we do, the language we use; indeed, in every minute of our waking hours we are leaving tracks. How much of this stamp is positive, creating increased happiness? How much of it is mean and below our highest selves? How many mean actions sneak into our lives? Let us not deceive ourselves: there is just a little of the criminal in us all.

Down through all history there have been and are those who try to serve themselves first, who put self before society, and there are those who feel that the real adventure of life is to serve others. Have you not seen a man who goes into business for personal aggrandizement and power? He is willing to foist inferior goods on the public or to get sure rake-offs from an obliging government. On the other hand, there is the man who will lose his position in order to expose corruption, who gives away money for the common good about as fast as he makes it. This contrast runs all through life. Few of us escape criminal selfishness at some point, all of us are generous somewhere. The task confronting humanity is to decrease the criminal in us and increase the power and love of God in our hearts until we, like Schweitzer of Africa, have sympathy for all mankind, even the lowest. This is a lifetime quest, and to rest on our laurels contentedly often means that we lose the goal.

Life that is healthy will be growing, it will be trying to find the things that it can do best and it will make sure that this best is in the service of others.

In our saner moments we know that evil lurks around the corner in us all. It is so easy to rationalize our actions and to believe that *we* are righteous, that the other fellow is evil. Each society tends to think it is good. Communism believes it is the most perfect society in the world. Capitalism believes it will last forever, it is so desirable. Those who are in power in either system, or who are the beneficiaries of a system, usually exalt it. This means that all mankind tends to succumb to the pressures of its own environment. How often one national group demands for itself conditions which it does not dream of granting to ignorant natives in the colony which it rules. All this goes to prove the truth of the inscription on the Supreme Court of Nebraska: "The eye and the ear are poor witnesses when the heart is barbarous." We would never dream that we have any element of barbarism in *us,* but Asians view us differently. The head of the Indian Delegation to the United Nations declared that headhunters were moral in contrast to the West: they merely take one head at a time, whereas we drop bombs slaughtering thousands in a single explosion!

In our hearts we know that truth alone triumphs. Prejudice kills. Let us try desperately to overcome dangerous rationalizations about ourselves.

We should be able to come to the realization that we are all infected with selfish rationalizations which are in large part spurious. Perhaps it will be easier for us to see the weakness in some of our mental processes if we consider for a moment the justifications which are sometimes given in the extreme South for racial discrimination against the Negro today. What are the real causes? What are the purported reasons?

First, it is said by some that the Negro is inferior biologically and cannot be changed since his characteristics are inherent in his germ plasm. Any one who considers notable Negro leaders such as Booker T. Washington, George Washington Carver, President Charles S. Johnson, and others, knows that this is an absurd theory.

Second, closely akin to this is the conviction of many whites, who are grossly ignorant about the Negro, that at any rate the Negro is an animal-like creature in his appetites and passions, far below the white master race and destined to remain so.

Third, in Alabama one of the political leaders said: "How can we possibly permit the Negroes to vote in this area? They are in the overwhelming majority. If we gave them equal rights they would take over political power." In other words, this leader believed in negating democracy rather than have the Negro rule.

Fourth, there is often a subtle financial advantage in racial discrimination. For instance, if you have a segregated small Negro district you can charge exorbitant rents for slum dwellings. It is nice also not to have competition from Negro department store owners or Negro restaurants.

Actually the costs of this evil in us, resulting in racial discrimination and prejudice, are enormous, although we may not realize it. What are these costs?

1. There is failure to use the full productivity and resources of the human factor in society. Many Negro college graduates must take inferior jobs when they could be contributing far more to the common good.

2. In many southern cities communicable diseases are spread far and wide because the Negro is kept in such dire conditions, with such limited medical aid that he comes down with various infections. These are then spread to the dominant white group and the cost to all is incalculable.

3. Oftentimes there is a willingness to tolerate evil conditions in a community as long as they apply primarily to the Negro group. For example, in Nashville, Tenn., as we have noted, there is the appalling smog which settles on the city in certain periods of the year. This is partly caused by selling low grade soft coal in the Negro slum areas. In these districts everything in a house has to be cleaned twice as often. The wealthy white group partly avoids this evil by living in other, restricted sections of the city. In St. Louis, where the use of this coal has been prohibited, all the leading eye, ear, nose and throat specialists testified that the change had reduced respiratory disease. But racial prejudice makes it easy to continue these evils.

4. The waste or duplication because of racial prejudice is unbelievable. In a Southern city still practising discrimination, the schools have to be duplicated for both white and black; there have to be separate Y.M.C.A.'s and Y.W.C.A.'s, separate churches, separate golf clubs. How long this will continue after the Supreme Court decision, remains to be seen. In Memphis, Tenn., only white taxi-cabs can carry white passengers, and only Negroe taxis can carry Negroes. The result is that if a

white woman and a Negro woman wish to take the same cab to the same destination they have to hire two separate vehicles. To all this must be added the cost of organizations peddling hate, such as the Ku Klux Klans and others attempting to perpetuate the status quo.

5. Racial prejudice creates barriers to communication. Negroes cannot attend white lectures, and whites hesitate to go to a Negro lecture. Discrimination creates psychological and personality diseases in the white personality just as it may do in the Negro.

6. Racial prejudice may cause groups to take wrong attitudes towards other measures, such as compulsory medical insurance or adequate medical aid for Negroes.

7. Racial prejudice may harm the trade union movement. For example, the Railroad Brotherhoods debar Negroes and so do eleven other A.F. of L. unions, not to mention some independent unions.

8. It creates fear and anxiety complexes in both groups too self-evident to need comment. In some areas a Negro who fears that he has come under the displeasure of some "unscrupulous" white person may flee the country.

9. Perhaps a more cogent argument than any other so far advanced is the moral effects of race prejudice. It creates a gap between creed and deed in the whole moral area. If we can ignore the Golden Rule here, we tend to do so elsewhere and our moral character becomes flabby. Oftentimes this racial prejudice brings disrespect for law and willingness to settle matters by violence. Even in the Chicago area houses have been blown up because some one did not wish a Negro to move into a neighborhood although he had a perfect right to do so.

10. Finally, the cost in hostility to the United States around the world is so colossal that it cannot be computed. It has probably cost the United States incalculable good-will, which in effect is worth far more than any monetary gain. Fully two-thirds of the people of the world today are members of races which are discriminated against on account of their color. They do not forget that the United States is one of the historic examples of this racial prejudice. This one defect in America has probably won the Communists more support than perhaps all the others combined. Not only that, but many Negroes feel like leaving the United States altogether on this account. Here, for instance, is a

letter from a Negro printed in the *Louisville Defender* in Kentucky, which is one example out of many which might be cited:

> I am leaving America because of segregation and monopolistic boxing. Since the time of my birth, in the state of Mississippi, I have been running to escape being segregated. Since the time my ancestors came here from Europe and Africa, the United States has segregated and mistreated my mother's people. As far as I can see the Negroes of America have never done any harm to the United States or any other country in the world.
>
> Being of five different nationalities, I can see the stupidity of segregation in the first place. While serving in the United States Marines in the service of Uncle Sam, I was discriminated against many times because of my race and I feel that I am an American and should be treated as such and given the same privileges as other citizens regardless of race, color or creed. As a parable, when you bring some one to your house you are to treat them with courtesy. . . . I say that the United States committed an international crime when they first made slaves of the Africans that they brought to America which has resulted in the present segregation situation.
>
> According to the Constitution of the United States each person born in America or naturalized is to receive the same inalienable rights.
>
> My great-grand uncle who was the former Governor of the state of Mississippi whose name was Anselm Joseph McLaurin was a leader of the people of Mississippi. If you will check the records, you will find that he was fair to all people and was kind; a great humanitarian. I feel that if he were alive today he would be proud of my decision when I say that the President of the United States should have Congress pass a law abolishing segregation entirely throughout the United States of America, placing America in the grace of the other freedom loving countries of the world.
>
> As it stands today, the United States and South Africa are the only two countries in the entire universe that have segregation. I will leave America July 2 and I will not return until segregation is completely abolished.
>
> Augustus C. Allen[1]

It is easy for those of us who pride ourselves on not practising racial discrimination to condemn others, but we in our turn are undoubtedly practising other forms of prejudice, self-interest, or callous disregard of the common good.

[1] Louisville *Defender*, July 1, 1954.

In the North, while prejudice against the Negro is not always so pronounced, we do have prejudice against Jews and discrimination of a serious nature against them.

In many parts of Asia the United States is condemned because it does not oppose Fascism. Here, for instance, is a lead article in *The Hindu Weekly Review* by T. B. Cunha:

> Every time I glance over the pages of the *American Reporter* and the hand-outs of the USIS and hear the voice of America hotgospelling over "democratic freedom" and condemning the dark acts of Communists, my thoughts take me to Portugal. . . .
>
> The American nation and people and their government trumpeting so loudly their "Free World," "mission of democracy," and righteously condemning "political slavery" of the Communists and "Iron Curtain" countries are actually supporting a regime in Portugal which is definitely worse than the one they are describing in their cold-war propaganda.[2]

Nearly all our military leaders have declared that Russia does not want a new world war. Robert R. Young, Chairman of the Board of the Allegheny Corporation, Chairman of the Chesapeake and Ohio Railroad, said in 1947 that Russia would "sincerely welcome preservation of the *status quo* long enough to arrange a sound solution in Europe, if our politicians will only stop edging up to [their] Mexico with their hands at their hips." Perhaps after all our military actions have repercussions.

We should always remember that anything new and different may be considered dangerous and "seditious." Susan B. Anthony, a century ago, dedicated herself to the cause of equal rights for women. For most of her life she worked for equal suffrage. For some forty years she appeared annually before Congressional committees pleading for genuine democracy, for the vote to be given to women. She wrote many articles and carried on a voluminous correspondence without a typewriter or secretary until almost the end of her life.

Today everyone acknowledges that her cause was righteous, that it was in the interests of true democracy and justice. Yet year after year Susan B. Anthony was subjected to the vilest abuse and called a traitor to her country. Here is what a Seattle editor said in 1871, "She is a

---

[2] T. B. Cunha in *The Hindu Weekly Review*, July 12, 1954, p. 10.

revolutionist, aiming at nothing less than the breaking up of the very foundation of society, and the overthrow of every social institution organized for the protection of the sanctity of the altar, the family circle and the legitimacy of our off-spring. . . . The whole plan is coarse, sensual and agrarian, the worst phase of French infidelity and communism."

Actually Susan B. Anthony was a Quaker and a devout follower of God who was one of the most patriotic and noble citizens of our Republic. Belatedly Americans see this. Yet how often today we, too, fall victims to prejudice. We, too, may use the same vile epithets at an Owen Lattimore who is truly patriotic and who is being tried and vilified because he dared to stand for international understanding even against some of the current shibboleths of our time.

The late J. Henry Carpenter, executive secretary of the Brooklyn Church and Mission Federation, one of our most consecrated Christians, was for a long time denied his passport to go abroad by the State Department.

These two examples are illustrative of the strange quirks in our mental processes. We rationalize that *our* way, *our* belief, is "patriotic" and the dissenter is un-American. Here again the criminal in us is exposed to view.

Many Americans are also highly prejudiced in favor of big business and capitalism. Murray D. Lincoln, the great cooperative leader in Ohio, not long ago proposed that the iron and steel industry of the Ruhr be run cooperatively for the benefit of the people. One of the key business leaders in the Administration, in a conference at the White House, then asked Mr. Lincoln if he were not a Christian. When Mr. Lincoln replied that he tried to be, the business leader retorted, "Then how can you propose doing away with the profit motive?" Incredible though it seems, Lincoln's Christian proposal making for peace was the one thing this business man labeled as "un-Christian." Selfish interest so often warps our viewpoint.

There is a criminal in each one of us. What are our unconscious prejudices? Where is the devil in us? Each of us must examine his own mind and heart. Perhaps, instead of getting angry at criticisms of ourselves or of America, we should welcome them. Perhaps, as Mrs. Roosevelt says, even criticisms by the Communists in the U.N. may be helpful in challenging us to overcome our own shortcomings.

In our American climate the press, the radio, television all too often play on our prejudices and accentuate them. If we all say that gray is black we do not realize that we are falsifying. Can we not determine to try to get *both sides* of every question involving other individuals, other groups, and other nations? When some one slanders us *we know* it is unfair. Why not then recognize that we should try to hear the positive side of the individual and nation that is being defamed? In America we hear so much of the better side of the United States that there is little danger, unless we belong to a minority race, that we will overlook the good side. But when it comes to Russia or the countries behind the Iron Curtain there is every danger that we will get an unbalanced view.

If we could only reverence the other personality, even the other nation, it would go far toward ending exploitation and oppression. Self-centeredness, class-centeredness, nation-centeredness, the feeling that *our* cultural pattern is the only right cultural pattern, all lead to exploitation by denying the sacredness of personality beyond our own circle.

If we would make America still better, if we would improve ourselves, then we must be alert to recognize our own weaknesses. We must not be quite so ready to adopt the "devil" theory about other groups and other nations. Instead we will accept the spirit, the teaching, and the practice of Jesus, who tried not only to love his neighbor but to love his enemy. If we followed His way of life what a difference it would make in international and domestic affairs!

> Is true freedom but to break
> Fetters for our own dear sake,
> And, with leathern hearts, forget
> That we owe mankind a debt?
> No! true freedom is to share
> All the chains our brothers wear,
> And, with heart and hand, to be
> Earnest to make others free!
>
> They are slaves who fear to speak
> For the fallen and the weak;
> They are slaves who will not choose

Hatred, scoffing, and abuse,
Rather than in silence shrink
From the truth they needs must think.
They are slaves who dare not be
In the right with two or three.

JAMES RUSSELL LOWELL

Prayer

O God, whose light shines into our hearts constantly whether or not we receive it, help us to throw open the curtains of our minds and hearts and let the full power of Thy healing rays enter into every nook and cranny.

In days of discouragement help us to turn to Thee with a certainty that we can always find Thy light and even in the darkest days Thy peace.

Deliver us from shallow thinking and from taking the wrong pathways to which we are peculiarly tempted when things go wrong.

May we cultivate the habit of daily listening to Thy voice, so that no matter what happens we may feel that Thy arms enfold and guard us and Thy light ever leads us on. Thus when opportunity beckons, help us to choose the pathway of service and sacrifice for Thee and for the people rather than for our own selfish pursuits. Grant us faith and courage and perseverance against the iniquities of our time.

All that we ask for ourselves we ask for every people around the world, even those who may consider us enemies but whom we in our highest moments recognize as those we too would love.   Amen.

If we work upon marble, it will perish.
If we work on brass, time will efface it.
If we rear temples, they will crumple to dust.
But if we work upon men's immortal minds,
If we imbue them with high principles,
With the just fear of God and love of their fellow men,
We engrave on those tablets something which no time can efface,
And which will brighten and brighten all eternity.
DANIEL WEBSTER, 1852.

The workers of the world are pushing up their heads out of the morass of poverty and ignorance which has engulfed them for so long, asking those who have occupied the seats of power and learning "What are you doing up there? Is there room for us also?" It is a movement of those who have been suppressed and exploited, and on the answer given their questions will depend the future influence of the church. Will the church give them a hand and help to pull them up, or will it pass them by or even support active measures to keep them down?

ERNEST H. BARKER, Secretary of the
Australian Labor Party.

We must give the laborers a life-pattern and purposiveness in life and push the lives of men farther up to the place of holiness and completion, abiding in eternity and departing from the phantom bubbles of life. The message of the church is there. Organize individuals in holier beings, into mutual aid, into social units, and into the life of mutual service and sacrifice, and so bring all those who are handicapped to a state of completion, a friendly brotherhood of all.

TOYOHIKO KAGAWA of Japan.

The purpose of the labor movement at its best, is to secure fullness of life, the opportunity of a complete development of manhood and womanhood for those who labor. It seeks to furnish a better world for people to live in . . . The labor movement can help the Church by bringing us into touch with activities, and increasing our discontent with pious aspiration, and assuredly the Church can help the labor movement by pointing the way to that spiritual power which can alone bring the law of righteousness and love into permanent action.

THE LAMBETH CONFERENCE OF BISHOPS OF THE
ANGLICAN COMMUNION, London, 1930.

Men were made to love one another, and to live as members of a community that transcends all barriers of race or nation or class. All economic institutions and practises that tend to divide men because they enhance false pride, covetousness, and bitterness, or encourage laziness or the selfish use of power, stand under Christian moral judgment. The Church should seek to influence the development of economic life.

THE GENERAL BOARD OF THE NATIONAL COUNCIL
OF THE CHURCHES, Sept. 15, 1954.

CHAPTER XIX

Through Organized Labor

In the United States the year 1955 saw the reuniting of the two great labor bodies the C.I.O. and the A.F.L. into one great organization of over fifteen million members. At the same time religious forces have been gradually solidifying their ranks through World Councils, National Councils and Federations.

Organized labor and organized religion should work together. At their best both are working for the same objectives. Labor leaders have frequently lived unselfish lives of service for the common good just as ministers have done. Both would be more effective if they joined forces wherever possible.

To change society we must make use of organized groups. One of the strongest in modern society is that of union labor. Most of the workers in coal, steel, automobiles, transport and other key industries are organized. Unions have become a powerful force in American life. Roughly one third of all workers are unionized and, in manufacturing, about sixty-five per cent.

Why do workers join these organizations? Primarily in order to better their conditions of work but this is not the only reason. Here they also find an outlet for self-expression, creativity and freedom of action. Here they get satisfaction from group activities which provide a feeling of adequacy, of community significance, of power, of solidarity, of welfare and service.[1]

Labor in America has not tried, to any considerable extent, to go into independent political action, rather it has tended to accommodate itself,

[1] Clinton S. Golden and Harold J. Ruttenberg, *The Dynamics of Industrial Democracy.*

as the Church has, to the existing two party system. Primarily labor leaders have sought for recognition of the union, higher wages, shorter hours, and better working conditions. In the history of their rise they have had to fight monopolistic industry, violence, prejudice, the opposition of the courts, injunctions and the indifference of the public including, too often, the churches.

In the early days the churches because of their middle class make-up and other reasons were hostile to trade unions. *The Advance,* the organ of the Congregational churches, at first opposed trade unions and in the Seventies even attacked the eight hour day as dishonest. This periodical felt it would be a waste of capital for men to work so little.

Alonzo Potter, Episcopal Bishop in Pennsylvania in 1840 opposed trade unions strongly. He said they inflamed the passions and poisoned the principles of labor.[2] T. DeWitt Talmage, the evangelist, in 1877 had this to say about the unions who were responsible for the railway strike, "For hundreds of miles along the track leading from the great West I saw stretched out and coiled up the great reptile which, after crushing the free locomotive of passenger and trade, would have twisted itself around our Republican institutions, and left them in strangulation and blood along the pathway of nations."[3] Gradually the attitude of religious leaders changed.

By 1908 the churches had accepted the Social Creed of the Churches which endorses, "The right of employees and employers alike to organize for collective bargaining and social action." The Catholic Church has also come out for trade unionism. In *The Christian Social Manifesto* approved by Pope Pius XI it says, "Without the unions the misery of the masses would be indescribable . . . Collective bargaining, under existing circumstances is not merely a right, but an absolute necessity . . . Destruction of labor unionism would be paramount to the destruction of democracy and liberty."

As we have noted, labor has not accomplished its task of organization in the United States for over half of all manual workers, and five-sixths of all employees remain unorganized. Too often labor organizations, themselves, have been willing to let some of the unorganized "stew in their own juice." Frequently union labor has not been too con-

[2] Alonzo Potter, *Political Economy,* p. 299.
[3] *Autobiography,* p. 84.

siderate of the consumer. They have been willing to have the wages of their members increased even if that meant an increase in the price of the product to the people. In the steel strike of 1949 when the companies granted pensions to the workers, it meant the price of steel was boosted four per cent, more than was necessary to cover the added cost, but the unions did not protest. Sometimes unions are too autocratic. Elections have been known to be stolen and conventions are not always held as frequently as necessary to maintain democracy. The irresponsibilities of unions even occasionally include social discrimination, but all of these evils are the exception rather than the rule. As Joel Seidman says, "Though in particular unions democracy may be seriously limited, moreover, [sic] it would be rare to find one in which the members, as a practical matter, have so little control over officers and policies as do the stockholders in many of our leading corporations."[4]

Labor has steadily increased its wages through collective bargaining but they have failed to reform the economic order. In most of the recent battles with the forces championing Big Business they have lost. The Taft-Hartley Law has not been abolished or amended.

Indeed the C. I. O. declared that President Eisenhower's proposals for amending the Taft-Hartley Act would even make it worse than before.[5] Labor has thus far made a serious beginning in securing the year-round wage, they lost the battle on price controls and have not yet attained the political rights of British labor.

These failures are partially due to the fact that labor has not had the united backing of church and synagogue. Often unions have fought each other rather than presenting a solid front to the monopolies.

Here then is a great opportunity for the church to help the labor unions to take a more far reaching and prophetic stand against the evils of our time. But church leaders can never do this unless they themselves are willing to speak out as did the prophets of old.

What are some of the principles which we should all recognize in a free society dedicated to liberty? They include in the labor area the following rights among others:

[4] Joel Seidman, *Union Rights and Union Duties*, p. 16.
[5] Congress of Industrial Organizations, *Worse than Taft-Hartley*, 1954.

1. The right to strike,—without which no society is free.
2. The free right of workers to join unions of their own choosing.
3. If the majority of the workers do join a union, the employer should be required to bargain collectively with that union as to wages, hours and working conditions.
4. In this collective bargaining the employer and the union should be left free to work out their own terms of agreement.

The C. I. O. Postwar Planning Committee declared labor's objectives to be:

1. "a job at decent wages, or a farm or business that pays;
2. "a well built, convenient home, decently furnished;
3. "good food, clothing, and medical care;
4. "good schooling for children with an equal chance for healthy, and happy growth;
5. "an adequate income through social insurance in case of sickness, old age, early death of the wage-earner or unemployment—not just for the worker, but for all people."

Labor unions have usually supported proposals which are in the interests of the public welfare, such as the consumers' cooperative movement. They favored the Federal Children's Bureau and the abolition of child labor. They strongly endorsed the Social Security Act with all its protection for maternal and child welfare. Community Chests and Councils are strongly supported by organized labor.

To show the extent to which unions are serving the public consider the fact that the C.I.O. is actually represented on over seven thousand community-service programs. Of course they supported FEPC legislation. All of organized labor has consistently favored price control to protect the public from sky-rocketing prices. How different this record is from that of many employers!

After World War II the National Association of Manufacturers wanted to abolish price controls. They printed large advertisements which said among other things, "If the O.P.A. (Office of Price Administration) is promptly discontinued, the production of goods will mount rapidly and, through free competition, prices will quickly adjust themselves to levels consumers are willing to pay . . . Prices will be fair and reasonable for all . . ."

Time has proved that these advertisements were fallacious and prices have advanced to the highest point in the history of the United States. In fact within one year after controls were abandoned prices rose 28% while output only went up 9%. Naturally the increase in the cost of living affected labor seriously.

Labor leaders often have many of the characteristics of the great preachers in standing for justice and serving the people. The late William Green, President of the American Federation of Labor, was a lay preacher who rose through the ranks of the United Mine Workers striving to do what he could for the workers throughout his life. He lived to see the abolition of the twelve-hour day and the seven-day week in steel, and the emancipation of labor.

Walter Reuther, President of the C.I.O. has had a colorful career. He was a shop foreman in a Detroit automobile plant who was discharged because of his union activities. From 1932 to 1935 he toured Europe including Russia working in industries and plants. On his return he became director of the General Motors Department of the United Automobile Workers of America, and helped to direct the sitdown strikes there. In 1942 he became Vice President of the U.A.W. and was elected President in 1946. In April 1948 he was severely wounded by an unidentified assailant and largely lost the use of one arm. In 1949 an unsuccessful attempt was made to dynamite his office at the U.A.W. Finally, Walter Reuther has emerged as President of the C.I.O. He is one of the labor leaders who has taken a constructive stand for an International T.V.A. and who has opposed the curbing of freedom of speech in the schools and colleges of America. In other words he has not simply tried to benefit his own workers but has endeavored to support a far-seeing policy for the betterment of all mankind. Ministers might be helped if they came to know him and studied what he has written. Every religious leader should ask himself, "Have I as effectively championed justice for the masses and sacrificed for the cause?"

The late Sidney Hillman is another leader whose life is an inspiring challenge. He was born in Zagare, a village in Lithuania, in 1887. He went into a "Yeshiva" or synagogue where the rabbi prepared his pupils for a rabbinical career. Only the Jewish scriptures or Talmud was taught. Some might call it a sort of Jewish Theological Seminary. When Hillman insisted on studying Russian and associating himself with the Socialist movement which was, under the Tsarist government a dangerous adventure, his father threatened to deprive him of the six roubles a month ($3.00) he sent him for maintenance. The result was Hillman left the Synagogue and went on his own. He became involved in revolutionary activities and was arrested. Then at the age of 17 he was first taken into custody for leading a band of workmen down the main street. In prison he was beaten into unconsciousness by the Tsar's police. Later when the reaction of 1906 threatened his very life he obtained a false passport and went to England. Thus in a sense it might be said that the revolutionary movement in Russia contributed Hillman to the workers of the United States. His first job in Chicago was at six dollars a week in a warehouse. Later he worked for Sears, Roebuck where 7,000 girls were toiling 70 hours a week at a low wage. Although he was a good worker he was fired when there was a slump in business in 1909. He promptly got a job at Hart, Schaffner and Marx where after a year of hard work he was getting a salary of $8 a week. But all these experiences had moulded his life work. He decided to go into the labor movement and improve conditions for all the workers.

In 1910 there was a garment strike in Chicago. Sidney Hillman became one of its leaders, and after the strike ended was employed by the union. Through successive steps he became chief clerk of the Cloak Makers Union in New York, and then President of the newly founded Amalgamated Clothing Workers of America. At the start he actually had to borrow money for an office. Today his union has total resources of a quarter of a billion dollars. It was not an easy post, since the union was in opposition to and independent of the powerful American Federation of Labor. Still he decided to sacrifice all for the cause. The union was embroiled in violent strikes before the ink was dry on the Constitution. Long afterwards in a testimonial to the workers of that period he said the struggle was so violent against the forces of special privilege and corruption that "In every city our dead are buried and I bow to them." Many workers had to pay the supreme sacrifice to get decent and equitable conditions of labor but gradually this struggle was fought and won. Eventually he led four hundred thousand workers who had obtained a good standard of living and social benefits of great significance.

Also, under Hillman's leadership not only was the clothing industry organized about ninety-five per cent but he was the architect of the collective bargaining machinery prevailing there. He is to be credited with the phenomenon that for over three decades there have been no major strikes in an industry where strikes were taking place at least twice a year, and some of them were disastrous, not only to the workers but to the employers as well.

As time went on when Hillman negotiated with an employer who was losing money he would even lower the wages of the workers and often would loan money to a company which was in financial difficulties when the banks refused to extend their credit. In one such case Hillman said, "Let's continue to have faith and confidence and trust in each other. Let us continue to build up a spirit of good will. Let us all pull together in a spirit of sincere cooperation."

Besides all this, Sidney Hillman pioneered in starting many new union practises such as cooperative housing and banking. He headed the Political Action Committee of the C.I.O. and was a valued friend of President Franklin Delano Roosevelt. He was founder and Chairman of the American Labor Party and in 1945 helped to create the World Federation of Trade Unions.

At the last Convention of the Amalgamated Clothing Workers of America before his death in 1946 he spoke these prophetic words:

"It is within the power of America to provide for our people conditions beyond the dreams of generations past.

"Not only do we have a tremendous productivity, but now is the time when we can open the door to the atomic age.

"This earth can be made a place where men and women can walk together in peace and friendship and enjoy all that this world can provide for: but we must see to it that the power of government is placed at the service of the people instead of in the control of the privileged few, selfish, greedy people who do not accept the right of the common man and do not understand what democracy means . . . Our program is not a class program. Ours is not a selfish program. Ours is a program for all America.

"We want a better America . . . an America that will carry on its great mission of helping other countries to help themselves, thinking not in terms of exploitation, but of creating plenty abroad so we can all enjoy it here."

In effect was not Sidney Hillman carrying on the work of the Lord just as truly as though he had become a Rabbi?

With great leaders like this the religious forces of the nation should be linked in partnership and mutual support.

Many other labor leaders might be mentioned. David Dubinsky is another who was given to America by the Tsar's autocracy. He was born in 1892 in Poland and early became involved in the trade union movement. Arrested several times he was exiled to Siberia and finally escaped to the United States. Today he is President of the the International Ladies Garment Workers Union. Walter Reuther in paying tribute to him made this comment, "Men of stature, regardless of the level of society from which they spring, are marked by one common and enduring characteristic: They are essentially selfless souls, driven more by an undying inner urge to help humanity forward to a happier future than by the narrower impulse of personal ambition. I am proud of this opportunity to say that my long-time friend, David Dubinsky, fits honorably in this distinguished category."[6]

Is it not clear from all this that the noblest labor leaders are working in the interests of bettering the conditions of the down-trodden and the exploited? For this reason, to the extent they are genuinely unselfish, they are carrying on the traditions of the prophets and other great religious leaders.

Because of all this we believe that Church and Synagogue should know the labor leaders, that they should help them in their struggles for every righteous cause. Labor and religion should march together towards the building of a new and better order in the world. Without this cooperation both will be handicapped.

All over the world the organized labor movement has helped to improve the conditions of labor. It has reduced exploitation. In England it has formed a mighty labor party which has several times taken over the government and ruled the country. No one disputes the fact of the

---

[6] *David Dubinsky, A Pictorial Biography*, 1951, p. 11.

human weaknesses of organized labor. Their leaders like to remain in power just the same as politicians and capitalists do. Nevertheless, in the main, trade unions do stand as a bulwark against exploitation. Church and Synagogue need to be aligned with the forces of labor wherever they are working for justice. Every community should have a fellowship representing organized labor and religion, which meets regularly. Unless your community has such a fellowship you should take action to see that one is formed.[7]

[7] The National Religion and Labor Foundation, 3392 N. High St., Columbus, Ohio will give concrete suggestions about starting such a fellowship.

Prayer

O God, master workman and creator of the Universe, we thank Thee for the life of Jesus, the carpenter, who was ever sympathetic to those who toil. We thank thee for those inspired souls who have suffered and persevered for the common people and for Thee, even when the trials and tribulations they faced threatened life itself; for the record of men and women through the centuries who have improved the lot of those who labor for their daily bread. We thank Thee for Moses and the prophets,—that Moses led the children of Israel out of the land of Pharaoh albeit on a strike.

We thank Thee for the inspiration which thus came to us out of the past. We sense Thy hand in the labor movement which has gradually cast off the shackles of slavery, serfdom, the twelve hour day and the seven day week. Help us too to catch the contagion and the kindling light from contemporary lives like William Green, Sidney Hillman, Albert Schweitzer and Kagawa of Japan. May we appreciate the great gifts that come to us from others, and for the life all about us. Above all we thank Thee for the example of Jesus who faced the hard, dark realities of life and yet met every difficulty and so became our leader and guide. Grant that we too may turn aside to everyone in need and so be true servants of Thine.

If the chance ever comes our way, help us to better the lot of the laboring masses even if this involves sacrifice on our part. Guard us from misunderstanding and ignorance of our fellows. Help us to free ourselves from selfishness, indifference, pride—and may we hear the voice of conscience and seek to follow Thee daily in our community life even if it costs time and reputation. Grant us today and every day a strong up-welling inner sense of Thy presence.   Amen.

Blaming the other fellow is sterile diplomacy; it is much more important to make a new start.

TOM DRIBERG, British M.P.

There never was a war that was not inward; I must fight till I have conquered in myself what causes war. . . .

MARIANNE MOORE, in *Distrust of Merit*.

International affairs is a field in which the pursuit of knowledge without understanding is peculiarly pointless and useless.

FORMER AMBASSADOR GEORGE F. KENNAN to the Alumni of Princeton University, Feb. 1953.

The honour of a country depends much more on removing its faults than boasting of its qualities.

MAZZINI.

CHAPTER XX

The Democratic Process in the Family of Nations

If we were intelligent we would recognize that the democratic process is well illustrated in the human body. Every part is tuned for the welfare of the whole. No one member gets a monopoly of development at the expense of the rest. In a well balanced body all parts are properly proportioned. It is true that the individual can dissipate his strength by catering to the lusts of the flesh. He can eat more than is good for him, for example. When he does this all the members suffer. But blood is furnished to every part of the body. The blood does not dictate to the eye and say "thou must function thus." Neither does it dictate to the foot and say "thou shalt not have a toe nail," for instance. Each is given its share in the common pool and in the by and large, responds by using it for the common good.

The same should be true of the family of nations in the one world organism. No part should dictate to another, giving commands such as "thou shalt become Communist," or, alternatively, "thou shalt not nationalize all the basic means of production and distribution." We can try to help another nation to produce more or to become more literate or to have more democracy, but never by using methods of mass murder such as bombs. This is self-defeating. It injures the entire world society.

In nature we find all forms and varieties of social organization—from the eagle, supremely independent and carnivorous, to the ant, which has a communistic way of life. In human society, in the long run, an organization which is ineffective will lag behind and be displaced, but every form of organization must be given its chance to prove its worth; and we can have faith that if it becomes too rotten it will in the end be displaced. This is not to say that we should not help the people of a foreign land to help themselves, but it is doubtful if military invasion from without is the answer.

If we are really to build a democratic world, it means that each nation must make sure that it practises liberty and freedom within, and, secondly, that the international organization representing all the nations is truly democratic. Are delegates elected, for instance? We might as well face it: every nation has shortcomings in its democracy. In the United States we debar Negroes in some states from voting, and in others we make it almost impossible for them to be elected to office. We have not entirely curbed the role of great wealth or boss rule. Perhaps even more vital to a free society is that every country should, in all its dealings with other nations, support democratic processes and never help to crush the will of other peoples.

In many ways the United States has a good record, but it is far from perfect. Claude G. Bowers, U.S. Ambassador to Spain, who was present throughout the overthrow of the democratic nationalist government of Spain and the seizure of power by Franco with the aid of Germany and Italy, states that the United States aided in this overthrow of democracy there. He asserts that both Secretary of State Hull and President Roosevelt recognized that they had made a terrible mistake. His report of what happened is as follows:

1. "That after the first days of considerable confusion it was plainly shown to be a war of the Fascists and the Axis powers against the democratic institutions of Spain.

2. "That the Spanish war was the beginning of a perfectly thought-out plan for the extermination of democracy in Europe and the beginning of a Second World War with that as the intent.

3. "That the Nonintervention Committee was a shameless sham, cynically dishonest, in that Germany and Italy were constantly sending soldiers, planes, tanks, artillery, and ammunition into Spain without interference or real protest from the signatories of the pact.

4. "That Germany and Italy were using Spanish towns and people for experimental purposes in trying out their new methods of destruction and their new techniques of terrorism. . . .

8. "That the attacks, ridicule, and insults aimed at the United States

and England by the Franco press left no possible doubt as to its position.

9. "That while the Axis powers poured in armies, planes, tanks, artillery, technicians, and engineers for Franco, the Nonintervention Committee of the European democracies and our own embargo were making a powerful contribution to the triumph of the Axis over democracy in Spain; that whereas the war on China was being waged by the Japs alone, on Czechoslovakia by Nazi Germany alone, on Abyssinia by Fascist Italy alone, the first country to be attacked *by the Axis —Germany and Italy together—was Spain*."[1]

We normally think that the West stands for democracy and that it is Russia, Asia, and Communist satellites who have defied it. But Arnold Toynbee, perhaps the greatest living historian, has shown that in the last five hundred years, on the whole it has been the West that has been guilty of aggression. In the thirteenth century the West seized the western fringes of the Russian world. Toynbee says: "It was not till 1945 that Russia recaptured the last piece of these huge Russian territories that were taken from her by Western Powers in the thirteenth and fourteenth centuries."[2] Furthermore, Russia was being attacked by the West over a long period. The Poles attacked in 1610, the French in 1812, the Germans in 1941, and combined token forces of the West, including the United States, in 1919. In historical perspective Toynbee maintains that "the Russians have had the same reason for looking askance at the West that we Westerners feel that we have for looking askance at Russia today."

It must not be forgotten, too, that if we condemn Communism we must reflect that "this is a weapon of Western origin." Karl Marx and Friedrich Engels were brought up in Germany but lived most of their lives in England. Russia, in using what Toynbee calls "spiritual warfare," is availing itself of a Western creed. Toynbee says that Marx's Communism was "a Western criticism of the West's failure to live up to her own Christian principles in the economic and social life of this professedly Christian society."

Now if we are really to practice democracy in the family of nations we must permit each group to have the kind of government, the kind of

---

[1] Claude G. Bowers, *My Mission to Spain*, pp. 411, 412.
[2] Toynbee, Arnold J., *The World and the West*, p. 5.

social ideology which it feels is fitted to its needs. We may believe rightly that Communism is a spurious panacea for the ills of humanity, but if the majority of any nation desire it they have the right to accept it. If England, for instance, permits the Communist Party to function along with other parties, that is her right.

Throughout American history until recently, it has been assumed that we must protect only our own borders from military attack. Now all this has been discarded as impractical fallacy and we are supporting military bases around the globe at fabulous cost. But is this really promoting democracy? Before the first World War we had almost no debt. Now, because of our new military global policy, it is approaching such an astronomical figure that the average citizen can hardly understand— three hundred billion dollars. Taxes are so high and inflation so great that the stage may be set for economic catastrophe. Actually President Truman collected more taxes than all the other Presidents of the United States combined.

America's fault is not lack of generosity. We expended over three hundred billion dollars in waging war against the Axis powers. Following the end of World War II we have spent approximately seven billion dollars for economic and military aid to Asia and over twenty-eight billion dollars in Europe. In 1954 Congress appropriated $2,250,000,000 for Europe and $1,959,000,000 for Asia. In the Korean War the United States bore the brunt of the struggle both in money and in men. Yet in spite of all this the reservoir of good-will towards our country has sunk to the lowest point in history. There must be some fault in our behavior pattern.

One wonders if our trouble has not been that we have relied too much on military rather than moral solutions. We have been violently against Communism but we have not been *for* the revolutions through which native peoples were trying to gain their liberty. If the democratic process is to work between nations we must always be on the side of the people, not of foreign interests.

Justice William O. Douglas of the United States Supreme Court has this to say of our record.

Many times in the past a great power has had one policy at home, another abroad. England, meticulous to respect every minority at home, promoted repressive policies abroad. France, whose proudest boast was

Democratic Process in the Family of Nations 277

liberty, equality and fraternity, squandered those ideals in her colonial policy. America, proud of her standards of freedom and justice at home, temporized with her principles in Indonesia and Vietnam. We threw our weight in diplomatic circles behind the Dutch and French. . . . Our neglect in Indonesia has been compounded in Vietnam. Not one official American voice has been on the side of the Vietnamese against the French.[3]

Dr. Harry Elmer Barnes describes our policy as follows:

Fantastic political boundaries are set up carelessly and arbitrarily, but once they are established, however carelessly and lightheartedly, they take on some mysterious sanctity; to violate them 'breaks the heart of the world.' Every border war becomes a world war, and world peace disappears from the scene. By this absurd policy, internationalism and interventionism invite and insure 'perpetual war for perpetual peace,' since any move which threatens petty nations and these mystical boundaries becomes an 'aggressive war' which must not be tolerated, even tho to oppose it may break the back of the world.[4]

The former editorial writer-in-chief for the *Saturday Evening Post*, Garet Garrett, describes our aid abroad in these words:

Just set down the names of the countries that have been receiving economic and military aid from the United States, either in alphabetical order or by continents and religions. Then what do you get? Certainly nothing you can imagine to be a table of essential political ingredients for a free world. It looks more like a queue, with at least one thing in common, namely, an appetite for American dollars. What is the bond of ideas between Burma or Siam on one side of the world and Belgium or Scandinavia on the other side? It is not even anti-Communist. A great deal of it is neutral, like India, and some of it teeters on the fence, saying, "Dollars, dollars, lest we fall into the hands of the Communists."

Perhaps, after all, George Washington was right for his day when he said: "Observe good faith and justice toward all nations; cultivate peace and harmony with all."

Europe has a set of primary interests, which to us have none, or a very remote relation. Hence she must be engaged in frequent controversies,

---

[3] William O. Douglas, *North from Malaya*, p. 325.
[4] Harry Elmer Barnes, *Perpetual War for Perpetual Peace*, p. 657.

the causes of which are essentially foreign to our concerns. Hence, therefore, it must be unwise for us to implicate ourselves, by artificial ties, in the ordinary vicissitudes of her politics, or the ordinary combinations and collisions of her friendships and enmities. . . .[5]

Louis Bromfield, the author, quotes from an article by J. R. Killian, Jr., President of the Massachusetts Institute of Technology, and A. G. Hill, director of the Lincoln Laboratory, in which they list five major tasks confronting the United States today:

1. Control of the high seas.
2. Defence of the North American continent.
3. Capability to mount a devastating counterattack on the enemy's bases and homeland.
4. Our share of the defence of Western Europe.
5. Control of sudden outbreaks such as the Korean attack.

He then says:

This is the perfect blueprint for the ultimate victory of Fascism or Communism, identical in their evils. It is the scientist-materialist's, the General's conception of an efficient and sordid world. It is also the perfect blueprint for the creation of a world and a life that I would abandon with indifference if I were forced to choose. It is a blueprint of ruin not only for ourselves but for the world. And together with the entire article, is as fine an example of the cold-blooded, inhuman detachment and materialistic laboratory science as I have encountered in the whole of this materialistic age. If this is our only choice as against destruction by the atomic bomb, I will lie down now and take the bomb.

On April 30, 1954, Sir Winston Churchill, speaking to the Primrose League of the Conservative Party in England, had this to say:

We should establish with Russia links which, in spite of all distractions and perils and contradictions, will convince the Russian people and the Soviet Government that we wish them peace, happiness and ever-increasing and ever-expanding prosperity and enrichment of life in their own mighty land and that we long to see them play a proud and splendid part in the guidance of the human race.

[5] George Washington in his Farewell Address.

Difficult as this suggestion may be, if it were followed it would enormously decrease the danger of war and increase our pattern of Christian action.

What America desperately needs is a rebirth of a profound faith in the principles of the prophets and of Jesus. We must be true to the highest conscience that God has given us. This means opposing colonialism, opposing injustice, opposing landlordism, opposing Communism in *all* our foreign policy but at the same time holding out hands of friendship to all governments, in building a peaceful world.

In the light of the realities we have sketched, perhaps we should apply the parable of Jesus that "it is harder for a rich man to enter the kingdom of heaven than for a camel to go through the eye of a needle" to nations as to individuals. If so, the United States, as the richest nation in the world, needs to take sober second thought. If we rely on military might, if we rely on our great wealth and material production, instead of on moral power and righteousness, then we face catastrophe.

Some Americans say, Cease giving injections of gold to the victims of poverty and disease. They have diagnosed the world malady as a cancer virus called "Soviet Russia." They say the remedy is drastic surgery. "Blow the Soviet rulers off the map. Co-existence is impossible."

On the other hand, some eminent Americans tell us that one characteristic of our national pattern is fear. Only a decade ago we were sitting on top of a world supposed to have been made safe for democracy. What makes us afraid today? Is it not because we are strong, rich, and powerful? The Bible says that the guilty are always afraid and they flee when no man pursues. Why are we afraid? Perhaps it is because we are rich in a starving world. We are trying to perpetuate our way of life when the victims of imperialism are crying for action. The poor, the exploited, the starving, the ignorant want justice and to some extent we refuse to heed their plea. The Communists, with a false dictatorial policy, have been sweeping forward because they purport to champion the poor and to oppose colonialism. The Bible says that the penalty for not loving our enemies is eternal death. We say we cannot love Communists, but why not *try* to follow the Christianity we profess?

To Jesus, ridding ourselves of fear means sacrificing our pride and our wealth and surrendering ourselves to faith and love.

Today the world is trembling on the brink of self-annihilation. If we go into a third world war our entire civilization could largely blow up. If the present cold war with Russia continues long enough, it may seriously impair freedom even in our own country, especially if we continue a negative policy of containment. The only alternative is to accept our highest moral principles and *act on them*. This means promoting justice and freedom both within our own country and abroad. It means the building up of the cooperative movement everywhere around the globe. It means support of the United Nations and letting every nation join that great body, not simply welcoming our friends.

Many Americans do not yet comprehend that this U.N. is perhaps the greatest international organization that mankind has yet devised. It is a body representing sixty nations and over 1,800,000,000 people. It is trying to find a way to solve world problems before the human race is annihilated through the explosion of hydrogen and cobalt bombs.

The organization has not had long to function, for it came into existence on October 24, 1945. The Preamble to the Charter affirms the following purposes:

> To save our children from any new wars.
> To assert our faith in basic human rights.
> To work for social progress, higher living standards, better standards of life in larger freedom.
> To practise tolerance and live with other people in peace as good neighbors.
> To unite and to work with other peoples to build and preserve peace and security.
> To ensure that armed force shall not be used save in the common interest.
> To work with other nations to promote the social and economic advancement of all peoples.
> To create conditions in which justice and respect for treaty obligations can be maintained.

The United Nations believes that all peoples are of worth and dignity and that all men and women have equal rights. It also stresses the sovereign equality of all nations, great and small, and believes we should have world friendliness and community.

The six main organs of the United Nations are:

1. The General Assembly
2. The Security Council
3. The Economic and Social Council
4. The Trusteeship Council
5. The International Court of Justice
6. The Secretariat

1. In the General Assembly everyone can listen to any speaker in any one of five official languages of the United Nations—Chinese, English, French, Russian and Spanish. By the use of head phones and simultaneous translation this miracle is achieved. Thus the General Assembly is a general forum for the nations of the world where any topic affecting the well-being of the peoples can be debated and voted on. The main power which the Assembly has is to recommend action, but this has great moral force. If the behavior of some nations is opposed by the vote of an overwhelming number of others, it acts as a powerful censure and an expression of world public opinion. This is a power of reasoned judgment over national interests.

Three United Nations organizations deal with refugees: the Office of the United Nations High Commissioner for Refugees, the United Nations Relief and Works Agency for Palestine Refugees in the Near East, and the United Nations Korean Reconstruction Agency.

In so many areas of the world wars, revolutions and crises of all sorts have made millions flee their homes and become stateless wanderers on the face of the earth.

The United Nations High Commissioner for Refugees gives international protection to some two million people all over the world. The Commissioner administers any funds he receives, both public and private, to aid the refugees. In April 1954, there went into effect a sort of "Magna Carta for Refugees," which establishes rights for refugees which must be observed by all governments signing the treaty.

As a result of the war between the Arabs and the Jews in Palestine there are now 880,000 Arab refugees. The United Nations Relief and Works Agency gives direct relief to these people, who are increasing at the rate of about 25,000 annually. The agency has been able to conclude agreements with governments in the area which should provide an opportunity for 200,000 of these refugees to become self-supporting.

Following the war in Korea there were vast numbers of orphan or abandoned children. Starvation was rife. The United Nations Korean Reconstruction Agency is handling this problem and trying to make the people once more self-supporting.

2. In some respects the Security Council (made up of five permanent members, China, France, the Union of Soviet Socialist Republics, the United Kingdom, and the United States) is even stronger than the Assembly, for these five, together with six elected for two year terms by the General Assembly, are the guardians of peace with power to look into all disputes between nations and can recommend peaceful settlement or enforcement action. Furthermore, the Security Council remains in session throughout the year, instead of meeting annually for a limited time only. In all except procedural questions, the vote of all five permanent members is necessary, so that in effect each of these nations has a veto power. While at times this veto has been strongly condemned, it was insisted on by the United States from the beginning, and it has the merit of forcing unanimous agreement among the "Big Five" before armed force can be used between them.

Under the charter, the Security Council has the primary responsibility for maintaining international peace and security. However, by a resolution adopted by the General Assembly in 1950, if the Security Council is unable to act because of a veto while a breach of the peace or act of aggression has occurred, the Assembly can recommend to its Members that they take action to restore peace even by the use of armed force. In this connection, the General Assembly also established a Collective Measures Committee to study methods of strengthening world peace and a Peace Observation Commission which reports on any area which is likely to endanger international peace and security.

3. The Economic and Social Council tries to promote justice, freedom, and plenty around the world. It investigates economic, cultural, health, and social matters and makes recommendations about solving the problems affecting different nations. It plans and works for higher standards of living, for full employment, and for human rights and basic freedoms. It works through many agencies and secures support even from non-governmental agencies. The United Nations International Children's Emergency Fund, or UNICEF, as it came to be called was established by the General Assembly but reports to the Eco-

nomic and Social Council. It has provided supplementary meals for millions of children in war ravaged and other areas as well as clothing for them, and also medical aid. As a result of its work more than nineteen million have been protected against malaria through spraying campaigns. It has immunized nine million children against tuberculosis; it has cured 1,500,000 children of the contagious tropical disease called yaws; it gives daily nourishment to four million children through schools, clinics, and emergency relief. In addition, it has provided safe milk for two millions more by setting up milk plants. Besides all this it has equipped over five thousand mother-child centers, chiefly in rural areas, and trained nurses, midwives, and workers to run them.

The Economic and Social Council also sets up regional and functional commissions. Seven of these latter specialize on specific economic and social problems such as world statistics, human rights, narcotics, transport and communications, population and the status of women. To show the magnitude of the narcotic problem, in the case of just one drug, heroin, 298,325 pounds of this illicit drug were seized in the one year of 1953 alone.[6] The Commission on Narcotics found that Lebanon and Turkey were the principal sources of raw opium.

The Economic and Social Council also deals with such problems as forced labor and slavery, women's rights and opportunities, welfare for the aged, the handicapped, the criminal, and the delinquent; the family, youth and child welfare, population, housing, taxation, freedom of information, and narcotic drug control.

It set up the Commission which drafted the Universal Declaration of Human Rights, which Mrs. Franklin D. Roosevelt says "ought to be ringing words that go out over the world." This declaration was adopted unanimously on December 10, 1948, by the General Assembly. Its 30 articles set forth man's inalienable rights in the civil, personal, economic, social and cultural fields: the right to life, liberty, and security of person; to freedom of movement and residence; to social security; to work; to education; to a nationality; to freedom of worship; to freedom of expression and of peaceful assembly; to his right to take part in the government of his own country; to hold public office; to seek and to be granted asylum; and to own property.

[6] See Commission on Narcotic Drugs, Report on the Ninth Session, 1954, Economic and Social Council, United Nations, pp. 58–61.

The Economic and Social Council is also concerned with technical assistance for the under-developed countries. Roughly 110 under-developed countries and territories have thus far received this aid in addition to about 74 countries which have taken students from needy areas and aided them in learning advanced skills or special techniques. Although this program has been in operation only a very few years, considerable results have been achieved. For example, small foundries in West Pakistan were able to cut down the rejects of castings from fifty per cent to ten per cent. In Afghanistan a tool expert introduced new types of agricultural implements, in particular, a scythe and a hoe, which would increase productivity from 250% to 500%. In some areas new irrigation has been introduced, thus transforming dry lands into rich farming soil.[7] In many ways the Economic and Social Council is the center of the most important welfare work that is now being done around the world through the United Nations.

4. Another aspect of the work of the United Nations is that of promoting the development of so called Non-Self-Governing and Trust Territories. Members of the United Nations responsible for the administration of over 150,000,000 people who do not govern themselves have undertaken to ensure the political, economic, social, and educational advancement of these peoples. About 17,000,000 of these people live in eleven Trust Territories and their administration is supervised by the United Nations Trusteeship Council which examines in detail annual reports sent by the countries administering them. For example, the Trust Territory of the Pacific Islands is under the administration of the United States. The Trusteeship Council, in addition to examining the annual report by the United States on its administration of the Trust Territory of the Pacific Islands, examines any petitions sent in from the inhabitants and others concerning those islands. The Council also sends visiting or special Missions to Trust Territories to survey conditions on the spot.

5. The Security Council and the General Assembly jointly elect fifteen judges from a variety of nations, who together make up the International Court of Justice which is located at The Hague. The court has decided many cases, which include a dispute between the United

---

[7] For a description of U.S. technical aid see *Technical Cooperation Programs,* Foreign Operations Administration, Washington, 25, D.C.

Kingdom and Albania arising out of mine explosions in the Corfu Channel, a case by France concerning the rights of United States nationals in Morocco and a dispute between Columbia and Peru over the case of a Peruvian citizen who was given asylum by the Columbian Ambassador.

6. The final one of the six main organs of the United Nations is the Secretariat. It embraces some 4,000 workers, some of whom are internationally recruited. While in the service of the United Nations a staff member is responsible only to the Secretary-General. Their offices are in the headquarters of the United Nations, a thirty-nine story building containing 5,400 windows and costing some $67,000,000.

The Secretary-General at present is Dag Hammarskjold of Sweden, who was appointed by the General Assembly upon the recommendation of the Security Council on April 7, 1953. He is the chief administrative officer. It is his duty to report to the General Assembly annually on the entire year's work of the United Nations, and he can also bring before the Security Council any matter which he thinks might threaten the peace and security of the world. The Secretariat can move at any time with the approval of the Assembly to deal with the new world problems which science and technology are constantly forcing upon us. Here is a center which is capable of calling on experts from the entire world to make investigations, to prepare plans, and to take action to meet need anywhere on the globe.

United Nations Specialized Agencies help to achieve the common purpose of securing better living conditions for all peoples. These agencies having wide international responsibilities in economic, social, cultural, educational, health and related fields are brought into relationship with the United Nations by individual agreements. Each agency has agreed to consider any recommendation made to it by the United Nations and to report to the United Nations on the action it takes on any such recommendation. In the case of the International Bank and the International Monetary Fund, the United Nations has agreed to consult with these agencies before making any recommendations to them. Co-ordination of the work of the United Nations and the agencies is the responsibility of the Economic and Social Council to which the agencies submit annual reports. Agreements with ten specialized agencies are now in force. It is proposed to bring the Inter-Governmental Maritime

Consultative Organization (IMCO) and the International Trade Organization (ITO) into relationship when they are fully constituted and in operation. The table (on page 287) gives a brief outline of the functions of these organizations.

Obviously the United Nations is only a slight beginning of the World Government that will sometime eventuate, but think of what this organization even in its initial stages has done! Without making an exhaustive summary, here are a few out of its many achievements:

1. When Iran complained to the Security Council regarding the presence of Russian troops in Northern Iran, the Soviet Union withdrew those troops.
2. The United Nations helped Indonesia secure independence.
3. It ended a shooting war in Palestine.
4. It is now working to solve the differences between the Arabs and Israel.
5. It has helped India and Pakistan to remain at peace.
6. It approved the Universal Declaration of Human Rights.
7. When North Korean forces launched a surprise attack on the Republic of Korea on 25 June, 1950 the United Nations used collective measures to restore peace. This was the first time in history that collective military measures had been undertaken by a world organization.
8. It has been an open forum where we could learn about other nations and they about us.
9. The United Nations' health agency has helped to check the spread of disease, and especially malaria, in many countries.
10. United Nations Technical Aid has helped "under-developed" countries reduce disease and illiteracy. Important irrigation and land reclamation projects have been inaugurated. Agricultural output has been increased.

All this has been done at a cost to the United States of only about sixty-two cents a year per capita. This is actually less than the cost of one meal or three packages of cigarettes. America probably gets more value for this expenditure than for any comparable amount spent by our Federal Government. But, of course, this is far too little. In many ways the United Nations could be described as the greatest adventure the

Short Name	Full Title	Fields or Areas in Which Agency Works	No. of Members	Headquarters
ILO	International Labour Organization	Labour problems	69	Geneva
FAO	Food and Agriculture Organization of the United Nations	Food, increase its production and distribution	71	Rome
UNESCO	United Nations Educational, Scientific and Cultural Organization	Education, science and culture	72	Paris
ICAO	International Civil Aviation Organization	Civil air transport—make it safer and easier to fly from one country to another	64	Montreal
BANK	International Bank for Reconstruction and Development	Lending for progress	57	Washington, D.C.
FUND	International Monetary Fund	Keeping national currencies stable	57	Washington, D.C.
WHO	World Health Organization	Health	81 3 associates	Geneva
UPU	Universal Postal Union	Postal Services between nations	93	Berne
ITU	International Tele-communication Union	Communication by telephone, radio, and telegraph between nations	90 4 associates	Geneva
WMO	World Meteorological Organization	Weather reporting	86	Geneva
IMCO	Intergovernmental Maritime Consultative Organization	International shipping by sea	—	Soon to be set up
ITO	International Trade Organization (Interim Commission)	Trade between nations	—	Soon to be set up

world has ever undertaken. Are we mature enough and moral enough to bring it to full fruition?

Even in the United States there are those who are seeking to destroy the United Nations. If they had their way they would have us withdraw from it entirely. To one who thinks soberly and maturely, these are people who are really endangering the safety of the United States itself. For if we withdrew we would be isolated, and in an age when we are all part of one small neighborhood world, such a course might mean our eventual extinction. Rather than to withdraw, the United States should seek to strengthen the United Nations at every point. How should this be done? Here is one suggestion out of many for action in the field of education:

Physically, we have demolished distance. Radio, television, and the jet plane have made us next-door neighbors to the world. Culturally and ideologically, however, we are today still separated by chasms as wide, as deep, and as impassable as man has ever known. This is both the great tragedy and the great challenge of our time.

One way to meet this challenge, one means of bridging the ideological distances as we have bridged physical space, is to create—now—a living, working University of the United Nations.

How to go about it? The mechanics, given that degree of good-will and common purpose which has marked the successes of some of the subordinate committees and councils of the United Nations, would not be difficult.

Agree to establish the United Nations University, like the United Nations headquarters itself, as an international enclave, but in a country away from the teeming centers of world power and conflict, a country which has historically distinguished itself for tolerance and freedom of thought. Norway, Sweden, or Switzerland might offer United Nations University a home.

The University Chancellor should be a world-renowned educator elected by the General Assembly. The students, who would be guaranteed freedom of entry and freedom of movement by the host country regardless of ideological attitudes, should be selected by the individual countries themselves; a nation's quota of enrollment would be based on its population. Should any land not fill its quota, the Chancellor and faculty could complete enrollment from students of other countries.

The faculty—and here would be the challenge for the nations to offer their best minds to the University—would not be limited in number. Each nation might send as many professors, in as many fields of academic study, as it chose.

Degrees granted by such an institution would be a mark of distinction, indeed! They would be awarded after comprehensive examinations closing each academic year. Regulations for the examinations could be established by the Chancellor and elected representatives of the faculty.

How would the expenses be paid? The United Nations would pay for the physical campus, the academic buildings and the housing facilities for the faculty and students. Each nation would assume responsibility for the tuition and other expenses of its students and the salaries of the men it sent to teach at the university. Tuition should be large enough to provide the institution, ultimately, with a great World Library.

Perhaps it will be said that, in a world at cold war, such a project will be dismissed by many as visionary. Yet might it not, by opening the minds of men, by creating a real market place of ideas, be one way to eliminate the conflicts which cause war, cold or hot?

A United Nations University would offer one oasis from the arid blasts of hysterical nationalism. Its students might still be subjected to propaganda, to be sure, but they would also be exposed to opposing ideas: they would be, at last, in a position to weigh conflicting ideologies against each other and to reach their own free intellectual choice.

Such a University would not, of course, bring us to the portal of Utopia. Yet it would be a real milestone along the road of man in his never-ending search for truth and progress.

If the United States could really act on the moral principles of the Declaration of Independence and the Golden Rule, we should learn to work together even with our enemies. Jesus' entire life was a demonstration of this principle. Again and again he enjoined his followers to follow the way of love and eschew violence.

No nation in our little world can build a mental and spiritual ghetto for itself or any other group. We are all brothers one of another. We need far less of sitting in judgment on Communists or any foreign government. If we love them, change may come as a by-product.

We come again to the necessity of the United States supporting and pushing through the United Nations a giant International Development Authority, with adequate financial means at its disposal to help underdeveloped nations achieve material and social well-being. We must really believe in and practise our faith that the God of truth is mightier than propaganda; we must really believe and practise our faith in liberty and economic justice for all subject peoples. We must not support dictators merely because they are on our side of the East-West struggle. That nation which first sincerely decides to follow moral principles rather than expediency, that nation which first dedicates her resources to freeing men everywhere from fear and hate, from exploitation and war, from dictatorship and materialism, and does it all through channels of peace, will in the long run go far towards aiding us all to build a world based on the rock of moral and spiritual values.

Prayer

God of all mankind, creator of man's conscience, to Thee we lift our hearts in fervent prayer for peace and brotherhood among all peoples of every race, creed, and belief.

Help us so to work together that we can achieve truth, justice, and good-will for all mankind. May we so harmonize our wills with Thy invincible love that we can genuinely free all humanity from tyranny, from hunger, from ignorance, and from disease.

Cast out from our hearts, our minds, and our behaviour the flaming intolerance which causes devastating conflict and breeds hatred and war.

We pray that all peoples may join together in beating their swords into plowshares and their spears into pruning hooks. Guard any of the nations from so hedging about disarmament with subtle restrictions that no agreement will be reached.

Make us all realize, including the rulers of every nation, that we are all brothers one with another and that we must live in concord and friendship, practising good works towards all men, even those whom we may, in our weakness, dislike.

May Thy blessing rest on this great and noble experiment in human coöperation, the United Nations. May it grow in wisdom and in stature until in truth and in deed, under Thy guidance, a world rule of law has come to pass, thus ending the bloody conflicts of men and beginning a true and lasting peace on the earth.

Help each one of us to realize our responsibility, that Thy law of divine love shall reign here and now in our hearts and everywhere in this Thy world.   Amen.

Never to have seen the truth is better than to have seen it and not to have acted upon it.

The Choice is always ours. "Do you not seek a light, ye who are surrounded by darkness?"

THE DHAMMAPADA

I am a man of peace, I believe in peace.
But I do not want peace at any price.
I do not want the peace which you find in stone.
I do not want the peace that you find in the grave;
but I do want that peace which you find embedded in
the human breast, which is exposed to the whole world
but which is protected from all harm
by the Power of the Almighty God.

Let then our first act every morning be
to make the following resolve for the day:
I shall not fear anyone on earth.
I shall fear only God.
I shall not bear ill will toward anyone.
I shall conquer untruth by Truth.
And in resisting untruth I shall put up
with all suffering.

MAHATMA GANDHI

It makes no sense whatever for a man to exert himself in behalf of peace on earth, if the roots of his life are grounded in disdain and contempt for God's will. At this point perhaps there is no great difference between East and West.

BISHOP HANNS LILJE

As a candle only shines when the wax of which it is made is being spent, so life is only real when it is being spent for others.

LEO TOLSTOY

Evil men really never get excited until the forces of freedom, justice and love begin to win. The Church should ponder this truth, that the nearer it comes to the mind, the spirit, the redemptive purpose of Jesus, the tougher will be the opposition of self-seeking individuals and groups. Yet at whatever cost the Church must bring every phase of contemporary life into the judgment hall and bring sentence.

D. R. Sharpe in the *Rauschenbusch Lectures,* 1948.

With the monstrous weapons man already has, humanity is in danger of being trapped in this world by its moral adolescents. Our knowledge of science has clearly outstripped our capacity to control it. We have many men of science, but too few men of God. We have grasped the mystery of the atom and rejected the Sermon on the Mount. Man is stumbling blindly through a spiritual darkness while toying with the precarious secrets of life and death.

The world has achieved brilliance without wisdom, power without conscience. Ours is a world of nuclear giants and ethical infants. We know more about war than we know about peace, more about killing than we know about living. This is our twentieth century's claim to distinction and to progress.

General Omar Bradley, Chief of Staff, Boston, Nov. 10, 1948.

CHAPTER XXI

What Will You Do With Your Life?

First things first. Will you decide to surrender your life completely to the will of God? Do you agree that *all* the moments of each day will be so dedicated? Paul said, "I am bound with the chain." (Acts 28:20) Are you willing to be bound with chains of love—chains that will make our life consecrated to justice and to peace in a warlike world? Are we willing to join the small group of contemporary apostles, prophets and saints who struggle for the exploited and degraded? Are we willing to face character assassination, misunderstanding, perhaps even imprisonment for God?

Men serve in two ways, by what they do in action, and in their spiritual communion with Him. Even the person who does not recognize that God exists may be serving Him if he lives a life of dedicated service to God's children, his fellow men.

Our lives take meaning from their interlacing with other lives. If you have irrevocably decided on surrender to God then you must renew your study of the prophets and Jesus. What did they mean, what did they do? But in another epoch, in another culture it is not always easy to apply the spirit and teachings of these leaders to your own life. We need interpretation. We need demonstration of what these lives mean today.

A good touchstone is to study the lives of contemporary leaders and prophets. We are going to list a random sampling of a few which may be rewarding for study. We make no pretense that these are the best for you to turn to. They are just random samples, a few lights from a galaxy of stars. You can easily call to mind others who may be even more effective servants of the living God as guides for you. We here give these names merely as illustrations of some lives, many of whom we have been privileged to know. Take Tolstoy for instance. He urged: a return to primitive Christianity, following the inner light, loving all men regardless of class or race, never resisting evil through violence or mass murder, and the renunciation of wealth. *Following the inner light meant focusing on one's own faults first.* He once said to an American friend, "You sweat too much blood for the world; sweat some for yourself first. You cannot make the world better till you are better."

Consider Washington Gladden,—he was a great preacher, editor and the author of some thirty-two volumes. He merged the personal and social into a blended gospel. He taught that in every business real Christianity must be applied to the very last detail. In 1879 he wrote that matchless hymn,

> O Master, let me walk with Thee
> In lowly paths of service free
> Tell me Thy secret; help me bear
> The strain of toil, the fret of care.

Take Richard T. Ely who wrote *Social Aspects of Christianity;* he saw clearly that most Americans simply do not understand the kind of social sermons which Jesus preached. He says, "A man who would talk as Christ did on the streets of Chicago or New York would be in danger of being clubbed by the police, if nothing worse."

Walter Rauschenbusch, a great minister and teacher of religion at Rochester Theological Seminary, was a socialist. He attacked the profit motive, championed the single tax, assailed war, worked for peace and economic justice. He declared, "The reign of competition is a reign of fear."[1] His *Prayers of the Social Awakening* will long continue to challenge the conscience of those who seek God's truth.

Jane Addams went into the slums of Chicago to found Hull House. She opposed war and all her life was creative in those things that made for peace. Graham Taylor, pastor, head of the department of Christian Sociology at the Chicago Theological Seminary, lived the life of a con-

---

[1] Walter Rauschenbusch, *Christianizing the Social Order,* Macmillan, 1921, p. 173.

secrated Christian. After his funeral, one of his former students wrote these lines:

> To him the way of injustice pointed the way to justice
> the way of despair pointed to the way of hope.
> Though he bore the sufferings of men,
> he linked it with the sufferings of God.
> Though he bore the defeat of the human
> he linked it with the victory of the spirit.
> Though men ridiculed and abused him,
> calling him a dreamer, a theorist, a rebel—
> He returned their misunderstandings with the understanding
> love of a neighbor and a friend.

Henry T. Hodgkin, Quaker, missionary in China, director of Pendle Hill, a Quaker school of graduate study, is another of this small band. The passion of his life was loyalty to Christ. He was one of the founders of the Fellowship of Reconciliation which opposes military violence and whose influence has spread around the world.

Consider Sherwood Eddy, great Y.M.C.A. Secretary, who went to India in 1896. No one can estimate the number of men who have been won to Christ through his influence. For as he won converts in India, they in turn went out and won others, the total thus going up in geometric ratio. He has always believed in combining the social and individual aspects of religion. Read his *Eighty Adventurous Years*. (1955)

He says, that from the year 1897, "I set apart a quiet time as regularly as I ate my breakfast. I had now to seek the full integration of the contemplative and active sides of existence, of inflow and overflow, of communion with God and service for man. I sought at the beginning of each day to relate my life to its Source, to live and move and have my being in God, as the Whole of Reality. Something happened that day thirty years ago, and it has been happening ever since, I have often failed God but he has never failed me."

Then there is Kirby Page, outstanding worker for peace and justice, author of over thirty challenging volumes, not to mention a host of pamphlets on Christian faith and action.

Bishop Paul Jones, socialist and pacifist is another prophetic leader. On the outbreak of World War I, he spoke against it in ringing terms in Los Angeles. His headquarters were in Salt Lake City, and the headlines in the local press read as follows:

SWARMS OF POLICE CHASE BISHOP JONES

and

PAUL JONES FLEES DECK OF BURNING PEACE SHIP

Some of his parishioners were so wrought up that they threatened to tar and feather him. The pressure was so great he resigned his diocese and was never assigned to one again although he remained a Bishop. Ever after this incident his effectiveness throughout the country as a dynamic religious leader was greatly increased.

George Landsbury lived from 1859 to 1940 in England. He was a tireless crusader for social justice and world peace. Nearly all his life he lived among the poor in East London always striving to help them. As soon as he finished his work on Saturday, he devoted the rest of the day and all Sunday to his efforts for social justice. He usually held one meeting on Saturday and three on Sunday.

In his first Parliamentary contest he polled exactly 345 votes in 1895. In his second campaign he had even less—only 204! During the Boer War he was soundly trounced at the polls and even in 1906 he only got 1200 votes. Finally in 1910 he was elected. By 1927, he had been made Chairman of the Labor Party. He made it a practise to go from one end of Britain to the other with friends from the Fellowship of Reconciliation, the Peace Pledge Union, the Women's Cooperative Guild and other labor organizations speaking on behalf of pacifism. He said, "In my opinion it would be quite easy to avoid war if nations were as willing to sacrifice imperialism, domination, and greed as they are to sacrifice human life in a vain endeavor to make the world safe for national aggrandizement." When the British Labour Party refused to follow a consistent peace policy he resigned. At the end of his life he wrote:

"I believe in the common people. 'The people, Lord, the people'— those who go down to the sea in ships, those who burrow in mine and quarry, who toil in docks and factories, railways and all the countryside, in counting houses and offices, all who make the wheels of life go round. Of all these and many others we have our share in East London, and it is they who with the toiling masses of the whole world will yet build the new Jerusalem." (George Lansbury, *Looking Backwards— And Forwards,* London.)

Do you know Muriel Lester of England? Allan A. Hunter writes of her, "What she professes in a way of life, is a way far more exciting, she insists, than the usual cement roads that lead to 'success' or 'victory' and it takes you more surely to where you want to go. If you are on it you really can't fuss about your own little self or what you feel, or what you imagine someone else feels. You're dealing with great world forces; your business now is to stop war, to purify the world, to get it saved from poverty *and* riches, to make people like each other, to heal the sick, to comfort the sad, to wake up those who have not yet found God, to create joy and beauty wherever you go, to find God in everything and everyone."[2]

Kagawa, Social Prophet of Japan, lived for fifteen years in the slums, ministering to any and all who cared to come to his center. Since then his books and his voice have reverberated around the world. Angela Morgan in a poem dedicated to him has this to say,

> You are my soul, made visible and strong;
> My heart that bled for those who could not speak;
> You are the flaming challenge to all wrong,
> God's answer for the torments of the weak.
> My deepest wounds, like rubies in the sun,
> Transfigured by your coming now rejoice.
> That cursing of my sorrow was begun
> With the first utterance of your brave voice.

Now to close these random specimens taken from a host of devoted men and women who have been serving God all over the world let us pay tribute to three leaders, a Protestant, a Jew, and a Catholic, who have but recently passed from our earthly sphere.

Bishop Francis J. McConnell was born on August 18, 1871 and was 82 years of age when he died. Rabbi Stephen S. Wise was born March 17, 1874 and Bishop Francis J. Haas was born on March 18, 1889.

First consider Bishop McConnell. He was President of De Pauw University nearly half a century ago. He became President of the Re-

[2] Allan A. Hunter, *White Corpuscles in Europe.*

ligious Education Association in 1916. A quarter of a century ago he was President of the Federal Council of Churches. By that time his reputation as a social prophet was so great that he was called to deliver the Lyman Beecher Lectures at the Yale University Divinity School. Besides all this he was President of the American Association for Social Security and a leader in a host of other organizations serving the public good. When the Religion and Labor Foundation was started over a quarter of a century ago he immediately accepted the Presidency, representing the Protestant faith.

Francis J. McConnell came from a labor ancestry; his grandfather was a stone mason and his father a preacher. McConnell is a Scottish name and someone studying the family history wrote that the McConnell clan was composed of "the most able minds and the most arrant rogues in Scotland." Be this background as it may, Francis joined the Church when he was only ten years old. It was his father's practice to issue an invitation at the close of every service. One morning, having carefully listened to the sermon, the boy went forward. Later he wrote "it seemed to me the only thoughtful thing to do."

Bishop McConnell was destined to attend the great world conferences of Jerusalem, Edinburgh and others, but he never forgot what he learned when he worked in the cotton mill in Lawrence, Massachusetts nor did he forget the rickshaw men who once pulled him along the road in China. Every now and then overcome by a fit of coughing these laborers would be forced to stop. The Bishop wrote "I could not get the rickshaw man out of my mind. He was coughing all the time." McConnell lived in a missionary home near much rickshaw travel and declared "I heard coughing all day and night. I wondered if I could get used to that distressing sound. How long do you think it did take me to cease noticing it? It took not much more than ten days." As a matter of fact, he *never* forgot that incident.

His amazing ability to put profound thought simply was seen in his statement, " 'The meek shall inherit the earth.' That's true, but the trouble is to keep them meek when they begin to inherit."

Students at De Pauw University while he was president, were deeply impressed by his sermons. Later, he would invite a brilliant student into the office and begin the conversation this way, "Can you give me one good reason why you should not enter the ministry?" Many decided to do so then and there.

Bishop Oxnam declares that at the meeting of the Council of Bishops when the going was tough, McConnell would rise and after a few moments, end the discussion in just the right way. Sometimes this was due to his humour, sometimes it was his satire, at other times his close reasoning, but always because of his Christian spirit and thought. He was a man of deep spirituality. "His pastoral ministry is replete with expressions of loving service which were unsung and unknown except to those who had been helped. He led the church in striking the shackles of illuminative literalism and thereby opened the Book of Books to intellectually honest believers. He took the social ideals of the Book and put them into the Social Creed of Churches. They came alive in social practice and the steel strike report was written."[3]

His rare sense of humor can be gauged in the following incident. He was urged to accept an appointment to China. Dr. Alva Taylor reports, "He got to the inter-church meeting late after adjournment. He sat down by me showing more hilarity than I had seen in him and began to tell me how they wanted to send him to China. 'The real reason,' he said, 'was to get me further away from my straight speaking.' He chuckled saying 'my wife's health is not good.' " He was excused.

The Methodist Church finally appointed Bishop McConnell to the Pittsburgh area where calmly as usual, but seriously he condemned the 12-hour day and low wages. He was always on the side of the common folk. Dr. Taylor says, "When we came to report to the Inter-Church Committee, Bishop McConnell was, of course, our spokesman. He presented our report in an almost nonchalant manner. The committee, mostly ordained ministers, sat silent until a wealthy businessman broke the ice saying such things were none of the church's business. Immediately, John D. Rockefeller sprang up and said it was the church's business and that he believed every word of the report, that he suspected that he held more steel stock than all the committee several times over, and he moved it be accepted, and it was accepted without a word."

Bishop McConnell became known as the greatest social prophet of the Methodist Church in America. Here are a few of the pointed remarks which characterize his leadership.

[3] See *Bishop Francis John McConnell* by G. Bromley Oxnam.

"Industry, politics and government need to be born again."

"Hope for the kingdom of God over yonder depends upon the practice of it here."

"Great financial success does not imply great success in the Kingdom of God."

"Church leaders do not consciously yield to Mammon. Mammon, nevertheless, plays too large a part in producing the social air which we breathe. The church inevitably suffers. They are not careful enough in receiving capitalists."

"War is a form of materialistic atheism, the common foe of belief in God."

"Especially should the entanglement of a church in the process by which its members make money always be kept in the full light—a complacent church is already dead."

"A Christian cannot be indifferent to the point of view of men by the million who are earning their daily bread by labor."

"If Jesus did not attack capitalism as such he did attack the vested interests and he once cleansed the temple in a vigorous demonstration. Labor has the same right to correct capital and business as the employer has to correct the working man who fails to give due service."

"Labor is right in expecting the church to state in living terms the ideals of Jesus with such effectiveness as to make social injustice impossible."

"If the business man has a right to require a margin of profit then Labor has a right to demand a living wage and to provide for the 'rainy day,' old age, a family, illness and all else nature requires."

"We are fortunate indeed if we have some ruthless questioner at hand young enough not to have any more sense than to make searching enquiries."

"Social radicals may be fools but they should be heeded because they may be the 'red of a danger lantern.'"

"Getting the labor radical in line is not more difficult than getting the oil, steel, meat and grain kings in line. Every epoch lives on the radicalism of yesterday."

"The early church was made up largely of working people and its sanity and its devotion and its simplicity defeated the powerful who sought to curtail or even destroy it."

"Any honest man who has followed the rise of the labor movement will testify to the fact that it was loyalty to the cause and willingness to pay a price for it, that won."

"The condition of labor today would be abject indeed if it had not been and it it were not now, for the leaders in their cause."

"The cause of labor is not safe with either the capitalistic class alone or with the church alone . . . the very social welfare that the labor unions practise, is Christian action."

"The spirit of profit for private gain will have to yield to the motive of service in all realms."

In conclusion we would characterize Bishop McConnell as a flaming prophet in an age of materialism, a devout seeker after divine truth in an era of Biblical platitudes, and an inspired follower of the social teachings of Jesus in a period when multitudes were harmonizing them with the flesh pots of prosperity.

Let us now turn to a great Jewish leader, Rabbi Stephen S. Wise. All down thru the years he was a friend who was ever ready to aid in every good cause for social justice. When the Religion and Labor Foundation was started he immediately accepted the joint Presidency with Bishop McConnell. When the author came under fire of financial interests because of criticism of some of the giant corporations who were working against the labor unions, Rabbi Wise not only supported him without limit but invited him to speak in the Jewish Free Synagogue in New York. His championship of labor was outstanding. As far back as 1912 he was asked to mediate a labor dispute in the textile mills. He found the majority of workers were mere children and they averaged only two and three dollars a week in compensation. Even the forelady received but six dollars a week for fifty-eight hours of work.

Rabbi Wise defended the steel workers. He was unalterably opposed to the twelve hour day and the seven day week and was wholeheartedly behind the efforts of the workers to organize. He preached a blistering sermon in defense of justice for the steel workers in which among other things he said, "I charge Judge Gary and the men associated with them with resorting to every manner of coercion, intimidation and violence . . . in order to avoid the organization of the workers." Before delivering this sermon Dr. Wise predicted it would mean the loss of the million dollar synagogue which he had hoped to build and he was right, it did.

In 1911 Rabbi Wise was invited to speak as he says "for the first and last time" to the New York Chamber of Commerce. Here were seated the great captains of American industry including Andrew Carnegie, James J. Hill, J. P. Morgan, Charles Schwab and George Baker. Stephen Wise showed magnificent courage as he always did, speaking right from the shoulder. Listen to just a few sentences:

> No business order is just nor can it long endure if it be bound up with the evil of unemployment on the one hand and over employment on the other, the evil of a man's underwage and a child's toil, and all social maladjustments incidental to our order which we lump together under the name of poverty . . . The conscience of the nation is not vital unless we protect women and children in industry, and protect them with half the thoroughness and generosity with which, for many decades we have protected infant industries.

A citation to Rabbi Stephen S. Wise given by the Religion and Labor Foundation reads:

"Inspired prophet of the Twentieth Century, fearless champion of justice for organized labor, believer in the trade unions as a defense against the exploitation of the workers, Founder and President of the American Jewish Congress which has helped to organize the Jewish community in the battle for civil rights and civil liberty, President and Founder of the World Jewish Congress established to secure and protect political and economic rights for Jews in all lands, Rabbi Wise takes his place among the greatest leaders of our age.

"His life-long devotion to the Zionist Movement has now borne fruit in the state of Israel which is demonstrating that it can build a model democracy in the midst of Arab feudalism. The heroic effort and courage of the leaders of Israel were in no small measure the result of the work over the years of Rabbi Wise.

"Founder of the Jewish Institute of Religion which has trained leaders for service all over the nation as prophets of tomorrow, friend of some of our greatest Presidents, implacable foe of Hitlerism, saviour of thousands of Jews in France, Roumania, Poland and other countries, Stephen S. Wise is a constant challenge to every sincere believer in religious justice around the world."

Bishop Haas was the son of immigrant parents and therefore early came to know the lot of the underprivileged. Few men in their lives have more effectively united efforts for labor and service to God. From the time when he wrote his doctoral thesis on labor arbitration in the men's garment industry until he was appointed Chairman of the Fair Employment Practices Committee established by President Roosevelt in 1943, his record was outstanding. Actually in his life he personally participated in the settlement of some 1500 labor disputes. Because of his record, he received in 1952, the Michigan C.I.O. Award "for distinguished service in the cause of Human rights." Because of his life-long fight against intolerance, in 1950 he received the award from the Jewish Workmen's Circle of Detroit and in 1952 he was given the interfaith award by the Michigan B'nai B'rith for outstanding work in interfaith, interracial, and intercultural relations. This is typical of the recognition in this field which he received during his lifetime. It is hard to see how any leader could more nearly embody the many facets of the ideal of combining religion and labor than Bishop Haas.

From the many tributes paid him at the time of his death consider but one. Martin P. Durkin, United States Secretary of Labor declared: "The death of Bishop Francis J. Haas is a great loss to the church and to the Nation. For the church he advanced immeasurably the doctrines of social justice. For the Nation he has awakened its wage earners to both their rights and duties.

"His counsel and guidance to labor and management will be surely missed. As a man he has distinguished himself not only by his intellectual attainments but also by his integrity, by his kindness and by his humility."

One of the most widely quoted talks of Bishop Haas was that given to the C.I.O. Convention in which he laid down the thesis that the "right to organize comes from Almighty God." In this address he charged that "the whole history of unorganized industries in our country is a history of degraded and enslaved men and women." Regarding the laws now on the statute books at Washington he declared in this address, "Accordingly, I can and do say that the Taft-Hartley Act which is designed not merely to put limits on the freedom of labor organizations, but to hamstring and destroy them, is a tyrannous usurpation by government of a worker's God-given rights."

In conclusion, Bishop Haas, was a teacher, crusader, arbitrator, and devoted follower of Christ. He gave his life unstintedly to the cause of suffering humanity—the downtrodden, the exploited. It was inevitable, therefore, that he should be a warm friend of organized labor. He was not content to utter religious platitudes. He applied his religion to life. As a teacher he instilled in his students a desire to work for humanity. He inspired them with a living passion for righteousness. He did all this with simplicity and self-effacement. He was a priest of great faith, love and humility yet Monsignor Ryan declared he was "one of the most competent authorities on labor questions in the United States and one of the most valued advisors to government officials in that field."

We have seen in these lives the great paradox: self-denial means self-realization. Just as when fruit decays, new fruit may spring forth, so as we give ourselves for others, new spiritual values are born. We must reshape all our interests, pleasures, comforts and fame so that they are part of God's plan. The people who desire religion but want it kept "in its place," that is separate from their business or their pleasures or what have you, are deluding themselves, they do not have genuine religion. Religion has to be lived, with one's whole life. It means a commitment to God. It means denying self-will. If we are willing to accept whatever God gives us in trial from within or without, then we will not be afraid of censure. When we give ourselves wholly to God, we are no longer our own. Our life should be a total response to the best in each situation. In what follows we seek to give a few hints for the development of one's own inner spiritual powerhouse.

The Way implies Choice. First, how do we get on *the Way to God?* How do we strengthen our moral and spiritual foundations? When we have made a choice towards God no matter where we are, we are in The Way. We may be in a dungeon or in a gambling den, the instant we set our face towards God, we are on the road to victory. The Way means purging ourselves first. When we have mastered ourselves then we have begun to achieve. If we desire nothing, we have everything. Our ego must be transformed into the soul that is seeking God's will at all points and at all times. Love can open the inner eye of the soul so that we can strip off selfishness. Purification is a perpetual process because illumination is never finished.

Man should realize that everything he does involves others. Just as a pebble thrown into the water makes larger and larger ripples, so our every action has its repercussions. We must strive after humility. We must be dead to the spirit and temper of a materialistic selfish world and live a new life in the spirit and mind of Christ. We must make life a consecration not a desecration.

Let us rise above physical selfish desires such as appetites and sex. Let us rise above social possessiveness, the wish for property and social position. In fact even pride and the desire for great social recognition compete with God's will for the center of our lives.

Second, since undoubtedly we all have many skins covering our inmost selves, we must learn to recognize and strip these off until our very souls are laid bare. Dwight L. Moody said, "I had more trouble with myself than with any other man I ever met." How can we then shed the various camouflages which disguise our real selves?

Here are two ways to find out your ego: One, ask yourself what it is you would rather have than anything else in all the world. Two, ask what is the greatest disaster that could possibly befall you. What would you hate most to lose in life? Now ask is the thing you really desire most the thing God would will for you? Is the thing you feel would be the greatest loss, what God would also rank as most disastrous? These questions may lay bare some of our weaknesses. We must beware of pursuing false goals. Let us get rid of our faults, blind spots, fears.

Third, if we would seek the way, the truth and the life, we must always have complete loyalty to the good. We must search our consciences by comparing our life with the life of Jesus. We must cleanse our hearts and cast out fear, hatred, selfish desire and no man can do this without the help of God.

Fourth, we must never accept any social ideals of our own contemporary society as final, we must give our supreme devotion to the better way which is not yet achieved. Think of how feudalism, slavery, colonialism have all gone down. Perhaps the institutions of our time may be defective also. Recognize that God is far beyond all present values. Hold fast to Him, and He will lead you on. "Man's sin is usually stamped upon man's universe," therefore beware of accepting the conventional standards of the society in which you find yourself. As the late George Albert Coe has well said, "Adherence to the status quo requires as a rule little reflection, while release from it to something better requires much." Recognize that what is called "the good" may be nothing more than "the prevalent."

We must always remember that serving God is a reciprocal relationship. Man must relinquish all that he wants to do for himself and place his will in the hands of God. His freedom must be moulded by God's will for him. When any individual does this completely, then he is infinitely stronger than the contemporary social "manners," "mores" or "morals." The latter are weighed in the light of God's judgment.

Fifth, if we love God with all our hearts and all our souls and all our minds, then we can no longer hate anyone, instead we sincerely endeavor to love everyone and try to help them. Would not the war against the people of Indo-China have been impossible if we were dominated by the love of God? Granted this is difficult for finite human beings to achieve. Still, it can be done. God can supplant our ego and take over but this can be accomplished only by disciplined lives, by patience, persistence and prayer.

We must develop a sensitivity of conscience until it is illumined steadily by the light which comes from God. If we do this, then God will guide us onward no matter how dark the night.

Sixth, shall we not remember that light in our inner spirit comes from every spark struck off from the anvil of God's love? It may be a sentence in a book, it may be a chance remark from a friend, it may be the song of a bird or the beauty of a flower but everywhere light shines in the darkness and we have only to tune ourselves to the current which is flowing all about us. In other words, we must see the invisible. A Persian parable puts it this way, "I was common clay until roses were planted in me."

Let us begin dying to self by being reborn in the love of God. This will bring light at all times along the road, there will be less stumbling. It brings peace, and joy and a faith that leaps ahead of present performance, present understanding. But don't imagine we can do this over night. As Francois Fenelon says, "People who are far from God think they are very near to him, when they begin to take a few steps to approach him. The most polite and most enlightened people have the same stupidity about this as a peasant who thinks he is really at court, because he has seen the King."

As Laotzu, Chinese philosopher, 6th century B.C. says, "A tree that it takes both arms to encircle grew from a tiny rootlet. A many storied pagoda is built by placing one brick upon another brick. A journey of three thousand miles is begun by one step."

As a first step, we must purge sin from the soul, then we must illuminate our spirits with divine love and finally we must unite our love with the will of God.

Seventh, let not our familiarity with the present social order blind us to its faults. Aldous Huxley says, "Our present economic, social and international arrangements are based, in large measure, upon organized lovelessness."

Do we not slaughter dumb animals, waste the earth's resources, ruin its soil, pour filth into flowing waters and poisonous fumes into the air we breathe? Pursuing wealth do not the methods of mass-production, mass-distribution and mass-financing sometimes lead to exploitation with God and brotherhood pushed back out of our consciousness? Professor Huxley says, "War and preparation for war are standing temptations to make the present bad, God-eclipsing arrangements of society progressively worse as technology becomes progressively more efficient." Carl G. Jung, Swiss psychotherapist concludes, "The great events of our world, which are planned and carried out by man, do not breathe the spirit of Christianity but of unadorned paganism." These judgments may be too sweeping but let us throw our weight on the side of a social order in which security, health and plenty will be the heritage of the world in which we live.

Eighth, *guard against self-righteousness*. We must beware of an enemy self which thinks itself moral, but which really is selfishly moral. We fancy that we are religious, we fancy that we are righteous when we are not. This is the basis of what Jesus spoke so often against as hypocrisy. A test as to whether we have this fault in any degree is the extent of our irritation when we are criticized. Everyone is hurt by unjust criticism but perhaps we should ask ourselves, "Is there a slight truth in this charge?"

Ninth, we should be willing to sacrifice ourselves in daily self-forgetfulness, which brings us to God-consciousness. In fact, we should get to the point where we recognize that every affliction may be a positive treasure. Sooner or later we will comprehend that every detail of life can be a means of bringing us nearer to God. When we suffer, we can surrender our souls to God. As Rabindranath Tagore says, "This surrender is our soul's free choice of its life of cooperation with God—cooperation in the world of the perfect moulding of the world of law into the world of love." God's crosses are always safer than any that are self-chosen. We can avoid a great many such as over-anxiety, self-will, self-pity and prolonged remorse. We should recognize with Brother Lawrence, "that all things are possible to him who believes, that they are less difficult to him who hopes, that they are easier to him who loves, and still more easy to him who perseveres in the practice of these three virtues."

Tenth, we should all recognize that different techniques and methods are needed by different individuals. Some may say that life itself will teach us. This is true. The spiritual life feeds on what surrounds it, the personalities it meets, the difficulties, the opportunities, the hardships, the suffering, but some people appropriate this food for the inner soul and some do not. Most individuals find that through prayer they open up themselves to God and their lives are changed. An analysis of the greatest mistakes made by individuals showed that they were nearly always made without genuine prayer. On the other hand, from Jesus down through our greatest contemporary leaders, right decisions were immeasurably helped if prayer preceded them. How difficult must have been Jesus' decision in the Garden of Gethsemane, but the stark rightness of his decisions are measured by their dynamic results.

Eleventh, let us recognize that we can grow into higher forms of prayer life. We can pray for various objectives for others as well as for ourselves. But a more advanced form of prayer is meditation and contemplation; it is opening all our thoughts and aspirations to review on the level of a higher divine will which makes for righteousness.

If any sincere soul goes into an inner room and shuts the door and then stripping himself of all egoism bows down in humility, he will grow in grace and wisdom. Supposing he then begins to ponder over what a brief span he is going to have here on earth and how feeble his efforts alone and then if he asks God's help to make him a more effective instrument of the divine will, he will certainly come forth to accomplish more in life. Inevitably the disease of self-love will be modified if not cured. Humility, penitence, contrition will make us rearrange our minds and make more effective our lives.

One can test out the value of prayer. Take time for meditation in the morning. See if it does not help to make us place first things first. Many times while in prayer, one has a new insight and when this is followed, it opens new vistas of effectiveness. If this is true in the ordinary day by day hurly burly of life how much more it is true in moments of crisis and anxiety. Prayer makes for self-change and this in turn makes for reshaping and remoulding the social life.

Some of us perhaps do not realize that even physical health can be changed by prayer. Listen to these words from the famous Alexis Carrel, the French surgeon, "Our present conception of the influence of prayer upon pathological lesions is based upon the observation of patients who have been cured almost instantaneously of various affections such as peritoneal tuberculosis, cold abscesses, osteitis, suppurating wounds, lupus, cancer, etc."

Brother Lawrence went through twelve long years of the practice of prayer before he felt that he had an habitual sense of the presence of God. Says he, "We are to be pitied, who content ourselves with so little. God's treasure is like an infinite ocean; yet a little wave of feeling, passing with the moment contents us. We are thus partially blind when we might be permeated with a living faith which would flood us with God's light at all times and in all places."

As individuals progress in prayer they speak less and listen more. A period of contemplation makes us always humble and prevents us from trusting in our own will which may cause grievous error. St. Augustine is a good example. He gradually worked himself out of the slavery of inner paralysis, brought on by conflicting desires, to a state where he really loved God with all his heart and soul and mind. Then he felt that he was free to do as he "pleased" because his every desire was to follow the will of God. One test of the effectiveness of prayer is whether it makes us go forth with a greater resolution to persevere in good works. Does it make us throw our energy all through the day in more effective channels? It is well to have a period of quiet at the start of the day when we try to listen to God's will. This should lead to that form of contemplation which is radiant to the heart. In the end our prayer life at its best should make us more effective servants of God.

All history shows that individuals who wish to appropriate added power from God must pray. To some degree we all have personal and social "darkness"; we must then seek the power of God within by concentrating on Him. This gives energy-radiation. This means seeking to make our lives in tune with the infinite and this in turn demands complete commitment to God. If we then wish to make our worship meaningful, we should relax and try to make ourselves receptive to love. We should ask forgiveness for our own mistakes, in other words we should have a spirit of humility. We should call to mind the vast potentialities for good which are possible if we integrate our lives with God. We then take up the chief problems which we are facing and ask God's help and guidance and that His will may rule our every act. Buddha may have something to teach Christians about meditation. He says we should practice benevolence or loving kindness in our devotions. This means we must also include our adversaries and our enemies, in our love. We should send thoughts of love to all including our enemies. How many religious leaders include the Russian Communists in their prayers, for instance? We should have pity for all suffering. This means our prayers should go out to the victims of warfare in French Indo-China or anywhere else. We should have joyous sympathy with the happiness of other human beings and finally we should have a state of serenity which can surmount all joy or sorrow.

Again one should seek to strip himself of all self-deception in this process so that he does not accept as light from on high his own lower aspirations.

Besides individual worship we must let group worship and fellowship with others inspire us, and we in turn may help them. It is extremely difficult not to have a self-centered life when one does not share in a wider group fellowship.

Finally spiritual devotion and contemplation are not enough. We shall come to God not only in prayer *but in every act of our lives. We must have the power to see it through all the way.* It is just as necessary to alter our lives in order to have true prayer as it is to alter our meditations and make them more in tune with God. It is simply impossible to live selfishly and be sincere in our prayers. Jesus supremely exemplified the life of action for others, but it was action fused with prayer. Jesus' prayer life can no more be separated from his teaching or action than character can be separated from personality.

We can come to God in countless ways. Some who are atheists end as believers through dedicating their lives to a cause which makes for righteousness. Angelo Herndon, the Negro labor organizer, was once given an opportunity to escape so that he would not be returned to a Georgia chain-gang and possible death. Here is the answer of this nineteen year old boy, "I cannot run away. There is too much at stake. If I run away and you run away, and everyone else who loves freedom and truth runs away, who will be left to fight the good battle? I am not afraid. Death itself is not the greatest tragedy that could happen to man. Rather, the greatest tragedy is to live placidly and safely and to keep silent in the face of injustice and oppression."

It is not right to say that men are *always* converted to God before they can do good. Some start doing good sincerely and are converted to God in the process. The religious life is a dual oneness of action and prayer, of devotion to God and to men. One without the other is always crippled and yet either is a step in the right direction.

There are many levels of action. One is the individual who is self-centered, who is unconcerned about those outside his immediate family and friends. The wealthy man wrapt up in his home, his club and his small circle of friends may be in this group.

Second, there are idealists who want to change society. They rebel against the injustice which is all about them but they are ready to use *any means* to change the situation. They grow to hate the rulers of the status quo. Some of them go Fascist, some go Communist, some of them into politics to change the evils but they are willing to use wrong methods to attain what they conceive to be noble ends. The militarist is willing to use violence. He will snuff out a million people to have "righteousness" prevail.

Third, there are the really great spiritual leaders of mankind, Jesus, Gandhi, Schweitzer, St. Francis. The Communist sweeps Jesus away as a deluded man of superstitious faith. The militarist of every nationality sweeps Gandhi aside as an impractical sentimentalist who would turn the other cheek and let the Communists take over the nation. Some great industrialists believe that Schweitzer is a half baked fool for wasting his great talents on the natives of Africa.

Oberlin, pastor of a poor parish in the Valley of Stone, Switzerland, believed in translating the gospel into action. When a Jew who was crossing the mountain above the valley was murdered, he insisted on sending on to the widow every year fifty francs. The woman was astounded at such generosity and asked how he came to do it. He answered that since the murder had been committed within his parish, he felt that they were all "blood-guilty" and that he wished to atone for the crime.

Later a Jewish pedlar who sold goods on credit to the villagers died, leaving his widow in poverty. Oberlin took over all the debts himself and paid for those who refused to settle their debts.

Once when Oberlin was in his study there was a great noise outside and people were shouting at some strange foreigner, "a Jew! a Jew!" Oberlin walked out and finally worked his way to the man's side and shouted, "Those who treat so cruelly one who is not a Christian, are themselves unworthy of that name." Oberlin then lifted the pedlar's pack on his own shoulders and took him to his house.

Oberlin's method of individual giving deserves to be studied by us all. He set up three boxes. In the first he placed one-tenth of his earnings for the church. In the second, he deposited another tenth for community improvements, entertaining strangers, help for school children, helping anyone who had been injured in the community and the like. In the third box he deposited another third of his income which was to be used for all the poor of his parish.

If a villager lost a cow, it was replaced. If the home of a poor widow was destroyed by fire, a collection was taken and the home was replaced. If any other action needed to be taken, Oberlin was there to inspire it.

Do we do as much in our communities as Oberlin did in his?

As we have already noted, St. Francis of Assisi demonstrated in his life that we must end hatred and build peace. He founded the Third Order where all were to make restitution for any injustice done, they were to be reconciled with their enemies, to live in peace with all men, to make prayer central in their lives and to do works of mercy and to give one-tenth of all they earned to the church. Everyone must agree to be free from slavery to things. Are we doing in our time what St. Francis did in his? Have we advanced towards God or retrograded?

"Slowly, through all the universe, that temple of God is being built wherever, in any world, a soul, by free-willed obedience, catches the fire of God's likeness. When, in your hard fight, in your tiresome drudgery, or in your terrible temptation, you catch the purpose of your being, and give yourself to God, and so give him the chance to give himself to you; your life, a living stone is taken up and set into the growing wall. . . . Wherever souls are being tried and ripened, in whatever commonplace and homely ways, there God is hewing out the pillars for his temple." Phillips Brooks, 1835–1893.

We take leave of each other here in the thought of complete surrender of self to God and His love. This means dedication of every moment, every day to His service. The world can never be rebuilt by individuals who are not dedicated souls. Neither can society be transformed by just creating "good" individuals unless the structure of society itself is changed,—social, economic, political and international. "The Kingdom of Heaven is within your reach." *We must change ourselves and change society also.* Building a just social order inevitably leads men toward God and changing our life so that it is really God-centered leads to civic righteousness: the synthesis creates the City of God.

Prayer

O God, sometimes our light grows dim and yet we know that we have but to turn to Thee and the light will come again. Forgive our shortcomings and help us increasingly to love all our neighbors both near and far. May we ever remember that small deeds done are better than untranslated dreams. May we grow to love Thee with all our heart and soul and mind and strength. Make us less fearful of facing facts and so guide us towards the truth and in support of what is genuinely right. Lead us here and now to dedicate our hearts, our lives and our all to Thy service. Guard us from lightly making this prayer of dedication that our supplication to Thee may be genuine and lasting. Amen.

Index

Action, test of, 193–201
Action to God, 312–3
Acheson, Dean, 37
Addams, Jane, 296
Aggression, 275
Air Bases, 42
American School, values, 207–8
Anthony, Susan B., 253–254
Atomic bomb, 40–41

Bach, Johann Sebastian, 15
Baiko San, 181
Barker, Ernest H., 259
Barnes Harry Elmer, 169, 277
Bevin, Ernest, 37
Bowers, Glaude, G., 274
Bradley, Gen. Omar, 294
Brain washing in America, 255
Bright, John, 37
Butler, Nicholas Murray, 75

Cadbury, Paul S., 97
Capitalism, 78
Chase, Stuart, 77
Chou Ch'u, 198
Church and vocational groups, 225
Churchill, Winston, 278
Cleanse ourselves first, 187
Communism, 99–108
Communism, fear of, 107
Communism, negative factors, 99–102
Communism, a secular "religion," 106
Community surveys, 226–7
Conservation of natural resources, 94
Cooperative, consumers—fundamental principles, 159
Cooperative movement, 156–162
Coon, Carleton S., 151
Corporations, billion dollar group, 84
Coumarin, 58

Crandall, Prudence, 142
Crime comics, 182–3
Criminal in Ourselves, 247–255
Criminal, scientific treatment of, 236–243

Davis, Elmer, 68
Declaration of Independence and fear, 69
Devil, 19
Dewey, John, 177
Disease, 59–60
Douglas, William O., 170–1, 276
Driberg, Tom, 271
Drinkwater, John, 149
Dyke, Henry Van, 23

Earnings, 86
Eckart, Meister Johannes, 76, 187
Economic democracy, 153–162
Economic Order, ethics of, 86 ff.
Eddy, Sherwood, 297
Eisenhower, Dwight, 98
Emerson, Ralph Waldo, 191
Equality, 137–148
Evans, Bergen, 26

Family, 205–214
Family of Nations, 273–290
Fascism, 72
Fear and domestic politics, 45
Fear and education, 68–9
Fear and foreign affairs, 279
Fletcher, Giles, 76
Fosdick, Raymond, 37
Flying saucer parable, 129
Four freedoms, 154
Freedom, 137–148
Franklin, Benjamin, 37
French Indochina, 43

317

Gandhi, 49–50, 233, 293
Garrett, Garet, 277
Garrison, William Lloyd, 193
Giovanni, Fra, 204
Gladden, Washington, 296
Goodwill, 180
Gray, John H., 65
Grenfell, Sir Wilfred, 15

Haas, Francis J., 305–6
Hagedorn, Herman, 125
Hillman, Sidney, 265–8
Hodgkin, Henry, 195, 297
Holmes, Oliver Wendell, 191
Home, changing, 208–9
Hughes, Charles Evans, 135
Human Rights, Declaration of, 154–5
Hutchins, Robert M., 53, 55
Hypocrisy, 247–9
Huxley, Aldous, 309
Huxley, T. H., 11

Imperialism, 34
Income, Distribution of, 91
International Development Authority, 173
Invincible Goodwill, 179–188

Jails, 235 ff.
James, William, 111
Jefferson, Thomas, 53
Jesus and poor, 114
Jesus and wealth, 115
Jesus and our enemies, 120
Jones, Bishop Paul, 297–8
Jones, E. Stanley, vii
Justice, 137–148
Juvenile delinquency, 184

Kagawa, Toyohiko, 259, 299
Keithan, Ralph, 228
Kempis, Thomas A., 245
Kennan, George F., 271

Labor, basic principles, 264
Labor, organized, 261–9
Lambeth Conference, 260
Landsbury, George, 298
Laubach, Frank, 200

Lay, Benjamin, 181
Lester, Muriel, 299
Levels of action, 313
Life on other planets, 128
Lilje, Bishop Hanns, 293
Lincoln, A., 75
Lincoln, Murray D., 98, 161, 254
Livingston, David, 196
Longfellow, S., 202
Lowell, James Russell, 126, 255–6
Loyalty investigation, 67

Malnutrition, 59
Marshall, George C., 245
Marshall, Peter, 175, 231
Masaryk, Jan, 37
Materialism, 90
Mazzini, 271
McConnell, Francis J., 299–303
Merrill, William P., 177
Mill, John Stuart, 135
Monopoly, 83–4
Missionary movement, 228–30
Moore, Marianne, 271
Moral force, 46

National Council of Churches, 260
National Religion and Labor Foundation, 269
Negro, 249–253
Neshima, Joseph, 18

Oberlin, 313–4
Our Own Faults first, 296
Overstreet, H. A., 152
Oxenham, John, 245

Pacifism, 184–5
Page, Kirby, 297
Parents, hints for, 213–4
Patriot, real, 8
Pelagius, 195
Penn, William, 191
Peters, Dr. John P., 146–7
Phillips, Wendell, 194
Poisoning, of the air, 55–6
Poisoning, of food, 56–58
Poisoning, of minds of men, 62–66
Pope Pius XI, 37

Index

Prayer life, 310–312
Preaching and practise, 194
Presbyterian Church, 72, 98
Prison, Denmark, 241–2
Prison reform, 235–243
Prophets, 25–32
Prophets and righteousness, 32
Prophets and wealth, 29
Purchasing power, 86

Racial intolerance, 137, 249–253
Rauschenbusch, Walter, 11, 217–8, 296
Religion, captive, 223
Religion, definition, 25
Religion, narcotic, 220
Religious leaders, action pattern of, 16–20
Reuther, Walter, 265
Revolutions, 104–5
Richards, Ned, 200
Robins, Raymond, 180
Rolland, Romain, 11, 233
Roman Catholic Bishops, 151
Roosevelt, Franklin D., 98
Roosevelt, Theodore, 75

Saint Francis of Assisi, 177, 314
Sayer, Dorothy L., 233
Schools, 211–2
Schweitzer, Albert, 14, 165
Security Council, 282
Seeking the best in others, 195–6
Servetus, Michael, 135
Sharpe, D. R., 294
Sheppard, R. H. L., 111
Smith, Lillian, 177
Smith, Margaret Chase, 54
Smog, 55–6
Social Christianity 113–122
Social Creed of the Churches, 262
Solidarity of mankind, 167–174
South Africa, 34, 82–3
Spain, 274
Spiritual power, hints for, 306–313
Stevenson, Adlai, 23
Symonds, John A., 202
Synagogue, 219–230

Tagore, Rabindrath, 151, 177
Tawney, R. H., 135
Taylor, Alva, 301
Technical advances, consequences of, 172–3
Test of action, 193–201
Tolstoy, Leo, 203, 293
Toynbee, Arnold, 97
Trueblood, D. Elton, 217
Truman, Harry, 53, 76

United Church of Canada, declaration of, 94–5
United Nations, 273–290
United Nations, Economic and Social Council, 282–4
United Nations, Secretariat, 285
United Nations, Specialized Agencies, 287
United Nations, University of the World, 288–9
United States, economically, 90–1
United States, pride in, 6
United States, some positive factors, 5–6
Universe, 127

Vietnam, 43

War, 39–50
War prevention, 46
Wealth, inheritance, 222
Webster, Daniel, 259
Wertham, Dr. Frederic, 182
Whitehead, Alfred N., 3
Wilson, Woodrow, 191
Wise, Stephan S., 303–4
Woolman, John, 186–7
World Health Organization, 61
World problem, 14

Xavier, 18

Your life, 295–315

Zwicker, General, 45